T0328555

Industrial and Development Economics

This book is a product of the CODESRIA Textbook Programme.

Industrial and Development Economics

An African Perspective

Stephen M. Kapunda

CODESRIA

Council for the Development of Social Science Research in Africa
DAKAR

Council for the Development of Social Science Research in Africa
Avenue Cheikh Anta Diop, Angle Canal IV
BP 3304 Dakar, 18524, Senegal
Website: www.codesria.org

ISBN: 978-2-86978-715-5

Typesetting: Alpha Ousmane Dia
Cover Design: Ibrahima Fofana

Distributed in Africa by CODESRIA
Distributed elsewhere by African Books Collective, Oxford, UK
Website: www.africanbookscollective.com

The Council for the Development of Social Science Research in Africa (CODESRIA) is an independent organisation whose principal objectives are to facilitate research, promote research-based publishing and create multiple forums geared towards the exchange of views and information among African researchers. All these are aimed at reducing the fragmentation of research in the continent through the creation of thematic research networks that cut across linguistic and regional boundaries.

CODESRIA publishes *Africa Development*, the longest standing Africa based social science journal; *Afrika Zamani*, a journal of history; the *African Sociological Review*; the *African Journal of International Affairs*; *Africa Review of Books* and the *Journal of Higher Education in Africa*. The Council also co-publishes the *Africa Media Review*; *Identity, Culture and Politics: An Afro-Asian Dialogue*; *The African Anthropologist, Journal of African Tranformation, Method(e)s: African Review of Social Sciences Methodology*, and the *Afro-Arab Selections for Social Sciences*. The results of its research and other activities are also disseminated through its Working Paper Series, Green Book Series, Monograph Series, Book Series, Policy Briefs and the CODESRIA Bulletin. Select CODESRIA publications are also accessible online at www.codesria.org.

CODESRIA would like to express its gratitude to the Swedish International Development Cooperation Agency (SIDA), the International Development Research Centre (IDRC), the Ford Foundation, the Carnegie Corporation of New York (CCNY), the Norwegian Agency for Development Cooperation (NORAD), the Danish Agency for International Development (DANIDA), the Rockefeller Foundation, the Open Society Foundations (OSFs), TrustAfrica, UNESCO, the African Capacity Building Foundation (ACBF), The Open Society Initiative for West Africa (OSIWA), The Open Society Initiative for Southern Africa (OSISA), Andrew Mellon Foundation, and the Government of Senegal for supporting its research, training and publication programmes.

Contents

Acknowledgements

I would like to thank the Council for the Development of Social Science Research in Africa (CODESRIA) for awarding and motivating me to write this book.

I am also grateful to my industrial economics students at the University of Dar-es-Salaam, Tanzania, MA students at Joint Facility for Electives (JFE)/ African Economic Research Consortium (AERC), Nairobi, Kenya and the industrial economics students at the University of Botswana. Although all of them contributed unknowingly to the development of this textbook, the more recent students contributed more since I taught them simultaneously with writing the book. Their feedback through questions and comments contributed significantly by way of inspiring the revision and hence the clarity of some of the material.

Thanks also go to the lecturers and administrators at various tertiary institutions for their valuable suggestions and/or other forms of co-operation. Special lecturers and administrators include Prof S. M. Wangwe, Prof A. Mbelle, Prof R. Mabele, Dr L. Rutasitara, Dr A. Mkenda, and Dr J. Aikaeli (University of Dar-es- Salaam); Dr F. Mutasa (Open University of Tanzania); Prof B. Ndulu, Prof D. Rwegasira and Prof. W. Lyakurwa (JFE/AERC, Nairobi); Profs H. Siphambe, N. Narayana, O. Galebotswe, I. Mogotsi and P. Makepe (University of Botswana); Dr E. Kaakunga and Dr Kakuja-Matundu (University of Namibia).

I am also grateful to all reviewers whose positive suggestions and guidance made me revisit and improve on the weak part of the book.

Great thanks go to all the other people not mentioned by name, who directly or indirectly contributed positively to the development of this book.

Last, but not least, my sincere gratitude goes to my wife, Judith, for her support through our joint prayer and her patience during my long absence while I was writing this textbook.

Preface

Most textbooks on industrial economics use examples from Europe, the USA, and other more advanced countries; very rarely from Sub-Saharan Africa. This book attempts to fill the implied gap.

The original material was first used by the author in a series of lectures mainly at the University of Dar-es-Salaam (1976-1999) and the University of Botswana (2000-2014). The material was expanded and modernised thereafter by updating it and enriching it through inputs from various lecturers of industrial economics, especially from the University of Dar-es-Salaam (Tanzania), Open University of Tanzania, University of Nairobi (Kenya), University of Botswana, University of Namibia, University of Malawi, and North-West University (South Africa). The book includes the most recent knowledge and research output in industrial economics and development. Some aspects of industrial development are included, firstly, to capture immediately some important development issues since traditional industrial economics should basically be regarded as an input to industrial development or industrialisation. Second, if the two discipline branches are separated, students tend, over time, to forget these links and material flow.

Third, some universities like the University of Botswana, University of Dar-es-Salaam and Open University of Tanzania follow this approach in teaching industrial economics.

Last, but not least, the new title was also accepted by the Council for the Development of Social Science Research in Africa (CODESRIA). Although the book is essentially intended for undergraduate students, some of the material can benefit postgraduate students. Most of the mathematical appendices and most of parts III and IV are primarily for postgraduate students; but some resourceful undergraduate students may find them useful too.

The general aim of the book is to provide comprehensive understanding of industrial economics and its applicability to African countries. The book is expected to serve as an intellectual and pedagogical support to teaching.

This textbook has four parts. The first part provides the theoretical foundations and has four chapters: Industrial Economics: An Introduction; Framework of Analysis of Industrial Economics; Theories of the Firm and Internal Organisation;

and Market Structure. Part two analyses firm strategies in two chapters: Pricing Practices and Strategies of Firms, and Non-price Strategies. The third part focuses on Industrial Theory and Practice with reference to Industrial Location and Finance as two distinct chapters. The last part analyses Public Policy and Industrial Development, each aspect forming a chapter.

Each chapter is arranged pedagogically, starting with learning objectives, followed by introductory remarks, then content and finally conclusion and review questions. Examples and case studies are provided from Africa, especially in the applied parts.

Professor Stephen M. Kapunda

2017

About the Author

Professor Stephen Miti Kapunda has taught Industrial Economics, among other economics courses, and has been an external examiner in various African universities. He has taught the course at both undergraduate and postgraduate levels for more than thirty years at the University of Dar-es-Salaam, Tanzania (1976-1999); the MA Joint Facility for Electives (JFE)/African Economic Research Consortium (AERC), Nairobi, Kenya (July-September 1996 and July-September 1997); and the University of Botswana (1999 to the time of writing this book). He has also been an external examiner of the course, among others, at the University of Malawi (1995-1996); University of Dar-es-Salaam, Tanzania (2007-2010, 2014, 2016); Moi University, Kenya (2002); University of Namibia (2007-2011) and North-West University, South Africa (2010-2016).

Professor Kapunda has won several awards for his outstanding teaching, research and writing, including the 2010 International Competition Award of Textbook Writing Programme organised by the Council for the Development of Social Science Research in Africa (CODESRIA); the 2004 International Competition Award organised by the Organisation for Social Science Research in Eastern and Southern Africa (OSSREA); and, the 1993 International Post-Doctoral Fellowship award at the United Nations Economic Commission for Africa (UNECA). The award for textbook writing organised by CODESRIA was, indeed, what motivated him to write this book.

The author has published over 50 refereed articles in journals and chapters in books in economics. He has also served on some editorial boards, including those dealing with industrial economics.

Professor Kapunda holds a BA (Ed) degree, majoring in Economics, from the University of Dar-es-Salaam, an MA (Economics), University of Toronto, Canada and a PhD (Economics) from the University of Dar-es-Salaam.

He is married and has three sons and one daughter.

I

Theoretical Foundations

1

Industrial Economics: An Introduction

Learning Objectives

The main objectives of this chapter are:
- To provide a brief historical note of industrial economics;
- To define and explain industrial economics and related concepts; and
- To give a brief scope and methods of industrial economics.

Introductory Retrospective Note

While the origin of industrial economics can be traced back to Adam Smith in the eighteenth century, the course became a separate economics discipline in the 1950s.

Adam Smith in his 1776 publication, *An Inquiry into the Nature and Causes of the Wealth of Nations*, explained the way to organise industrial production more efficiently, through division of labour. Later works include Marshall's 1899 publication, *The Economics of Industry*, which explained the factors of industrial localisation and conditions for an efficient organisation of industry. Later on, Chamberlin (1933) and Robinson (1933) underlined the competition and performance aspects. Such works led to development of the current analytical framework of industrial economics: *structure – conduct – performance* (S-C-P) paradigm which was developed by the American economists, E.S. Mason (working in the 1930s and 1940s) and later his student J.S. Bain (working in the 1950s and 1960s). It is during the 1950s that industrial economics developed as a separate economics discipline.[1] Apart from the works of Bain, the name 'Industrial Economics' was possibly adopted in the early 1950s through the writing of P.W.S. Andrews and the rise of the *Journal of Industrial Economics*.[2]

Concepts and Definitions

Since its infancy in the 1950s, industrial economics has been defined in various ways. Definitions worth considering include that of Clarke (2000:7), i.e.:

By tradition, industrial economics deals mainly with manufacturing and mining industries, although some of its ideas can also be applied to the service sectors. Sectors such as agriculture, financial markets and so on are usually treated in other specialist economics courses.

Note that mining (mainly coal) traditionally used to be a major source of energy in the manufacturing sector; hence it was regarded as a component of the industrial sector. Currently, electricity is the main source of energy and supports the manufacturing sector.

Andreosso and Jacobson (2005:1)[3] define simultaneously *industrial economics and industrial organisation* as, 'a distinctive field of economics that deals with the functioning of markets and industries in a specific business, institutional and legal environment'. This definition underlines the function of markets and industries.

Church and Ware (2000:7) also define simultaneously *industrial economics and industrial organisation* as, 'the study of the operation and performance of imperfectly competitive markets and the behaviour of firms in these markets'.

However, Pepall *et al.* (2009:4) simply define industrial organisation as, 'that branch of economics that is concerned with the study of imperfect competition', while Ferguson-Ferguson (1994:1) views industrial economics as, 'the application of micro-economic theory to the analysis of firms, markets, and industries'.

In this book the working definition of *industrial economics* is, 'a branch of economics dealing with the organisation of *industry* and the links between market structure and business conduct in determining market performance'.

Unlike the other cited definitions, this definition underlines the industrial organisation and the link among structure (S), conduct (C), and performance (P). In this book the S-C-P relationship is the foundation and basic method or approach to industrial economics as will be elaborated in the subsequent chapter.

Implied in the working definition are some key related concepts to which we now turn.

An *industry* is the aggregation of units of production manufacturing and selling similar goods. This is a narrow definition. The *industrial sector* is, therefore, regarded as the *manufacturing sector* in a narrow sense. The broad definition of the industrial sector includes manufacturing plus its direct supporting sectors, especially mining, construction and public utilities (electricity, water and gas).[4] As pointed out earlier, traditionally coal mining was a direct supporting component and source of energy of the manufacturing sector. Electricity, however, is the modern source of energy of the sector. Many authors, therefore, consider mining as a separate sector and exclude it in the broad definition of the industrial sector (Kapunda and Akinkugbe 2005:149). This book does the same, especially in the case of economies like Botswana where the mining sector is dominantly diamond or non-coal. In fact, even the Botswana Government supports this approach. Botswana's ninth National Development Plan (NDP 9), for instance, defines industrial sector in Botswana as:

business or individuals engaged in the transformation of raw material inputs into semi-finished or finished products for domestic sale or for export, e.g. manufacturing, and construction (Republic of Botswana 2003:111).

Industrial development is regarded as economic development with reference to the industrial sector. Industrial development is an essential part of economic development.

In Africa and possibly elsewhere, *industrialisation* may simply be viewed as a process of intensifying and developing more industries over time. Sutcliffe (1971:16) views industrialisation as the process by which a non-industrialised country becomes an industrialised one. Although this definition is somewhat tautological, it raises important questions such as: 'How is industrialisation measured?' and 'When should a country be considered industrialized?'

Two main criteria are usually employed in gauging the degree of industrialisation of a country: the percentage contribution of the industrial sector to GDP, and the industrial percentage contribution to total employment or population. Measurement may include other criteria, such as the industrial contribution to total exports (Kapunda and Akinkugbe 2005:151).

Sutcliffe (1971:18), for instance, used some of these criteria in defining arbitrarily an industrialised country as a country where at least 25 per cent of GDP comes from the industrial sector, of which at least 60 per cent is in manufacturing, and at least 10 per cent of its population is employed in industry. Sutcliffe considered the broad definition of the industrial sector covering manufacturing, mining, public utilities and construction.

If the criterion of industrial contribution to GDP alone is applied to Botswana using the broad definition of industry, for instance, the country, using 2009 data, would be considered highly industrialised as its industrial contribution to GDP was about 50 per cent (double the minimum 25 per cent suggested by Sutcliffe). However, the manufacturing sub-sector contributed only about 8 per cent to industrial GDP (compared to 60 per cent level suggested by Sutcliffe). The rest of the contribution came from other sub-sectors, predominantly mining. Furthermore, only 4 per cent of the country's population was employed in the industrial sector (compared to Sutcliffe's 10 per cent). Thus Botswana is not an industrialised country when all Sutcliffe's criteria are considered.[5]

In fact if the criterion of industrial contribution alone is applied, Zambia would have been considered industrialised in the 1960s when the ratio was above 50 per cent (Sutcliffe 1971:21).

The *Structure-Conduct-Performance* concepts will be explained in the process of discussing the S-C-P relationship in the next chapter.

Scope and Methods of Industrial Economics

Although some studies like Andreosso and Jacobson (2005:1) and Church and Ware (2000:7) tend to regard industrial economics and industrial organisation as the same concept, slight differences in terms of use, location and coverage are worth noting. Firstly, 'industrial economics' is a term which has mainly been used in Europe, while Americans tend to use the term 'industrial organization'.

Secondly, according to Hay and Morris (1991) and Ferguson-Ferguson (1994), whereas industrial organisation underlines the structure of industries at a particular point of time, industrial economics includes also the dynamics of industrial structure. Industrial economics, therefore, examines the evolution of industry as a process in time at the macro level, the sector or industry level, and the firm level.

However, both industrial economics and industrial organisation use the S-C-P paradigm as a basic framework of analysis. Other alternative schools of thought include Harvard and Chicago school approaches and the 'new Austrian' school of economic thought.

The Harvard school of thought is closely comparable to the S-C-P approach adopted in this book as it dates back to the traditional S-C-P paradigm developed by Mason (1939) at Harvard University and later by Bain (1956). The approach, in general, underscores the importance of monopoly linked to certain market structures as a general issue in industrial economic analysis.[6]

The Chicago school essentially uses price theory which employs microeconomic models to explain market structure and the behaviour of firms.

The 'new Austrian' school generally opposes government intervention in industry but agrees that political support for a free market economy is important.[7]

There are also aspects of emphasis which may be generally regarded as approaches to industrial economics analysis; they include economic geography, game theory and contestable market theory. Although this book also employs some of these aspects such as economic geography (see Chapter 7 on industrial location), it supports Kay's (2002) position that the S-C-P approach remains dominant in industrial economics analysis.

Conclusion

This chapter has provided the historical note of industrial economics – indicating that it became a separate economic discipline in the 1950s. The chapter has also defined various concepts related to industrial economics or industrial organisation – whose scope and methods have been explained.

Review Questions

1. Explain the evolution of industrial economics indicating when the course became a separate economics discipline.

2. What would you consider to be a superior definition of industrial economics? Why?

3. How would you differentiate industrial economics from (i) micro-economics, (ii) industrial organisation?

4. (a) Differentiate between broad and narrow definitions of industry.

   (b) State the criteria which may be useful in gauging the degree of industrialisation.

5. Consider the following data for the Botswana economy for the year 2010:

Table 1.1: Botswana's GDP and Employment (2010)

Sector	GDP[a] (P[b] million)	Employment[c]
Agriculture	500	6 000
Mining	10 000	10 000
Manufacturing	1000	35 000
Public Utilities	700	3 000
Construction	1 300	25 000
Others	11500	221 000
Grand total	25,000	300,000

Notes:

a. Constant 1993/94 prices

b. P = Pula (US$1 = P7 in 2010)

c. Population for Botswana = 1.8 million in 2010

Use the data to decide whether Botswana was industrialised or not in 2010. State the criteria you use.

6. Consider the following data for Tanzania's economy in the year 2010 (Tables 1.2 and 1.3)

Table 1.2: Tanzania's GDP at Market Prices (2010)

Serial Number	Sector	GDP (sh million)
1	Agriculture	4,060,554
2	Mining	402,331
3	Manufacturing	1,639,050
4	Public Utilities (Electricity, gas and water)	430,689
5	Construction	1,182,581
6	Others	9,113,358
	GDP	16,828,563

Table 1.3: Human Resource (2010)

Human Resources	(2010)
Population	43,000,000
Labour force	23,000,000
Total Employment	20,000,000
Industrial Employment	330,000
Manufacturing employment	110,000

Source: United Republic of Tanzania – URT (2011), *The Economic Survey*, URT.

Use the data selectively and apply preferably Sutcliffe criteria to decide whether Tanzania was industrialised or not in 2010.

Notes

1. See also Clarke (2000:1).
2. For details see Andrews (1951,1952), and Barthwal (1985).
3. Andreasso and Jacobson (2005:1) also consider industrial economics and industrial organisation as the same subject. Whereas the former is common in Europe and Africa, the latter is common in the USA.
4. See also Clarke (2000:7); Kapunda and Mbogoro (1989:147) and Sutcliffe (1971:16).
5. Source: Botswana Central Statistical Office data.
6. For details see Clarke (2007:5).
7. For details see, for instance, Littlechild (1978).

2

Framework for Analysing Industrial Economics

Learning Objectives

The main objectives of this chapter are:

- To provide the simple / basic one-way causation framework analysis of industrial economics;
- To describe how the basic framework can be modified closely to reality; and
- To explain the criticism of the S-C-P framework of industrial economics.

Introduction to the Basic Structure-Conduct-Performance Paradigm

As noted in Chapter One, the traditional methodological approach in industrial economics or industrial organisation is the Structure-Conduct-Performance relationship or the S-C-P paradigm. This has been the centre of analytical framework of the discipline since the 1950s. The paradigm underscores theoretically and empirically the links between market structure and business conduct in determining performance.

The Essence of the Basic Structure-Conduct-Performance Paradigm

The fundamental S-C-P paradigm underlines a one-way relationship showing a causal link running from market structure through conduct to performance.

The outline of the S-C-P paradigm is shown in Figure 2.1.

Figure 2.1: The Basic S-C-P Paradigm
Source: Adopted from Clarke (2000:3)

The basis of the paradigm is a set of basic conditions: costs, demand and technology. These are important in determining the paradigm which runs from market structure to performance via conduct.

According to the simple form of the S-C-P paradigm, *market structure* (such as oligopoly) determines market conduct or behaviour (such as collusion) which in turn determines performance (such as profitability). More specifically, a number of factors such as the number and sizes of buyer and seller, degree of product differentiation and barriers to entry form the elements of market structure. Market structure determines *conduct* which forms, broadly speaking, the policies and strategies of firm such as pricing behaviour, investment, research and development (R & D), advertisement and various types of strategic alliances with other firms.[1] Pricing, for instance, is determined by the collusive behaviour induced by high market concentration. Advertisement may be linked to market structure if, for instance, moderate concentration leads to increases in mutual offsetting advertisement expenditure.[2]

Finally, *performance* in given industries is generally determined by conduct. The element or indicators of performance such as profitability, efficiency, technical progress and growth may be used to explain the links. Profitability, for instance, depends on advertisement, R & D, pricing and other business strategies included as elements of performance. The business strategies form the basis of competitive practices and are guided by business goals.

As noted earlier, this analytical framework was popularised by Bain (1958). However, the roots may be traced back in the works of Mason (1939, 1949) and Clark (1940).

The advantage of the approach was that this simple S-C-P paradigm enabled analysis to deduce easily policies either empirically or theoretically.

With time, however, the one-way S-C-P approach was criticised and has led to the more recent approach or the 'new industrial economics or organisation' which focuses on development and testing explanations of firm conduct (Church & Ware 2000:10).

Criticism of the One-way S-C-P Paradigm

The simple one-way causations running from structure through conduct to performance has been criticised over time from several angles.

As Clarke (2000: 4) underscores, the paradigm is too simplified as there are cases where reverse or two-way causations may operate. For example, technical developments induced by R & D activity determine the cost and demand conditions and may affect market structure in the long run. More immediately, successful advertising campaigns affect market shares and hence concentration, so that not only may concentration affect advertising intensity in industry, but a reverse effect may also apply.[3]

Other examples are in order. Although conduct strategies such as advertisement and R & D determine profit, profit may also determine the strategies. Higher profits enable further advertisement and more expenditure on R & D. These again lead to more profits. Two-way or double causation is thus possible.

Using the financial/commercial banking which promotes the industrial sector in Botswana through provision of loans and other related services, a study by Kapunda and Molosiwa (2012) revealed empirically that there were two-way causations between profitability (performance) and market concentration (market structure). For details see Appendix 2.1.

In modern industrial economics or organisation, however, the S-C-P model is modified to underscore supply and demand basic conditions; indicate the possibility of two-way causations; and show the interaction with government policies or intervention4 (see also Appendix 2.2). Government regulations, for instance, may affect the number of sellers in an industry and firms may influence government policy to achieve higher profits.[5]

Despite the modification of the S-C-P paradigm, the Chicago school criticises it for having diverged too far from the basic neoclassical price theory.[6]

As noted in Chapter One, the Austrian economists generally oppose government intervention and hence view skeptically the modified S-C-P paradigm.

With the advent of more research, empirical work and knowledge, a new approach has been developed, leading to new industrial economics or organisation with the following salient features:

- Development and test on explanations of firm conduct.
- Emphasis on specific industries.[7]

This book also considers to some extent these development aspects.

Conclusion

This chapter has underscored the development of the basic-conduct-performance paradigm from its basic one-way relationship to two-way causation or reverse relationships. Critical arguments have also been advanced.

Review Questions

1. Explain the simple S-C-P paradigm.
2. Outline the main criticism of the S-C-P paradigm.
3. 'A reverse or two-way causation may occur in S-C-P paradigm'. Explain this proposition with support of three examples.
4. Explain the S-C-P modified model with reference to your country.
5. Using the S-C-P approach a researcher estimated the following two models:

$\pi = 0.41 + 2.02\ AD.................................(1)$

t   (0.14)   (3.96)

$R^2 = 0.95$ n = 31

$AD = 2.48 + 0.25\ \pi ....(2)$

t   (2.58)   (3.57)

$R^2 = 0.90$ n = 31

where:

   π = profit

AD = advertisement expenditure

   (a) Explain the two-way causations between performance and conduct.

   (b) Interpret the parameters 2.02 and 0.25.

   (c) Evaluate any of the models using both economic and statistical criteria.

6   Explain the double or two-way causations implied from the following two
    equations and interpret all the coefficients including the coefficient of
    determination.

$\ln PR = -4.0 + 2.1\ln CR4$; $R^2 = 0.69$ (1)

SE   3.0)(0.5)   n = 15

$\ln CR_4 = 2.5 + 0.3\ln PR$; $R^2 = 0.61$ (2)

SE   (0.9)(0.1)n= 15

where

PR = profit

CR_4 = four-

firm market concentration

Appendix 2.1: Banking Sector in Botswana: An Empirical Illustration of Two-way Causation in the S-C-P model

Using the financial/commercial banking sector which promotes the industrial
sector in Botswana through provision of loans and other related services, a study
by Kapunda and Molosiwa (2012) showed empirically that there were two-way
causations between profitability (performance) and market concentration (market
structure). Formally, in general

   PR = f(CR) and CR = f(PR)

   where:

   PR = Net interest profit margin

CR = 3-firm concentration ratio: the three major firms (banks) being Barclays Bank, First National Bank and Standard Chartered Bank. More specifically:

$\ln PR = -0.41 + 2.02\ln CR + 6.71\ln LR - 0.23\ln KA_{t-1} + 0.03\ln GR_{t-1} - 3.22\ln BSS_{t-1}$.-

SE   (2.99) (0.51) (0.71) (0.05)   (0.01)   (0.36) $0.59\ln Rt-1$ (0.04)

$R^2 = 0.99$

DW = 2.53

n = 15(1992 – 2006)

The additional supporting variables are defined as follows:

LR = lending rate

KA = capital adequacy

GR = the average annual growth rate

BSS = bank size and share

R = reserves

(NB: Numbers in brackets are standard errors).

In this case concentration is positively and significantly related to profit as expected from economic theory. If concentration increases by one per cent, net interest profit margin increases by about two per cent.

On the other hand, if profit increases by one per cent, concentration increases by 0.25 per cent as shown in the equation below. Profit could have increased due to mergers and take-overs over time.

$\ln CR = 2.48 + 0.25\ln PR + 0.77\ln LR + 0.08\ln KA_{t-1} + 0.30\ln BSS + 1.67\ln R_{t-1}$

SE   (0.96) (0.07)   (0.28)   (0.02)   (0.12)   (0.05)

$R^2 = 0.90$.

DW = 2.04

n = 15

For details, see Kapunda and Molosiwa (2012).

Appendix 2.2: The Modified S-C-P Paradigm

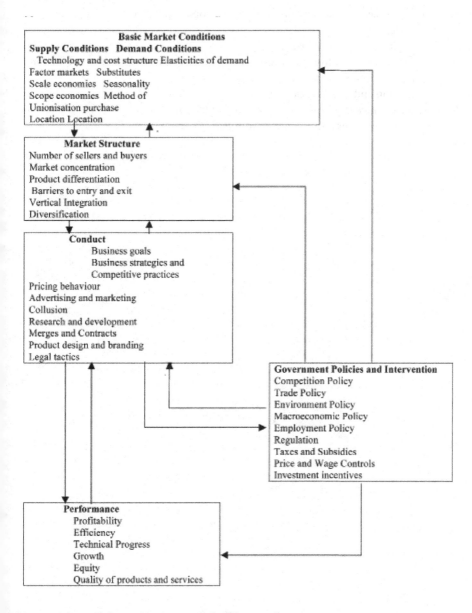

Source: Adopted from Carton & Perloff (2005:4)

Notes

1. For details see, for instance, Andreasso and Jacobson (2005:13).
2. See Clarke (2000:3).
3. For detail see Clarke (2000:4)
4. See, for instance, Carlton and Perloff (2005), Lipczynski *et al.* (2009) and Waldman and Jensen (2007).
5. See, Carlton and Perloff (2005:3).
6. See, for instance, Andreasso and Jacobson (2005:15).
7. For detail see, for example, Church and Ware (2000:10).

3

Theories of the Firm and Internal Organisation

Learning Objectives

The main objectives of this chapter are:

- To review the traditional neoclassical theory of the firm with a specific focus on profit maximisation;
- To examine the development of neoclassical theory; and
- To consider and outline modern theories of the firm.

Introduction

Theories of the firm and internal organisation have evolved from the traditional neo-classical theory of the firm to the modern theory of the firm which emphasises business conduct behaviour that includes pricing and non-price strategies with reference to profit maximization or new industrial economic organisation

Traditional Neoclassical Theory of the Firm

Despite the debate on the origin of the theory of the firm, many scholars trace it back to the 1930s mainly through the works of Chamberlin (1933) and Robinson (1933). It represented a sharp change of focus from the 'theory of value' which dominated Orthodox economics (Devine *et al.* 1985:71). However, some aspects of the theory may even be traced back to Marshall (1892) or even Smith (1776).[1]

The 'theory of the firm' was created in the 1930s. It represented a sharp change of focus from the 'theory of value' which dominated orthodox economics (Devine *et al.* 1985:71).

The traditional neoclassical theory of the firm assumes a purely profit maximising automaton or '*black box*', operating in a spaceless and timeless environment. The owner is also the manager of the firm whose primary goal is to maximise profit (minimise costs). In the traditional neoclassical paradigm, profit maximisation (cost minimisation) is performed in the light of perfectly known cost and demand conditions.[2] Imperfect information, uncertainty and time are irrelevant.[3]

Profit (π) is defined as the difference between total revenue (TR) and total cost (TC), i.e. $\pi = TR - TC$. The firm will increase output if the revenue obtained from the last unit produced (marginal revenue) is greater than the cost of producing the last unit (marginal cost). Profit is maximised when the last unit no longer adds to profit, i.e. marginal revenue (MR) is equal to marginal cost (MC).

Formally, $\dfrac{\Delta\pi}{\Delta Q} = \dfrac{\Delta TR}{\Delta Q} - \dfrac{\Delta TC}{\Delta P} = 0$

where $\dfrac{\pi\Delta}{\Delta Q}$ = change in profit resulting from a unit change in output

$\dfrac{\Delta TR}{\Delta Q}$ = marginal revenue (MR)

$\dfrac{\Delta TC}{\Delta P}$ = marginal cost (MC)

Thus profit is maximised when $MR - MC = 0$ or $MR = MC$.

Historically, five main assumptions form the basis of the traditional view that the firm maximises profit (minimises cost).

1. There exists something unambiguous and potentially measurable called profit which can be maximised.
2. A firm acts as an individual decision-taking unit, behaving in the same way an individual entrepreneur does ('*black box assumption*').
3. The utility of the firm is influenced only by profit.
4. The decision-taker is rational and aims at maximising utility.
5. There exists complete and certain information.[4]

Two main reasons are normally given to justify the profit-maximising assumption of the firm: *subjective motive* and *objective motive*.

In the case of the subjective motive, the owner-manager is regarded as an 'economic person' who takes risks, makes decisions and receives rewards. The interest of the owner-manager is solely to maximise profit.

In the assumed competitive markets, profit maximisation is a *survival condition*. Profit maximisation is, therefore, an objective motive.

Other supporting justification include simplicity (based on the already stated assumptions), *precision* and *convenience* – which give room for application of profit maximisation models and various mathematical techniques.

It should be emphasised that according to the traditional neo-classical theory, the firm is a simple atomistic or idealised form of business described by a simple and static production function which shows the relationship between inputs and outputs.[5]

Development of Neoclassical Theory

Overview

Over time, the firm was viewed as a more complex organisation where management and ownership may be different. Both may not focus on pure profit maximisation. Furthermore, the size of the firm may increase over time. Time and uncertainly were no longer ignored. Other related developments focus on the *managerial theory and the principal-agent theory*. The two types of theories are elaborated hereunder.

Managerial Theory

The *managerial theory* emphasises that modern firms are *organisationally complex* since they no longer assume certainty and timelessness. The complex structure and size of organisations form the basis of an objection to regarding the modern entities as profit-maximising. Furthermore, multi-plant operations and the resultant multiple divisions such as research and development, production, marketing, accounting and finance departments enhance bureaucracy which make decisions consistent with the profit-maximisation assumption more difficult to enforce. Managers with an accounting background, for instance, may lean towards cost- constraining decisions, while those from an engineering, production or scientific background may prefer process- or product-improving decisions.[6]

Corporate and complex organisations need good corporate governance. Corporate governance is increasingly becoming important in Africa. In Botswana, for instance, Corporate governance increased its importance since its 'codification' by the Botswana Institute of Directors in 2017.[7]

Codes of corporate governance are a set of 'best practice' recommendations with regard to the behaviour and structure of the board of directors of a firm.[8]

Furthermore, the separability hypothesis which maintains that there is separation between ownership and control gives room for non-profit maximisation objectives. Unlike owners (shareholders) salaried managers who control firm operations may hold no or few shares. They may, therefore, give priority to other objectives apart from profit maximisation. Managers may seek prestige, for instance, by adhering to the following managerial objectives: (i) the need for large sizes of firms (ii) growth of firms (iii) maximum sales or revenue but high costs (iv) large employment and (v) 'high status' companies with prestigious offices, expensive cars and other prestigious items. These are mostly conflicting objectives to profit-maximisation especially in the short-run. These objectives have been elaborated elsewhere. Baumal (1967), for instance, elaborated that hired managers may be more interested in sales or revenue maximisation than in profit maximisation for the following reasons:[9]

- An executive would typically like to assess his/her firm's performance by sales rather than by profitability.
- The financial market and retail distributors are more responsive to a firm.
- If sales fail to rise, this is often associated with decrease in market share and market power, and consequently, with increased vulnerability to the action of competitors.[10]

According to Marris (1963, 1966) managers may also be interested in growth of firms. These works led to the widely cited hypothesis: 'Managerial Control would lead to growth maximisation rather than profit maximisation'. The latter is the common objective of owners of firms or shareholders.

In spite of the conflicting objectives, the theory of the firm assumes that the firm tries to maximise its *value*. Since the firm's value can be defined in a variety of ways such as wealth, book value, liquidation value, among others, to avoid confusion, in managerial economics, the *value of a firm* is usually regarded as the present value of its expected future net cash flows. If net cash flows are assumed to be equal to profits for simplicity, the value of the firm today or its *present* value may formally be expressed as follows:

Value of the firm (V) = present value of expected future profits.

Using symbols:

$$V = \frac{\pi_1}{(1+r)^1} + \frac{\pi_2}{(1+r)^2} + \frac{\pi_n}{(1+r)^n} \qquad (3.1)$$

where π = profit

r = appropriate interest, or

discount rate. Equation (3.1) may be expressed as:

where Σ = summation

t = time horizon (n being the highest value of t).

$$V = \sum_{t=1}^{n} \frac{\pi_t}{(1+r)^t} \qquad (3.2)$$

Since profit is equal to total revenue (TR) minus total cost (TC), equation (3.2) may be expressed as follows:

Because time, uncertainty and risk may be incorporated in the model, the

$$V = \sum_{t=1}^{n} \frac{TR_t - TC_t}{(1+r)^t} \qquad (3.3)$$

adjusted discount rate, ra, may be used instead of r:

ra = rf + rp   (3.4).

where: ra = risk adjusted discount rate

rf = r = risk – free discount rate

rp = risk premium

Despite the earlier explained conflicts of objectives of owners and managers especially in the short run, profit maximisation remains the guiding objective of the firm. This is the key to management *optimal decision.* Management and workers are expected to be involved in profit maximisation, especially in the long run. The marketing manager is responsible for maximisation of sales or total revenue (TR); the production manager is expected to contribute positively to the minimisation of product development costs (TC); the financial manager is responsible for acquiring capital at appropriate discount rate; and workers are expected to work hard towards profit maximisation.[10]

In general, maximisation of profit is determined by conduct's firm pricing and non-pricing, given total revenue (TR) is equal to the product of price (P) and quantity demanded (Q):

TR = PQ   (3.5)

Principal-Agent Theory

The *Principal-agent theory* may be stated in a very simplified manner as follows: It is a theory that examines situations in which there are two main actors: a principal who is usually the owner of an asset or firm, and the agent who makes decisions which affect the value of that asset or firm, on behalf of the principal. The manager is usually the agent, but the principal could also be the manager.[11] Unlike the managerial theory, the principal-agent theory emphasises contracts relevant to profit maximisation, and hence firm's value maximisation. The contract may include, for instance, a defined salary based on the manager's marginal product plus a bonus based on performance. In general, the theory focuses on contractual aspects and sometimes uses *game-theory methods.*[12]

Modern Theories of the Firm

Overview

The modern theories of the firm attempt to incorporate some aspects of neoclassical theory of the firm, technology, and the 'new economy' or 'new industrial organisation'. These theories are subsequently elaborated.

Recent Theory Development: Neoclassical Theory, Technology and the 'New Economy'

One of the recent developments of theories of the firm is based on the incorporation of aspects of neoclassical theory of the firm, technology, and the 'new economy' based on the success of micro- and macro-economics during the 1990s and early 2000s. The theoretical analysis is essentially centred on growth models and neoclassical theory-based Walrus's model, which examines the economy as a myriad of exchange activities on different markets for goods, services, factors of production, as well as money and credit. Technology is subsumed into several types of capital such as machines, instruments and tools. Equilibrium analysis is done through several systems of equations.[13] However, this approach does not explain well the technological change or innovation.[14]

New Industrial Organisation

Another recent theory of the firm hinges squarely on '*new industrial organisation*' or '*new industrial economics*'. The focus here is the theory of business strategy based on the conduct of firms in imperfectly competitive markets. This modern theory of the firm emphasises business conduct behaviour that includes pricing and non-pricing strategies with reference to profit maximisation. The emphasis is on the C in the traditional S-C-P model which had been questioned since the late 1970s due to lack of consensus empirical support, irregularity and double causations.

The salient features of the 'new industrial organisation' are as follows:

- Focus on developing models of firm behaviour.
- Empirical work based on well-founded models of firm behaviour.
- Emphasis on specific industries.

Development of good theoretical explanation of firm behaviour such as the non-cooperative game theory in the 1970s and optimal choices or decisions played an important role in shaping the theory.[15]

Conclusion

This chapter has examined retrospectively the traditional neoclassical theory of the firm and the subsequent theories including the one emphasising 'new industrial organisation' or 'new industrial economics' which underline strategic business behaviour. In summary, the major theories may be summarised as done in Table 3.1

Table 3.1: Major Theories of the Firm

Theory of the firm	Emphasis
Neoclassical	Black box
Managerial	Owners vs. managers
Principal-agent	Contract (employer vs. employee)
Modern	New industrial economics organisation

Review questions

1. Explain the salient features of the traditional neoclassical theory of the firm.
2. Outline briefly the evolution of the theory of the firm.
3.   (a) What is meant by present value of the firm?

   (b) Suggest how managers and workers can positively influence the present value of the firm.

   (c) Under what conditions might salaried managers not want to maximise profit or value of the firm?
4. Compare and contrast managerial theory and the principal-agent theory of the firm.
5. What is meant by the 'new industrial organisation'?

Notes

1. For details see, for instance, Lipczynski *et al.* (2009:54).
2. Cf. Basic conditions in the S-C-P paradigm.
3. See, Andreasso and Jacobson (2005:46).
4. For details see, for example, Hay and Morris (1991:292).
5. See, Andreasso and Jacobson (2005:44).
6. For more examples, see for instance, Andreosso and Jacobson (2005: 50), and Baumol (1967).
7. For details, see Rhodhers and Edmond (2013).
8. See Millstein and Cadbury (2005).
9. See, especially, Andreasso and Jacobson (2005:53).
10. For details see, for instance, Hirschey (2009:7) and Manfield et al (2002: 11).
11. See, Andreasso and Jacobson (2005:58).
12. For details see, for instance, Andreosso and Jacobson section 3.3.2. For examples of game- theory methods, see section 5.5.3.6.
13. For details see, for instance, Andreosso and Jacobson (2005: 60).
14. For details, see especially, O' Sullivan (2000).
15. For details see, for example, Church and Ware (2000: 10).

4

Market Structure

Learning Objectives

The main objectives of this chapter are:
- To clarify the meaning of market structure and related concepts;
- To compare and contrast the various types of markets;
- To explain and illustrate measurements of market concentration; and
- To provide examples relevant to market concentration from Africa.

Aspects of Market Structure and Competition

Introduction: Conceptual Framework

It should be underscored that despite the possibility of double causation, firm or business strategies and behaviour under conduct (C) essentially depend upon the market structure (S) under consideration as implied in the simple S-C-P paradigm. The structure of the market essentially affects the process by which price and output are determined. In this book we define a *market* as, 'a nexus of interaction among actual and potential buyers and sellers of a particular product'[1].

Mutasa (2011) views a market as an interpersonal institution which brings together buyers and sellers of commodities or services.

Markets can be perfect or imperfect. The perfect market structure is composed of perfect competition, while the imperfect market structure is made up of monopoly, oligopoly and monopolistic competition (Mutasa 2011:90).

Market structure in the S-C-P paradigm was defined by Bain (1958) as, 'The characteristics of the organization of a market that seem to exercise an influence on the nature of competition and pricing within the market' (Andreosso & Jacobson 2005:90).

Koch (1980), however, views market structure as: 'the relatively permanent strategic elements of the environment of a firm that influence, and are influenced by, the conduct and performance of the firm in the market in which it operates' (Koch 1980:90).

Whereas Bain's definition implies only one-way causality, that of Koch underlines double-causation.

Boyes (2012) defines briefly markets structure as: 'a selling environment in which a firm produces and sells its product'.

In this book we define market structure as:

> the way markets are organised in a competitive environment involving the interactions of individuals, firms and other organisations and influencing or being influenced mainly by the conduct and performance of the firm.[2]

Market Structure and Degree of Competition

Market structure is examined mainly by viewing four industry characteristics: the number and size distribution of sellers (and buyers); degree of product differentiation and substitutability; conditions of entry and exit; and nature of information dissemination related to price and quality of goods and services. Four main forms or types of market are normally examined in economics: *perfect (pure) competition, monopolistic competition, oligopoly,* and *monopoly*. These are normally covered in details in standard micro-economic textbooks. However, a brief review is in order:

Perfect competition and *monopoly* are two extreme types of market. For pedagogical reason they are examined first.

Perfect competition is a type of market where individual firms have no absolute power to influence market price: they are price *takers*. This can be deduced from the following characteristics of perfect competition: (1) there are very many sellers and buyers; (2) the product is homogeneous or equivalently identical or (perfectly) standardised; (3) there is no meaningful barrier to entry or exit; (4) sellers and buyers have free access to market information, i.e. there is perfect information dissemination; and there is perfect mobility of resources, no transaction costs and no externalities.

The other extreme type of market is monopoly.

Monopoly is a type of market where there is a single firm or seller of a unique product which has no close substitute. Entry into the industry is very difficult (blockaded) due to very high barrier. Furthermore, there is very imperfect dissemination of information. All these characteristics support the proposition that the single firm has very great ability to set prices, and is referred to as a *price setter or price* maker.

Between these extreme types of markets are monopolistic competition and oligopoly, to which we now turn.

Monopolistic competition refers to the market where there are many sellers of heterogeneous or equivalently differentiated product. Other basic characteristics include relatively low barrier to entry and imperfect information dissemination.

Oligopoly is the type of market where there are few sellers of homogeneous or differentiated product. Other basic salient characteristics include high barrier to entry and relative imperfect information dissemination.

For illustration see Table 4.1.

Table 4.1: Characteristics of the Main Types of Market

Characteristics	Perfect Competition	Monopolistic Competition	Oligopoly	Monopoly
No. of Sellers/producers	very many	many	few	one
Type of product/substitutes	homogeneous (identical, standardised)/ identical substitutes	heterogeneous (differentiated)/ very similar substitutes	homogeneous (standardised or differentiated)/ close substitutes	unique/ no close substitutes
Barriers to entry	practically none	low	high	very high
Information dissemination	perfect	imperfect	imperfect	very imperfect

Source: Compiled by the author.

It should be noted that while definitions and characteristics of types of market have been presented essentially with reference to sellers/producers, analogous types of market can be defined in terms of buyers as follows:

Monopsony refers to the type of market where there is a single buyer of product or input and there are no close substitutes.

Oligopsony is the type of market involving few buyers. *Monopsonistic competition* refers to the case involving many buyers. Sometimes examples may be drawn from a labour market dominated by one or few large employers (buyer) to illustrate monopsony and oligopsony respectively; government as the only buyer of defence electronics may be regarded as an example of monopsony.

This book, however, focuses on the four types of market elaborated earlier with reference to firms (producers) or sellers: the main concern of industrial economics.

Other deduced characteristics like power of firm over price (market power), pricing and non-price competition strategies may be deduced from the four main characteristics indicated in the table. This is elaborated in the subsequent two chapters.

Market Concentration

Concepts and Definitions

As noted in the previous sub-section, one key element or characteristic of market structure is the number of sellers (and buyers). This is closely related to the degree of seller (buyer) concentration or market concentration.

More often than not, market concentration focuses on sellers and hence many authors[3] tend to use the term market concentration and seller concentration interchangeably. In this regard, *market concentration or seller concentration* may be defined as the degree to which production for a particular market or industry is concentrated in the hands of a few large firms.[4]

In some cases, the term buyer concentration may be viewed as the degree to which a product or market is concentrated in the hands of a few large buyers. Both types of market concentration measure the intensity of competition or market power.

Measures of Market Concentration

There are several measures of market concentration or market structure[5]. The simplest of all is the reciprocal of firm numbers. Other common ones are the concentration ratio, Hirschman-Herfindahl index, Hannah and Kay index, Gini-coefficient, entropy index, and the Lerner index. The basic ones are explained hereunder.

Reciprocal of firm Numbers

The reciprocal of firm numbers is expressed as:

$$C = 1/n \qquad (4.1)$$

where C = concentration index

n = number of firms

Clearly the concentration index is 1 for monopoly (n = 1) and 0 in the case of perfect competition when sellers are assumed to be infinitively many (n = ∞). Thus the index lies between 0 and 1 inclusively. The index, however, is too simple to take into account the production (output) share for each firm. However, it remains a good theoretical measure of concentration especially when dealing with symmetrical models which assume equal-size firms.

Concentration Ratio

This is the *r-firm concentration ratio or index* which consider the sum of the output or sales shares for the largest r firms. Formally:

$$C_r = \sum_{i=1}^{r} \frac{x_i}{x} \qquad\qquad 42$$

Where Cr = r-concentration ratio

x_i = output or sales from firm i

x = total industry output or sales

Equating the shares x_i with si, equation 4.2 may be expressed as:

$$C_r = \sum_{i=1}^{r} s_i \qquad (4.3)$$

If the shares in a textile industry, for example, are 0.28, 0.12, 0.11 and 0.09, the four-firm concentration ratio (C_4) is 0.6 or 60 per cent. This means that 60 per cent of the textile industry output or sales comes from the four largest firms. The reader may wish to find and interpret C_1 and C2.

The r-firm concentration index is most popular among researchers as it takes care of the production or sales shares (unlike the 1/n index), easy to understand intuitively, not involving too much data and its calculation is not complicated.

Although many researchers prefer to use r* = 4, the main critique is centred on the arbitrary selection of r* or any other r. Furthermore, the concentration ratio may not reveal the extent to which one or more firms within the first four dominate a particular industry.

If the output shares of the 24 firms in two industries X and Y are given, for instance, as shown in Table 4.2, the four-firm concentration ratio for industry X is 0.70 + 0.05 + 0.03 + 0.02 = 0.80. Similarly, C_4 = 0.80 for industry Y. Both have equal concentration! However, C_1 = 0.70 for industry X and only 0.22 for industry Y. Industry X, therefore, dominates the market. One could argue similarly using C_2, and C_3. Ideally, nevertheless, the concentration index should be one figure. The subsequent index tries to solve the problem.

Table 4.2: Output Shares of 24 Firms in Two Industries

Industry	Firm 1	Firm 2	Firm 3	Firm 4	Firm 5	Firm 6 ... Firm 24
X Y	0.70	0.05	0.03	0.02	0.01	0.01 ... 0.01
	0.22	0.21	0.20	0.17	0.01	0.01 ... 0.01

Hirschman-Herfindahl Index (H)

This is the second most widely used concentration index. It is actually the square of the n-firm concentration ratio explained above. Formally:

$$H = \sum_{i=1}^{n} (x_i/x)^2 \qquad (4.4)$$

equivalently:

$$H = \sum_{i=1}^{r*} s_i^2 \qquad (4.5)$$

The notations are essentially the same, but r = n.i.e. all firms are considered in the computation.

It should be underlined that the H index combines information about the size of all firms in a market and takes into account the dispersion. It varies inclusively between 0 and 1. If the index is 0 it points to the existence of a large number of equal-sized firms in the given industry.[6] If H=1 the market is dominated by one large firm. In short, the higher the H, the higher the concentration or dispersion and the largest firms contribute significantly to the high magnitude of H. From Table 4.2 information:

$$H = \sum_{i=1}^{24} s_i^2 \qquad\qquad (4.6)$$

For industry X,
    H = 0.4900 + 0.0025 + 0.0009 + 0.0004 + 0.0001 + ... + 0.0001 = 0.4958
For industry Y,
    H = 0.0484 + 0.0441 + 0.0400 + 0.0289 + 0.0001 + ... + 0.0001 = 0.1634
Sometimes the H index is expressed as

$$H = \sum_{i=1}^{r}(100s_i)^2 = 10,000 \sum_{i=1}^{n} s_i^2 \qquad (4.7)$$

The reader may wish to express the calculated

H-indices using equation (4.7).

Employing the H index, it is deduced that industry X has higher concentration than industry Y as may be expected from the mere observation of the output share distribution in Table 4.2.

The H index is also important in analysing some oligopolistic pricing models and incorporates the market share inequality as shown in Appendix 4.1.

The previous two explained indices are the most popular. In special cases, the Hannah and Kay's indices, Gini co-efficient, entropy index, and Lerner index may be viewed as indices of concentration. For concept clarity, see Appendix 4.2.

Market Concentration: Theory and Empirical Evidence

There are various hypotheses on market concentration. Weiss (1963), for instance, hypothesised that market concentration is related positively to economies of scale. Formally:

$$C_4 = f(E) \qquad\qquad (4.8)$$

where C_4 = proportionate change in the four-firm concentration ratio.

E = economies of scale (the proportionate change of the ratio of plant minimum efficient scale – MES).

empirically:

$C_4 = 70.2 + 0.3E; R^2 = 0.30$ 4.9)

(3.1)

(*t* ratio in parenthesis)

Thus the variables are positively correlated at 1 per cent level of significance, with co-efficient of determination equal to 30 per cent.

Market concentration may also influence other variables such as costs and profitability. An example is in order:

$\pi = f(C_4, A, W)$ (4.10)

where π = profit margin

C_4 = four-firm market concentration ratio

A = advertisement

W = wages

Specifically;

$\pi = 16.0 + 0.1C_4 + 1.2A - 0.2W; R^2 = 0.75$ (4.11)

t (2.1) (3.5) (2.5) (3.2)

The specified model shows a positive influence of market concentration on profit margin. If market concentration increases by 1 unit, profit will increase by 0.1[7].

Market Structure and Concentration in Africa

Market Structure

Hitherto, we have learnt theoretically about market structure and the types of market. Let us now consider examples from Africa.

As noted in sub-section 4.2.2 perfect competition involves very many sellers and buyers and homogeneous products. Examples in real-world markets are essentially only approximations of perfect competition. In Africa, and possibly elsewhere, they include agricultural markets and non-specialised input markets (unskilled labour). Nevertheless, perfect competition is rare in manufacturing and mineral extractions.

Monopoly involves one seller and unique product. Examples at national level involve public utility companies such as the Botswana Power Corporation (BPC) and Water Utilities Corporation (WUC), also in Botswana. For details and more examples, see Table 4.3.

Table 4.3: Selected Public Utility Companies in Africa

Country	Public Utility Company	Abbreviation
Botswana	Botswana Power Corporation	BPC
	Water Utilities Corporation	WUC
Malawi	Electricity Supply Commission of Malawi	ESCOM
Rwanda Sierra	Rwanda Electricity Corporation	RECO
Leone	National Power Authority	NPA
	Guma Valley Water Company	GVWC
South Africa	Electricity Supply Commission (South	ESKOM
Tanzania	Africa) Tanzania Electricity Service Company	TANESCO
Uganda	Electricity Regulation Authority	ERA
Zambia	Zambia Electricity Supply Corporation	ZESCO
Zimbabwe	Zimbabwe Electricity Supply Authority	ZESA

Source: Compiled by the author from various sources including M.R. Bhagavan (ed.) 1999.

Oligopoly involves few sellers. Many African countries have few firms in the textile industry and cement industry. Typical examples include Tanzania and Botswana. In some countries, oligopoly cartels may be found. The cement industry in South Africa, for example, is dominated by three producers, i.e. Portland Cement, Anglo-Alpha and Blue Circle. These firms form a cartel.[8]

Monopolistic competition involves many sellers with heterogeneous products. Examples in many countries in Africa include the many firms of the food industry.

Market Concentration

Regarding market concentration, a few examples from Africa are in order. Kapunda and Molosiwa (2012) found a positive significant relationship between concentration and profitability in the banking sector. For details, see Appendix 2.1 Agu (1992), however, found no significant relationship between concentration and profitability in Nigeria.

Market concentration indices in Botswana measured by three-firm concentration ratios (C_3) decreased from 0.77 in 1995 to 0.70 in 2000 in the chemical and chemical product industry. The average C_3 in the manufacturing sector, however, increased from 0.33 in 1995 to 0.50 in 2000 – an indication of decrease in competition (BIDPA 2002). For detail, see Table 4.4.

Table 4.4: Market Concentration in Selected Sectors in Botswana

CR$_3$			
Sector	1995	1997	2000
Chemical and Chemical Products	0.77	0.72	0.70
Manufacturing	0.33	0.44	0.50
Construction	0.59	0.38	0.40

Source: BIDPA (2002)

In Ghana, for example, industries with concentration ratio 1.00 included tobacco, petroleum, iron and steel, non-ferrous metals and professional and scientific goods in 1974 for concentration ratio C_2 and C_4, implying that these industries were not competitive but had highest degree of monopoly. One hundred per cent of total sales came from the two and four largest firms in those industries. The average for all manufacturing was 0.68 and 0.79 for C_2 and C_4 respectively. For details, see Table 4.5.

The reader is encouraged to deduce which industries are proxies or real examples of monopoly, oligopoly and monopolistic competition.

Table 4.5: Concentration Ratios for Ghanaian Manufacturing Sector

Industry	C_2	C_4
Food	0.48	0.71
Beverages	0.44	0.62
Tobacco	1.00	1.00
Textiles	0.45	0.75
Clothing	0.60	0.71
Leather	0.44	0.65
Footwear	0.55	0.01
Wood	0.21	0.38
Furniture	0.43	0.62
Paper	0.88	0.94
Printing and Publishing	0.65	0.80
Chemicals	0.65	0.83
Other Chemicals	0.69	0.82
Petroleum	1.00	1.00
Rubber	0.79	1.00
Plastics	0.68	0.75
Non-metallic mineral products	0.69	0.91
Iron and Steel	1.00	1.00
Non-ferrous metals	0.27	0.55
Metal products	1.00	1.00

Non-electrical	1.00	01.00
Electrical machinery	0.79	0.94
Transport	0.80	0.94
Professional and Scientific goods	1.00	1.00
Miscellaneous	0.58	0.87
All manufacturing	0.68	079

Source: Calculated using data provided by the Ghana Central Bureau of Statistics. For details, see Baah-Nuakoh 1997: 159.

Conclusion

This chapter has made the foundation of the strategic firm behaviour by examining important aspects of market structure and concentration. Despite the existence of some double causation cases between market structure (S) and business conduct (C) in the S-C-P paradigm, it remains cardinal in explaining the pricing and non-pricing strategies.

Review Questions

1. (a) What do you regard as a good definition of market structure? Explain briefly.
    (b) Describe the characteristics of the main types of market structure.
2. (a) Explain briefly the advantages and limitations of the following concentration indices
    (i) Reciprocal of firm numbers;
    (ii) The r-firm concentration index;
    (iii) The Hirschman-Herfindahl index.
    (b) Which index is the (i) simplest (ii) most popular? Explain briefly.
3. a) Use Table 4.2 to find and interpret (i) C_1 (ii) C_3 (iii) C_{23} and C_{24}. (b) Why may the H index be considered superior to the r-firm index?
4. Show that:
    $0 \leq H \leq 1$.
5. Suppose an industry consists of three firms. Two firms have sales of $10,000 each, and one firm has sales of $80,000.
    (a) What is the two-firm concentration ratio? Interpret your answer.
    (b) What is the three-firm concentration ratio? Interpret your answer.
    (c) What is the H-index? Comment on your answer.
6. (a) Comment on the effect of all explanatory variable in equation 4.11
    (b) The cost function was estimated as follows:
    $$C = 20.5 + 0.6Y - 0.9C_4; \qquad R^2 = 0.50$$
    SE (9.0) (0.1)   (0.1)
    n = 50 industries

where:

C = costs

Y = operating income

C_4 = four-firm concentration ratio

Comment on the impact of concentration and income on costs.

7. Using the S-C-P approach researchers estimated the following two models for the three largest Botswana banks treated as firms using annual data (1992 – 2006):

$\ln PR = 0.41 \ + 2.02\ln C_3 \ + 6.71\ln LR................(1)$

SE (2.99) (0.51) (0.71)

$R^2 = 0.94$

$\ln C_3 \ = 2.48 \ + 0.25\ln PR + 0.77\ln LR.................. (2)$

SE (0.96) (0.07) (0.28)

$R^2 = 0.90$

where:

PR = net interest profit margin.

C_3 = 3-firm concentration ratio.

LR = lending rate

a) Explain the two-way causation between performance and conduct.

b) Interpret the parameter 2.02, 6.71, and 0.94.

c) Evaluate the second model using both economic and statistical criteria.

8. Using the concept of market concentration or otherwise, give and elaborate on examples (from Africa or your own country) of monopoly, oligopoly and monopolistic competition.

Appendix 4.1: Inequality Measure and the Hirschman-Herfindahl Index

The Hirschman-Herfindahl index (H) can be expressed as:

$$H = \frac{v^2+1}{n}$$

Where v^2= the square of the co-efficient of variation (of firm size)

n = the number of firms

The proof is as follows:

Let the average firm size be:

$$\bar{x} = \frac{1}{n}\sum_{i=i}^{n} x_i$$

and the firm size variance (σ^2) be

$$\sigma^2 = \frac{1}{n}\sum_{i=i}^{n} x_i^2 - \bar{x}^2$$

The co-efficient of variation of firm size v, may be expressed as $v = \sigma/x$

This is a unit-free measure of the inequality in the shares of firm market.

$$\therefore v^2 = \sigma^2/\bar{x}^2 \quad \text{or}$$

$$v^2 = \frac{1}{n}\sum_{i=i}^{n} x_i^2/\bar{x}^2 - 1$$

Thus $H = \frac{v^2+1}{n}$

NB: The index is a function of both the market share inequality (v^2) and the number of firms n.

For monopoly ($v^2 = 0$ and $n = 1$).

H = 1 (maximum value), for firms under pure competition, and existence of extremely many small equally-sized firms, ($v^2 = 0$, $n - \infty$.

$H = \frac{1}{\infty} = 0$, minimum value.

Thus the index, H, lies between 0 and 1 inclusively i.e. $0 \leq H \leq 1$. For details see Clarke (2000:15)

Appendix 4.2: Other Measurements of Concentration

Hannah and Kay's Indices

The Hannah and Kay's indices (HK) are based on the general relationship:

$$D = \sum_{i=i}^{n} s_i^{\alpha} \qquad \alpha > 0$$

It clearly follows that, when $\alpha = 2$, $D = H$.

A set of Hannah and Kay's indices is expressed as follows.

$$HK = \left(\sum_{i=i}^{n} s_i^{\alpha} \right)^{1/(1-\alpha)} \qquad \alpha > 0, \qquad \alpha \neq 1$$

The indices satisfy important conditions relevant to market concentration such as concentration curve ranking criterion, sales transfer principle, entry condition, and merger condition. For details see, especially, Clarke 2000: 12 - 16.

The Gini Index

This is a co-efficient popularly used in income distribution and sometimes in market concentration and other variables. It is based on the Lorenz curve. The index ranges inclusively between 0 and 1; 0 for perfect equality and 1 for perfect inequality. For details see, for instance, Andreaso and Jacobson (2005: 99).

Entropy Index

This is essentially an inverse measurement of concentration based on the market share weights $_{\ln}(1/s_i)$. The entropy index (E) is formally expressed as follows:

$$E = \sum_{i=i}^{n} s_i \ \ln(1/s_i)$$

For the monopoly case $E = 0$; and in a case where there are n firms of equal size $E = \ln(n)$.

For details see, especially, Clarke (2000: 16) and Andreosso and Jacobson (2005: 100)

Lerner Index

This co-efficient (L) is more frequently used to measure market power than concentration. It is formally expressed as:

$$L = \frac{P\text{-}MC}{P}$$

where P = price

MC = marginal cost

When L = 0 it implies P = MC, the case of perfect competition. For a monopolist firm, however,

L = $\frac{1}{\varepsilon p}$, εp being the price elasticity of demand for the product under consideration. The proof is as follows: For a monopolist

MR = MC (profit maximisation condition)

But MR = P*(1 - $\frac{1}{\varepsilon p}$) (to be proved in the next chapter)

where P* = price which ensures that profit is maximised

εp = price elasticities of demand

Thus the Lerner index, L, will be given by

$$L = \frac{P_* - MC}{P_*} = 1 - \frac{MC}{P_*}$$

$$L = 1 - \frac{P_*(1 - \frac{1}{\varepsilon p})}{P_*} \qquad \text{since MC=MR= i.e. } L = \frac{1}{\varepsilon p}$$

i.e.$|L| = 1/\varepsilon p$

Notes

1. Cf. Andreasso & Jacobson (2005:90), and Hirschey (2009:379).
2. Cf. Andreasso and Jacobson (2005:96), Hirschey (2009:379) and Koch (1980:90).
3. For more details see, for instance, Clarke (2000:10).
4. See, Clarke (2000:9).
5. Measurement of market structure and measurements of market concentration are sometimes used interchangeably (see, for instance, Besanko *et al.* 2010: 210) and Pepall *et al.* 2009:44).
6. The H-index has a minimum value when the n firms in the market have identical shares. Thus:

$$H = \sum_{i=1}^{n} (1/n)^2 = \frac{1}{n}$$

When sellers are assumed to be infinitively many (n = ∞), H = 0. This is comparable to the reciprocal of firm members explained earlier (see, also, Barthwal 1985: 152).
7. Cf. Clarke 2000:31, 102.
8. See, Regent Business School (2007:74)

II

Analysis of Pricing Practices and Strategic Firm Behaviour

5

Pricing Practices and Strategies of Firms

Learning Objectives

The main objectives of this chapter are:

- To briefly review neoclassical price theory;
- To explain pricing under perfect competition;
- To examine various pricing practices and strategies under imperfect competition; and
- To examine pricing in Africa.

Introductory Note

It should be underscored from the onset that strategic firm behaviour is normally examined through pricing and non-pricing strategies implied in the business conduct (C) of the S-C-P model. The strategies normally depend on the type of market and market power.

This chapter examines various pricing practices and strategies starting with a neoclassical price theory framework. Non-pricing strategies will be the focus of the next chapter.

A Brief Review of Neoclassical Price Theory

Background Explanation

The neoclassical price theory maintains that price is paid in exchange for a commodity and depends on the type of market and market power. For measurement of market power, see previous chapter (Appendix 4.2).

The neoclassical theory of the firm assumes profit-maximisation (cost-minimisation), and price is determined by employing the behaviour rule: marginal revenue equals marginal cost (MR = MC). The price that each firm charges is derived from the quantity produced under profit-maximising conditions.

The elaboration of pricing under various types of market is examined hereunder.

Pricing under Various Types of Markets Structure

Pricing under Perfect Competition

Under perfect competition individual firms have no market power. Firms are therefore not *price makers* but *price takers*, in the sense that they have to accept the prevailing *market prices* or *industry prices* determined by the market force of supply and demand.

The individual firm demand curve, however, is horizontal (perfectly elastic demand curve) at the market-determined price. This is the price to be charged by each competitive firm and is equal to both Marginal revenue (MR) and Average revenue (AR). For illustration, see Figure 5.1.

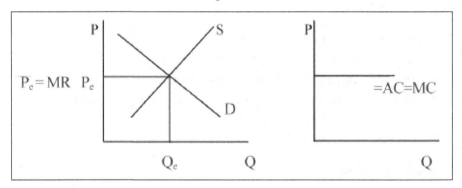

Figure 5.1: The Industry and Firm's Equilibrium Price under Perfect Competition

Using the neoclassical approach (MR = MC) the equilibrium price Pe may be expressed as:

$$Pe = MR = AR = MC \qquad (5.1)$$

At this price equilibrium quantity is Qe

Note that in the short run, however, firms can make abnormal profit or economic profit (MR>MC). In the long run, as more firms enter the market the *abnormal (economic) profits are reduced until they become break–even profit*; average cost is at its minimum point and P =MC=MR.

Pricing under Monopoly

Under monopoly, pricing also follows the neoclassical approach, i.e. determining the price by employing the behaviour rule: MR = MC in order to maximise profit.

In this case

$$MR = MC = P^* \left(1 + \frac{1}{\varepsilon p}\right) \qquad (5.2)$$

where

εP* = optimal price, which ensures profit maximisation.

= price elasticity of demand of the product under consideration.

(For details, see Appendix 5.1).

Thus, optimal price, $P^* = \dfrac{MR}{1+\frac{1}{\varepsilon p}}$ (5.3)

Therefore, optimal price, $P^* = \dfrac{MC}{1+\frac{1}{\varepsilon p}}$ (5.4)

The firm (which is also the industry faces a downward sloping demand curve. The monopolistic firm is a *price maker*, unlike the perfect competitive firm which is a price taker.

Since the monopolist has market power is $\dfrac{1}{\varepsilon p}$, as shown in Appendix 4.2, it makes economic profit both in the short and long runs. In general: p> MC

Pricing under Monopolistic Competition

Like monopoly, monopolistic competition is a form of imperfect competition. It has, however, the qualities of both monopoly and perfect competition.

In the short-run a monopolistic competitive firm resembles a monopolist in the sense that it is a price maker and can set price in line with profit-maximisation at MR = MC while making economic profit.

In the long run, nevertheless, the economic or abnormal profit will attract new entrants since, unlike the case of monopoly firm, the barrier to enter in the market is low. As competition increases due to more firms in the market, the economic profits are exhausted. The firm will thus behave almost in line with perfect competition; it will make normal profit and price will be almost equal to marginal cost.[1]

Pricing under Oligopoly

Consider the simple case of oligopoly with two firms (duopoly) producing a homogeneous product. In this case, three options for the two firms may be identified: competing against each other on the basis of price; colluding and forming a cartel; and competing against each other on the basis of quantity (Cournot Strategy).

If the firms were to compete on the basis of price, they would be willing to lower their price up to marginal cost.[2] Other options and pricing strategies will be explained in the subsequent section.

Pricing in Practice

Background Information

In the real world markets are imperfect and have some market power. In this case, data on marginal cost and marginal revenue may be difficult and expensive to obtain so as to set prices in the neoclassical way: MR = MC. Markup pricing and other practical pricing techniques are therefore, used in practice.

Markup pricing

General Approach

This is setting prices to cover direct cost plus a percentage profit contribution. Formally:

P = C + m (5.5) where

P = price

C = direct cost

m = profit margin

The direct cost (C) is estimated using *cost-plus pricing (full-cost pricing)*. Although there are many methods of estimation, the cost (C) typically the average variable cost (AVC) of producing or purchasing a product for a normal or standard level of output is estimated. This level is normally between 70 and 80 per cent of capacity. The AVC and an average overhead charge (a percentage of AVC) are summed up in estimating the *fully allocated average cost or direct cost* (C).[3]

There are two main types of markups, namely: markup on cost and markup on price. These are explained in the next sub-sections.

Markup on Cost

This is the profit margin for a product expressed as a percentage of unit cost. It is used by very many firms. Markup on cost is expressed algebraically as:

$$MOC = \frac{(P-C)}{C} \qquad (5.6)$$

where

MOC = markup on cost

P = price

C = cost

If the price of a product is $10 and the unit cost is $8, the markup on cost can easily be calculated using equation (5.6) as follows:

$$MOC = \frac{\$10-\$8}{\$8} = 0.25 \text{ or } 25\%$$

Since P-C is the profit margin (m), the markup on cost may also be expressed as

$$MOC = \frac{m}{C} \qquad (5.7)$$

Using the numerical example:

MOC = 2/8 = 0.25 or 25% (as expected).

The price can be expressed in terms of C and MOC using equation (5.6), i.e.

$$P = C(1 + MOC) \qquad (5.8)$$

Continuing with the previous numerical example:

$P = \$8(1 + 0.25) = \$10$ as expected.

Markup on Price

Sometimes *markup on price* (MOP) is used by some firms. This is the profit margin for a product expressed as a percentage of price. Formally:

$$MOP = \frac{P \cdot C}{P} = \frac{m}{P} \qquad (5.9)$$

Using the previous numerical example,

$$MOP = \frac{\$10 - \$8}{\$10} = 0.2 \qquad (5.10)$$

The price, P, expressed from equation (5.9) is

$$P = \frac{-C}{MOP - 1} \qquad (5.11)$$

Applying the previous numerical example

$$P = \frac{-\$8}{(0.2 - 1)} = \$10$$

as expected.

Markup on cost and markup on price are related as follows:

$$MOC = \frac{MOP}{1 - MOP} \qquad (5.12)$$

and

$$MOP = \frac{MOC}{1 + MOC} \qquad (5.13)$$

The reader is encouraged to prove these relationships algebraically or using numerical examples.

Optimal Markup Pricing

Optimal markup pricing is profit-maximising markup pricing. It is a pricing strategy for firms with market power, especially monopolists. In this case, optimal price (P*) which ensures profit-maximisation is set.

As we noted in equation 5.1, for a firm under monopoly to maximise profit (even under monopolistic competition):

$$MR = MC = P^* \left(1 + \frac{1}{\varepsilon p}\right)$$

and

$$P^* = \frac{MC}{1 + (1/\varepsilon p)} = \left(\frac{\varepsilon p}{1 + (1/\varepsilon p)}\right) MC \qquad (5.14)$$

This relationship can be expressed as:

$$P^* = \left(\frac{\varepsilon p}{1+(1/\varepsilon p)}\right) MC \qquad (5.15)$$

$P^* = KMC$

where

$$K = \left(\frac{1}{1+\frac{1}{\varepsilon p}}\right) = \left(\frac{n\varepsilon p_*}{1+n\varepsilon p_*}\right)$$

K can be viewed as the *profit-maximising markup factor*, and

εp is the price elasticity of demand for the firm.

If the manager's best estimate of the price elasticity of demand for a pair of shoe is -2, K = -2/(1-2) = 2. Thus the manager should set the optimal price for the pair of shoes at

$P^* = 2MC$

i.e., price should be double the marginal cost.

Note that for *Cournot Oligopoly*[4], the profit-maximising markup factor K^* is:

$$K^* = \frac{1}{1+(1/n\varepsilon p_*)} = \frac{n\varepsilon p_*}{1+n\varepsilon p_*} \qquad 5.1\,6)$$

where εp = market elasticity of demand in the industry with homogeneous firms. This may be compared with firm elasticity of demand for monopoly where n=1 and the firm is the industry ($\varepsilon p = \varepsilon p^*$)   .

The corresponding optimal price P is:

$$\overline{P} = \left(\frac{1}{1+\frac{1}{n\varepsilon p_*}}\right) MC \qquad (5.17)$$

or

$$\overline{P} = \left(\frac{1}{1+\frac{1}{n\varepsilon p_*}}\right) MC \qquad (5.18)$$

For details, see Appendix 5.2.

As was with the case of markup on cost and markup on price in the case of monopoly or monopolistic competition, optimal markup on cost and optimal markup on price may similarly be expressed. For optimal markup on cost (OMOC), the expression is:

$$OMOC = \frac{P_*-MC}{MC} \qquad (5.19)$$

where OMOC = optimal (profit-maximising) markup on cost.

P^* = profit-maximising (optimal) price.

MC = marginal cost. (This is the appropriate cost for optimal cost plus pricing as implied in equation 5.1. Optimal markup on cost is sometimes referred to as optimal markup on marginal cost).

But

$$P^* = \frac{MC}{1+\frac{1}{\varepsilon p}}$$

Thus

$$OMOC = \frac{MC}{1+(1/\varepsilon p)} - MC)(\div MC$$

$$OMOC = (\frac{MC}{1+(1/\varepsilon p)} - MC)\frac{1}{MC}$$

Therefore

$$OMOC = \frac{1}{1+(1/\varepsilon p)} - 1$$

After simplifying, the optimal or profit-maximising markup on cost can be expressed as:

$$OMOC = \frac{-1}{\varepsilon p+1} \qquad (5.20)$$

Thus, optimal markup on cost is essentially the inverse of the absolute price elasticity of demand (εp) of the product under consideration.

Similarly, the optimal markup on price can be presented formally as:

$$OMOP = \frac{P_* - MC}{P_*} \qquad (5.21)$$

where

OMOP = optimal markup on price.

P^* = optimal price.

MC = marginal cost.

Thus OMOP is

is written as follows;

$$\frac{P_* - P_* 1(+\frac{1}{\varepsilon p})}{P_*}$$

After simplifying, the formula for optimal markup on price is:

$$OMOP = -\frac{1}{\varepsilon p} \qquad (5.22)$$

Note that the optimal markup on price is exactly equal to the inverse of the absolute price elasticity of demand.

The Role of Demand in Markup Pricing

Markup pricing depends essentially on price elasticity of demand of the product under consideration. The price elasticity of demand, however, depends heavily on availability of close substitutes. If a product has a close substitute, its demand is normally price elastic. An increase in price of the product will make most buyers purchase the close substitute. In this case, the higher the price (P), the lower the revenue (PQ) as quantity demanded (Q) will fall more than the rate of increase in price. Therefore, products whose demand are price-elastic should be given relatively low markups (normally 0 – 20 per cent). Examples of such products are Fanta, coffee and milk.

On the other hand, higher markups (greater than 20 per cent) may be set to products whose demand is price-inelastic. The demand for products with no close substitutes like alcohol, cigarettes, and fresh fruits (in season) is normally price- inelastic. The higher the price, the more the revenue as quantity demanded will fall relatively slightly compared to the rate of increase of the price. Products whose price forms a relatively small fraction of consumers' budget like salt and spices also tend to have inelastic demand. Higher markups may be set to such products (see also Hirschey).

The role of demand indicated by the magnitudes of price elasticities is easily noted in the case of optimal pricing since absolute elasticities are inversely related to the optimal markups as shown in Table 5.1.

Table 5.1: Price Elasticities and Optimal Markups

Source: Computed by the author

Price Elasticity of Demand	Optimal markup on cost (%) $\left(\dfrac{-1}{\epsilon p + 1}\right)$	Optimal markup on price $\left(\dfrac{-1}{\epsilon p}\right)$
-1.2	500.0	83.3
-1.5	200.0	66.7
-2.0	100.0	50.0
-5.0	25.0	20.0
-10.0	11.1	10.0
-21.0	5.0	4.8

From the table it is clearly noted that the higher the absolute price elasticity of demand, the lower the optimal markups (on cost or on price).

Other Techniques of Pricing in Practice

Background Information

Apart from markup pricing, there are other simple and practical techniques which do not need accurate data required to fulfil the neoclassical approach of ensuring that MC = MR. Examples are incremental analysis in pricing, prestige pricing and promotional pricing. These are explained briefly below.

Incremental Analysis in Pricing

The rule for this practice is that a firm should change the price of a product or its output, introduce a new product, or a new version of a given product, etc., if the increase in incremental or total revenue from the action is greater than the incremental or total cost.[5] If a firm wants to add a new product line and change price, for example, it should make sure that the total cost or incremental cost of taking the action (extra cost resulting from the additional product line) is greater than the total or incremental total revenue (extra revenue resulting from the decision).

It should be noted that incremental cost is not the same as marginal cost. The former refers to extra cost from an output increase that may be very substantial (e.g. doubling the output), while the latter refers to extra cost from a very small (one unit) increase in output. Incremental revenue and marginal revenue may be differentiated in a similar way.

Prestige Pricing

Prestige pricing involves firms deliberately setting high prices to attract prestige-oriented consumers. These consumers normally relate high price to high quality even if the relationship is not perfectly direct. This may apply to highly priced shirts, high prices of certain brands of cars and other goods.

Promotional Pricing

Promotional pricing or dealing is charging a temporary reduced price by placing the product 'on sale' for a specified period.[6] This may be practiced simultaneously with other strategies such as 'buy two and get one free' strategy or quantity discount and block pricing to be explained later in this chapter. Promotional pricing is common globally, and is widely practiced in Africa.

Psychological Pricing

Psychological pricing is the practice of charging prices ending with 9's and similar figures, such as $9.9 or $19.9 instead of just $10 or $20, for a product in the belief that such pricing will create the illusion of significantly lower price to the consumer.[7]

Pricing Strategies of Firms

Background Information

Pricing as a strategy occurs when there exists a high level of concentration with the emergency of a dominant firm (monopolistic or oligopolistic firm with strong control of the market) which uses various strategic techniques in pricing.[8]

A firm's strategic pricing behaviour is displayed by different price strategies such as price discrimination, the limit price, price leadership, predatory pricing, and collusive pricing. Such strategies are explained in the following sub-sections.

Price Discrimination

Definitional Introduction

In its simple but somewhat general definition, price discrimination is a strategic technique of charging profitably different prices to the same product in different markets. Alternatively, price discrimination is setting strategically and profitably different prices (markups) for the same product, or different quantities of a product, at different times, to different customer groups, or in different markets. The former definition is useful in simple practical illustrations. The latter is ideal in explaining the various degrees of price discrimination as will be done in due course.

For price discrimination to be very profitable three conditions must be met. First, the firm must have substantial market power (monopolistic power). Second, different demand conditions must exist. Specifically, different price elasticities of demand for the product must be there across different market segments. Thirdly, market quantities of the product, the times when they are used and the customer groups must be separable. In short, the firm must be able to segment or separate the market.

There are three degrees of price discrimination: first-degree price determination, second-degree price discrimination and third-degree price discrimination.[9] These are explained in the sections following here below.

First-degree Price Discrimination

First-degree Price Discrimination is strategic behaviour of a monopolistic firm which charges each consumer the maximum price which that consumer is willing to pay, for each unit. In so doing, the firm extracts all the consumers' surplus and maximizes total revenue, hence profit.

Consider the demand curve faced by a monopolist (Figure 5.2):

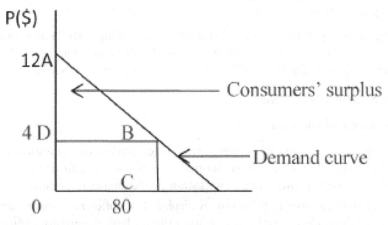

Figure 5.2: First-degree Price Discrimination

If the equilibrium price is $4 and equilibrium quantity is 80 units. Consumers will actually pay $640 (Area of rectangle ABCO). The first consumer, however, may be willing to pay the maximum price ($12) for the first unit. The second one, third and so on will be willing to pay a maximum price less than $12, for each additional unit, in descending order of prices (guided by the demand curve) such that all consumers will be willing to pay $640 (the area of the rectangle BCOD plus the area of triangle ABD). This will be the revenue of the monopolist. Note that the area of the triangle ABD is called the *consumers' surplus* and is equal to $320.

Note also that in short *first-degree price discrimination* is charging different prices to each customer; therefore it is sometimes referred to as *personalized pricing or perfect price discrimination*.

First-degree price discrimination, however, is theoretical as it is rarely encountered in the real world. One situation where this seems to be approximately practiced is at some independent universities, especially in the USA, where they collect information such as family income, mortgage payment, savings and the like and try to charge the highest price/fee for each applicant.[10] A proxy example in Africa would be the case of a traditional doctor in a small village who charges patients on the basis of assessment of their ability to pay.[11]

Second-degree Price Discrimination

Second-degree price discrimination is a strategic pricing technique of charging profitably different prices based on the use of quantities or rates purchased. A monopolistic firm may charge a uniform price per unit for specific quantities or blocks of the product sold to each customer, a lower price per unit form for an additional block or batch of the product. In so doing, the firm does not extract all the consumers' surplus but part of it.

Unlike the first-degree price discrimination, the second-degree price discrimination is useful in practice. Examples are the case of public utilities where the first kilowatt-hours of electricity consumption, for instance, are charged higher rates than the second kilowatt-hours. A similar case may be applied in the case of water and gas using cubic metres. Other examples may be the case of number of copies duplicated charged in batches or blocks and use of computers based on time spent.

There are various forms of second-order price discrimination such as block pricing and quantity discounting, two-part tariffs and the like. These are explained hereunder.

Block pricing and Quantity Discount

Block pricing and quantity discounts represent two forms of second-degree price discrimination as illustrated above in the case of public utilities and others. It essentially entails a decreasing average price with increasing use. The underlying assumption in this definition is that the costs are the same whether the sale is in blocks or in units.[12]

Two-Part Tariffs

Another form of second-degree price discrimination is a *two-part tariff*. It is used mainly by monopolistic and oligopolistic firms to discriminate profitably between high- and low-demand users of a product. All consumers first pay an initial price or fee for the purchase of the product (first tariff), then they pay additional or usage price or fee for each unit of the product they purchase (second tariff). The second tariff is targeted mainly to high-demand users. Examples include the case of computer firms which charge monthly rentals plus usage fees for renting their mainframe computers; and the case of telephone firms which charge monthly fees plus message-unit fees.[13]

Two-part tariffs are directly or indirectly related to other forms of pricing especially tying. For details, see Appendix 5.3.

Third-degree Price Discrimination

Third-degree price discrimination is the strategic behaviour of a monopolistic firm which charges different prices for the same product in different sub-markets until the marginal revenue of the last unit of the product sold in each sub-market equals the marginal cost of producing it.[14] Therefore, third-degree price discrimination is based on the neoclassical profit-maximising rule of $MR = MC$. For a market segmented into n – sub-markets

$$MR_1 = MR_2 = \ldots = MR_n \qquad\qquad (5.23)$$

For third-degree price discrimination to be very profitable the three earlier generalised main conditions must be met. First, the firm must have substantial market power (monopolistic power). Second, the firm must be able to separate the sub-markets. Third, each sub-market should have a different demand function.

Third-degree price discrimination is profitable since it allows the firm to increase revenue without increasing costs. A quantitative example is in order:

Consider the case of a manager of a monopolistic firm who has isolated two distinct sub-markets whose demand functions are:

$Q_1 = 12 - P_1$ (sub-market 1)   1)
$Q_2 = 12 - 2P_2$ (sub-market 2)   (2)

where Q_1, Q_2 = quantity demanded for sub-markets 1 and 2 respectively.
P_1, P_2 = price of the product in sub-markets 1 and 2 respectively.
and the cost function (C) for the market is specified as:
$C = 6 + 2 (Q_1 + Q_2)$ (3)

In this case the price to be charged in each sub-market and the respective quantities can be obtained as follows:

For sub-market 1

$Q_1 = 12 - P_1$ or $P_1 = 12 - Q_1$

But Revenue $= P_1 Q_1 = (12 - Q_1)Q_1 = 12Q_1 - Q_1^2$

Therefore marginal revenue $(MR_1) = 12 - 2Q_1$

From equation 3, marginal cost $= dc/dQ_1 = 2$

Since $MR_1 = MC$

$12 - 2Q_1 = 2$

and $Q_1 = 5$ and $P_1 = 12 - 5 = 7$

For sub-market 2

$Q_2 = 12 - 2P_2$ or $P_2 = 6 - \frac{1}{2}Q_2$

and revenue $= P_2 Q_2 = (6 - \frac{1}{2}Q_2)Q_2 = 6Q_2 - \frac{1}{2}Q_2^2$

Therefore, $MR_2 = 6 - Q_2$

But from equation 3, $MC = dc/dQ_1 = 2$

Since $MR_2 = MC$

$6 - Q_2 = 2$

$Q_2 = 4$ and $P_2 = 6 - \frac{1}{2} \times 4 = 4$

In summary, the monopolistic firm should sell the product for 7 units in the first sub-market where the quantity demanded $Q_1 = 5$. For the second sub-market where quantity demanded $= 4$, the firm should sell the same product for 4 units.

It can also be shown that the firm charges a higher price where the absolute elasticity of demand of the product under consideration is lower but the market power is higher.

For sub-market 1:

The absolute price elasticity of demand $| \varepsilon p |$ is given by

$$\left| \varepsilon p\, 1 \right| = \left| \frac{dQ1}{dP1} \cdot \frac{P1}{Q1} \right| = \left| -1 \cdot \frac{7}{5} \right| = 1.4$$

and the market power $L_1 = \frac{1}{\varepsilon p1} = \frac{1}{1.4} = 0.7$

For sub-market 2

The absolute price elasticity, $\left| \varepsilon p\,2 \right| = \left| \frac{dQ1}{dP1} \cdot \frac{P2}{Q2} \right| = \left| -2 \cdot \frac{4}{5} \right| = 2$

and the market power, $L_2 = \frac{1}{\varepsilon p2} = \frac{1}{2} = 0.5$

This clearly shows that the firm charges higher price in the sub-market 1 where the absolute elasticity is lower but the market power is higher.

Since with price discrimination total profit (π) of the firm is given by:

$\pi = R_1 + R_2 - C$

where

R_1 = Revenue in sub-market 1

R_2 = Revenue in sub-market 2

C = Total cost

$R_1 = P_1 Q_1 = 7 (5) = 35$

$R_2 = P_2 Q_2 = 4(4) = 16$

and C = 6 + 2(5+4) = 24

Therefore π =35 + 16 – 24 = 27

Without price discrimination: $P_1 = P_2 = P$

and $Q = Q_1 + Q_2$

$= 12 – P_1 + 12 – 2P_2$

$= 24 – P – 2P$

Thus Q = 24 – 3P or P = 8 – 0.33Q

Total revenue = R =PQ = (8 – 0.33)Q

i.e. $R = 8Q – 0.33Q_2$

Marginal revenue, MR = 8 – 0.66Q

But MR = MC

8 – 0.66Q = 2

$Q \approx 9$

P = 8 – 0.33Q = 8 – 0.33(9) $\approx$ 5

Therefore total revenue R is PQ = 5 (9) = 45

Thus Profit π = R – C

$\qquad\qquad$ = 45 – (6 + 2Q)

$\qquad\qquad$ = 45 – 6 + 2(9)

$\qquad\qquad$ = 45 – 24

$\qquad\qquad$ = 21

Clearly, this is lower than the profit, 27, in the case of price discrimination. Therefore, the firm actually makes more profit when it practices price discrimination than when it does not.

Other Pricing Strategies

Predatory Pricing

Predatory pricing is a pricing strategy where a firm uses the profits earned in one market (at home) to sell a product below its marginal cost in another market (abroad) in order to knock out competitors and discourage new entrants, but subsequently increases the price to acquire monopoly profits. Predatory pricing is sometimes referred to as *international price discrimination or predatory dumping.*[15]

Botswana, Tanzania, and many other African countries have come up with competition policies and laws to protect domestic industries from such unfair competition.

Cross-subsidy Pricing

Cross-subsidy pricing is a pricing strategy in which profits obtained from the sale of one product are used to subsidise sales of a related product so that its price is low.[16]

This is comparable to predatory pricing but it is generalised and may be done within the same economy or country.

Market Penetration Pricing

Market penetration pricing or just penetration pricing is a pricing strategy of charging very low initial price for a product in order to create a new market, thereby grabbing the market share. Computer firms, for example, have used this strategy in many parts of the world, including Africa, to sell the initial versions of software programmes at promotionally low prices to create a bigger market but subsequently increased their prices.[17]

Skimming may be regarded a special form of market penetration pricing for a newly introduced brand or product. For details, see Appendix 5.4.

Limit Pricing

Limit Pricing is a competitive strategy for a dominant or monopoly firm to set less than the maximum monopolistic price (P_1) sufficiently low to prevent competitors' entry into the market. In so doing, the dominant firm obtains less than maximum profits in the short run.

In the long run, however, the maximum monopoly price (P_m) is maintained to maximise profit. For illustration, see Figure 5.3.

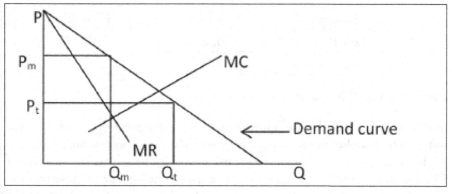

Figure 5.3: Limit Pricing

Notes: P_t = Limit price.

P_m = maximum (monopoly) price.

Q_t and Q_m are the respective outputs.

Price Leadership

Price leadership is a strategic form of market collusion in oligopolistic firms whereby the leading firm initiates a price change and other firms in the industry accommodate the price change.

The leading firm is normally a dominant firm in the industry. This is referred to as *dominant firm price leadership*. The leading firm, however, may not necessarily be the dominant but it may be a low-cost firm or a particular firm which is accepted by other firms in the industry as the best judge regarding when to change price. Other firms believe that the leading firm has enough knowledge and ability to suggest change in prices while others do not have. In this case, the firm is normally called a barometric firm and the leadership is referred to as barometric price leadership.[18]

Collusive Pricing

Collusive pricing is charging the same or similar prices for the same or similar products through collusive agreement among oligopolistic firms. In this case collusion could result in charging higher prices at the expense of consumers. This is done essentially to attempt to increase profits by avoiding competition at least in the short run.

In the long run, however, cheating (selling secretly at low prices) may be possible. The game theory approach is normally used to illustrate this tendency. Consider Figure 5.4 where a duopoly case of two firms X and Y is shown.

		Firm Y	
	Strategy	Low Price	High Price
Firm X	Low Price	(20, 20)	(50, 10)
	High Price	(10, 50)	(30, 30)

Figure 5.4: Payoff Matrix for a Pricing Game

In this case, if firm Y charges a low price (say $5), the *payoff* (profit) for firm X will be $20 if it also charges a low price, and $10 if it charges a high price, say $7. If, however, firm Y charges a high price (say $7), firm X will get a profit of $50 if it charges the low price and $30 if it sells at the high price. Note that the *dominant strategy* (a strategy that results in the highest payoff regardless of the opponent's action) for firm X is to charge a low price.

Similarly, if firm X charges the low price, firm Y's payoff will be $20 if it also charges the low price; otherwise it gets $10. If firm X charges the high price, firm Y will get a profit of $50 if it charges the low price and $30 if it charges the high price. Charging the low price is also the *dominant strategy* for firm Y.

Note also that if the agreement of selling the high price was adhered to, each firm would get a profit of $30.

This is an example of a *simultaneous-move* game where each player (firm) makes a move on price setting without the knowledge of the other player and is often called the *Betrand duopoly game*.

In practice, however, collusive pricing is illegal in many countries.[19]

Pricing in Africa

A Retrospective Note

After independence, many African countries practiced *price control* (centrally-fixed prices). The practice was essentially an attempt to protect consumers from capitalist profit-seekers. This was in line with the socialist approach which was by then common in the USSR, China and Eastern Europe. The early 1980s economic crises in many African countries due to the escalating price of oil and other external and internal factors was also used as another explanation for *price controls*.

In an attempt to mitigate the negative impact of the economic crises, many countries opted for recovery and *structural adjustment programmes* (SAPs) guided by the International Monetary Fund (IMF) and the World Bank. Countries like Burundi, Ghana, Ivory Coast, Kenya, Malawi, Nigeria, Senegal, Tanzania and Zambia went through SAPs which essentially promoted liberalisation of markets and anti-price control prices.[20]

Countries like Tanzania and Zambia which were significantly involved in socialism had to struggle relatively hard to evolve from intensive 'socialist price control' to market liberalisation and price regulation. For details, see Case Studies 5.1 and 5.4.

Case Study 5.1: Price Control and Deregulation in Tanzania

At independence in 1961 Tanzania (Tanganyika by then) inherited essentially a market-oriented economy which enhanced pricing based mainly on market forces. In 1967, however, major changes were made through the Arusha Declaration. The economy was gradually transformed in line with socialistic central planning and price control. African socialism (*Ujamaa*) was the guiding political road map.

Price controls were intensified in the 1970 and early 1980s. These controls, however, led to acute shortage of goods and illegal pricing (black market pricing or parallel market pricing). Despite an attempt of stabilisation and other measures it was difficult to change the situation.

In 1986, however, the government opted for liberalisation of the economy. A series of recovery and structural adjustment programmes (SAPs) supported financially by IMF and the World Bank, were implemented thereafter. By 1984 the SAPs had reduced price controls to only 50 locally manufactured product groups and 6 imported product categories. The government deregulated prices. By 1989 industrial price controlled items were less than 15 per cent of the consumer price index weights, and many of the controlled prices were set according to international prices. By 1994 only 3 items were subject to price control: sugar, fertilizer and petroleum products. The latter two are still regulated by the government.

Sources: Mans (1994) and Rweyemanu (1973).

In another East African country – Kenya – there was a need for price control before adjustment period in the 1970s. For details, see Case Study 5.2.

Case Study 5.2: Price Control and Deregulation in Kenya

Like Tanzania, since independence in 1963 Kenya inherited a market-oriented economy which promoted pricing based on market forces. However, the oil price shocks in the 1970s and the disintegration of the East African Community changed the policy to more government intervention including price control based on the Price Control Act of 1972. Manufactured goods prices were controlled, and parastatals controlled wholesale trade in a number of goods.

Although the first adjustment period was 1980-1984 it was during the subsequent (1985-94) adjustment period price control limited as per the Restrictive Trade Practices, Monopolies, and Price Control Act of 1988. However, controlled prices felt significantly since the 1986 Session Paper which had policy statements on reducing protection of industry, reforming agricultural marketing, and controlling prices and public spending. During 1983-1991 the number of controlled products under the general order fell from 56 to 6. Price decontrols were mostly geared primarily toward manufactured goods. However, controls on consumer prices of staples continued to exist, except on such items as sugar and milk. Nevertheless, cost-plus pricing continued to guide price setting in the manufacturing sector. To date prices of very few products like petrol and petrol products are controlled.

Sources: G. Swamy (1994)

Price control in Burundi was also common prior to the reform initiated in 1986. For details, see Case Study 5.3.

Case Study 5.3: Price Control and Deregulation in Burundi

At independence in 1962 Burundi inherited essentially a poor but stable economy. By the late 1970s, however, there was an abrupt fall in coffee prices, oil shocks, and adverse weather conditions. Government interventions and price controls were then intensified.

Adjustment funding was approved in 1986 by the World Bank and the IMF. This was the beginning of the reforms in Burundi. Prior to the programme, all prices of imported and locally manufactured goods were subject to controls exercised by the ministry of commerce and industry. Prices were set on a cost-plus basis, with the manufacturing receiving a net profit margin of 10 to 20 per cent. Price controls sought to prevent producers and traders from reaping expensive profit in a monopolistic market.

At the outset of the reform programme the government decided to deregulate both consumer and producer prices except food crop producer prices and consumer prices of certain essential products such as flour, sugar and powdered milk. The list of price controlled items decreased over time throughout the reform period.

Sources: P. Englebert and R. Hoffman (1994).

The case of Zambia in Southern Africa is very similar to that of Tanzania (Case 5.1). Both countries practiced African Socialism: Ujamaa for Tanzania during President J.K. Nyerere regime and Humanism in the Case of Tanzania under President K. Kaunda. For detail see Case Study 5.4.

Case Study 5.4: Price Control and Deregulation in Zambia

After independence in 1964 Zambia followed African Socialism (humanism) similar to the Ujamaa of Tanzania. Socialist central planning and price control became increasingly practiced. This was discredited by the Bretton Woods institutions in the early 1980s. This led to the introduction of structural adjustment programmes (SAPs).

The early implementation of the SAPs began in 1983, but due to internal socialist inertia and macro-economic instability it created, it was discontinued in 1986. In 1991, however, the new multi-party system government re-introduced them. This led to radical policy reforms which included market liberalisation, price deregulation and rapid privatisation of the public sector.

Sources: Funjika (2010) and Mulikita (2000).

The African socialism ideology, government intervention and price control also existed in some West African countries, but not at the same intensity as in the case of the East African ones like Tanzania and the Southern African country of Zambia.

In Senegal, for example, the long tradition of 'African Socialism' characterised by government intervention and regulatory of prices existed in the 1960s and1970s to some extent. For details, see Case Study 5.5.

Case Study 5.5: Price Control and Deregulation in Senegal

At independence in 1960 Senegal inherited a relatively well developed economy with modern physical and social infrastructure resulting from the prominent role Dakar played as the capital of the large French West African colony. Over time, Senegal, however, maintained a long tradition of 'African Socialism', government intervention, and price control institutions. Nevertheless, the severe crisis resulting from poor financial and investment policies, worsening of terms of trade and successive droughts in the late 1970s led the country to opt for structural adjustment programmes.

In 1980 the government started liberalising the market and decontrolling prices. In 1987 and 1988 prices for all but 16 consumer goods were decontrolled. By 1988 all prices except of essential goods were decontrolled. They included sugar, salt, tea, wheat, flour, pharmaceutical products, cement, electricity, petroleum products, water, transportation, broken rice, tomato and tomato concentrates and cooking oil. Furthermore, fertilizer subsidies were eliminated for all commodities except cotton. In 1990 the price control office was closed.

Source: Rouis (1994).

Nigeria too practiced significant government intervention, social planning, and price control in the 1960s and 1970s. By 1986 the SAPs were inevitably implemented in an attempt to mitigate the economic crisis of the late 1970s. For details, see Case Study 5.6.

Case Study 5.6: Price Control and Deregulation in Nigeria

After independence in 1960 the Nigerian economy was transformed from a subsistence one into a largely monetised economy. The discovery of oil fields in early 1970s intensified the monetisation. In the late 1970s, however, the country experienced economic crisis resulting from internal and external sources. As was the case elsewhere in Africa many industrial commodities were subject to price control and distribution controls. With further intensification of the crisis in 1986 the government inevitably opted for implement economic recovery measures under structural adjustment programme. This led to market liberalisation, price deregulation and privatisation of public enterprises.

> In 1987 private enterprises were allowed to set their own prices, thereby taking the rents away from traders. However, for some time, prices of special goods, (fertilizers and petroleum and gas products) remained controlled officially.

Source: Faruquee (1994).

Ghana also practiced socialist government intervention and price control in the 1960s and 1970s; but started liberalising the economy and deregulating prices in 1983. For details, see Case Study 5.7.

Case Study 5.7: Price Control and Deregulation in Ghana

> In spite of the various civilian and military regimes since Ghana's independence in 1957 to the early 1980s the country to some extent practiced government intervention, socialist or central control including price controls. Between 1961 and 1962 the Ghanaian economy was virtually converted from market oriented to a controlled one. The Price Control Act was endorsed in 1962. In general, the economy was controlled throughout the 1960s and 1970s.
>
> As has been the case with many other African countries the economic crisis of the late 1970s also affected Ghana negatively. A solution had to be sought through the IMF and the World Bank. An Economic Recovery Programme (ERP) was introduced in 1983, followed by various Structural Adjustment Programmes (SAPs) to remove the distortions in the economy. Serious implementation of SAPs actually took place in 1986. This led to the abolition of the price control system, effective liberalisation of the economy and privatisation.

Sources: Baah-Nuakoh (1997) and Leechor (1994).

In short, most African countries practiced direct government intervention and price controls in the 1960s and 1970s. The late 1970s and early 1980s intensified the intervention and price controls.

With the assistance of the IMF and the World Bank the African countries opted for structural adjustment programmes which promoted market liberalisation and price deregulation. The list of price regulated items dwindled over time.

Contemporary Pricing

The most common current pricing practices and strategies in Africa and elsewhere include markup pricing in various types of markets, block pricing and quantity discount, tying, penetration pricing, promotional pricing, psychological pricing and prestige pricing.

Limited price control is practiced for very special products and services like petrol and petroleum products and public transport fares in Botswana, Tanzania, Kenya and some other African countries.

Markup pricing is most common in industrial pricing in Africa. The role of demand, through various price elasticities, plays a key role in firms' pricing decisions. This is illustrated further by estimated markups on cost by the Imalaseko Supermarket (Dar-es-Salaam) shown in Table 5.2.

Table 5.2: Markups on Cost Charged on Some Grocery Items by Imalaseko Supermarket (2011)

Item	Type of Demand	Markup on Cost (%)
Cigarettes	Inelastic	30 – 60
Coca Cola	Elastic	0 – 10
Coffee	Elastic	0 – 10
Colgate toothpaste	Elastic	5 – 10
Fanta	Elastic	0 – 10
Milk	Elastic	5 – 10
Salt	Inelastic	30 – 50
Tea	Elastic	0 – 10

Source: Compiled by the aurthor

Items with substitutes like Coca Cola, coffee, Fanta tend to have elastic demand. They are price-sensitive, and hence were given low markups (0 – 10), while items like cigarettes and salt had inelastic demand and were given relatively high markups. Note that cigarettes are price-insensitive because they are essentially addictive and may be regarded as having no close legal substitutes. However, salt may be regarded as a necessity and its share in total household expenditure is very small; hence it has inelastic demand.

Price discrimination is practiced to some extent in Africa. As noted earlier, first-degree price discrimination is essentially theoretical. A proxy example, however, may be that of a private doctor in a small village who tends to use first-degree price discrimination by charging each patient for medicine and service on the basis of ability to pay.[21] In some small villages in Mwanza and Shinyanga regions (*Sukumaland*) in Tanzania, for instance, some traditional doctors (*bafumu*) tend to use first-degree price discrimination by charging each patient a different price or fee depending on one's level of income or property including livestock since the traditional doctor (*mfumu*) is able to know the property and income status of each villager given the small size and strong communal links among villagers. Where enough information or data is not readily available the assistants to the traditional doctor (*bahemba*) go around households informally and secretly to collect such information.

Block pricing and quantity discount forms of second-degree price discrimination are very common in the case of electricity and other public utilities in Botswana, Tanzania and some other African countries.

Third-degree price discrimination is common among groups or sub-markets involving, for instance, students and non-students, large commercial consumers of electricity and water and small household consumers in Botswana, Tanzania and some other African countries.

Regarding oligopolistic collusive pricing, its control is not very clear. In Ghana, for instance, open collusion, price fixing and other anti-competitive acts were not forbidden by 1997. This made it easier for firms to co-ordinate their actions for price fixing. For example, the Prices and Income Board could fix identical prices for beer, whether it is from Accra Brewery, Achimota Brewery or Kumasi Brewery.[22]

In South Africa, the cartel of three main cement industries (Portland Cement, Anglo-Alpha and Blue Circle) determined prices and controls cement production to ensure economies of scale.[23]

Illegal pricing practices and strategies are, however, generally discouraged globally, including in Africa. As noted earlier, African countries like Botswana and Tanzania have recently introduced competition policies and laws to protect domestic industries from predatory pricing and other unfair competition and illegal pricing practices.

Prestige pricing is also widely practiced in Africa. More often than not, higher prices are set in prestigious stores or shops in market places like Samora Avenue in the centre of Dar-es-Salaam as compared to lower prices in Kariakoo or Manzese shops for the same quality shirt, for instance.

Promotional pricing, tying, penetrating pricing, and psychological pricing are also common in many African countries.

Conclusion

This chapter has reviewed the neoclassical price theory focusing on various types of markets. Pricing practices and strategies have been examined in general before spelling out pricing in Africa. The chapter has concluded by underscoring, with examples, that most of the pricing practices and strategies are applied in Africa.

Review Questions

1. (a) Explain the main features of the neo-classical price theory of the firm.
   (b) Why should pricing under perfect competition differ from pricing under imperfect competition?
2. (a) What is meant by optimal price? Derive its formula for a monopolist.
   (b) The market manager of Jambo firm operating under monopoly must formulate a recommendation for the price of a new product. It is estimated that

the marginal cost of producing the product is $20. What recommendation should the manager make to ensure that profit is maximised?

3   (a) Why do many firms prefer markup pricing to the neo-classical approach: MR=MC?

    (b) Show mathematically the relationship between markup on price and markup on cost.

4   (a) Explain, with examples from your country or any specified African country, the different types of price discrimination.

    (b) The Hakuna Matata monopolistic firm has isolated two distinct sub-markets for its product. The demand functions for the two markets are:

$Q_1 = 12 - P_1$ (Sub-market 1)

$Q_2 = 8 - P_2$ (Sub-market 2)

Its total cost function is:

$C = 5 + 2(Q_1 + Q_2)$

where

Q_1, Q_2 = quantity demanded for sub-markets 1 and 2 respectively.

P_1, P_2 = price of the product in the sub-markets 1 and 2 respectively.

C = Total cost.

   (i) Find the quantity demanded and price in each sub-market.

   (ii) Show that the firm will charge higher price in the market where the absolute price elasticity of demand is lower but market power is higher.

   (iii) Show that it makes economic sense for the firm to price- discriminate.

5   (a) Is there any difference between pricing practices and pricing strategies? Explain briefly.

    (b) With reference to examples from African countries or otherwise differentiate between the following pairs of pricing practices and strategies:

   (i)   markup pricing and full-cost pricing.

   (ii) prestige pricing and psychological pricing.

   (iii) market penetration pricing and skimming pricing.

   (i)   block pricing and tying.

   (ii) predatory pricing and cross-subsidy pricing.

6   (a) What is meant by

   (i) collusive pricing?

   (ii) price leadership?

(b) Are the two types of pricing strategies common in Africa?

(c) Why do some countries in Africa or elsewhere have policies and laws against anti-competitive pricing strategies like collusion, limit pricing and predatory pricing?

Appendix 5.1: Mathematical Relationship Between Marginal Revenue and Price

From the revenue (R) definition:

$R = PQ$

where P = own price

Q = quantity demanded

Marginal revenue MR is given as

$MR = \dfrac{d(PQ)}{dQ}$

By the rule of differentiation of a product

$MR = P + \dfrac{d(Q)}{dQ} + Q\,\dfrac{dP}{dQ}$

Since dQ/dQ = 1

$MR = P + Q\,\dfrac{dP}{dQ}$

Therefore $MR = P\left[1 + \dfrac{Q}{P}\dfrac{dP}{dQ}\right]$

But price elasticity of demand εp is defined as

$\varepsilon p = \dfrac{dQ\,P}{dP\,Q}$

Its reciprocal, $\dfrac{1}{\varepsilon p} = \dfrac{Q}{P}\dfrac{dP}{dQ}$ which leads to εp

$MR = P\left(1 + \dfrac{1}{\epsilon_p}\right)$

For profit-maximising price P*

$MR = MC = P^*\left(1 + \dfrac{1}{\epsilon_p}\right)$

Appendix 5.2: Optimal Markup for Cournot Oligopoly

The Cournot Oligopoly in this case assumes n homogenous (identical) firms. The optimal or profit-maximising price (P) for a firm in the market is:

$P = \left(\dfrac{n\varepsilon p*}{1 + n\varepsilon p*}\right) = MC$

Where $\varepsilon p *$ = market elasticity of demand

MC = marginal cost.

In this case, the price elasticity of demand for the product of an individual firm is n times that of the market price elasticity of demand, i.e.

$\epsilon_p = \epsilon_p *$

Appendix 5.3: Tying and Bundling

Tying

Tying is strategic pricing where a consumer is charged a 'tying price' for two or more goods by a dominant (monopolistic or oligopolistic) firm or dealer. When computers were introduced consumers were charged for computers and their tabulating or punch cards. Similarly, when the Xerox Corporation was the only producer of photocopiers in the 1950s, one had to purchase some paper from the company, for leasing a photocopier (Salvatore 2006). More current examples include (i) the case of a franchise operation firm tying the use of its brand name to the purchase of franchise inputs (Church and Ware 2000:168) (ii) the case of manufacturers or dealers of certain machines who tie service contracts of the machine and charge as a 'tying price' or 'package price' (iii) the case of dealers of certain types of cars, e.g. some dealers of cars who tend to monopolise the sale and services of such cars as the case of Toyota Motors Company in Botswana.

Tying may be regarded as a form of two-tariff pricing as it may discriminate between high-demand users and low-demand users, thereby qualifying to be also a form of price-discrimination. This is normally the case when the average price for the services of the good varies inversely with the intensity of use, i.e., the high-demand users tend to pay a lower average price than the low-demand users (Church and Ware 2000:169).

Bundling

Bundling or commodity bundling or bundle pricing is a pricing strategy practiced normally by a dominant firm of selling two or more different commodities/products at a single '*bundle price*'. It is a form of tying in fixed proportions or fixed packages like left and right shoes; or car body is bundled with engines and tyres (Church and Ware 2000:169) as a fixed package.

Although bundling is a form of tying, it is not closely related to price-discrimination as the case of tying per se.

Appendix 5.4: Skimming Pricing

Skimming pricing or simply skimming is a strategic practice of setting high prices when a new product or a special new brand is introduced and gradually but profitably lowering the price. This may occur in the case of a new brand of cars, refrigerators, and personal computers.

Skimming may be viewed as a special form of market penetration pricing. Skimming may also be regarded as subset of value pricing – a pricing strategy where the price is adjusted from time to time in line with the value and elasticity of demand (Douglas 1992:467; Salvatore 2006; Regent Business School 2007:83).

Notes

1. For details see, for example, Allen et al (2005:430).
2. See, for instance, Allen et al (2005:536).
3. For details see, for example, Salvatore (2006).
4. In the Cournot Oligopoly there are few firms in the market servicing many consumers. The firms produce either differentiated or homogeneous products. Each firm is assumed to believe that rivals will hold their output constant if it changes its own output (Baye 2010:400).
5. For details, see, for instance, Salvatore (2006).
6. Cf. Douglas (1992:446).
7. For details see Keat and Young (ch. 14).
8. Cf. Andreasso and Jacobson (2005:218).
9. This is in line with the early works of Pigou (1932).
10. For details, see Salvatore (2006).
11. For details, see Pricing in Africa (in the subsequent sections) also Lipczynski *et al* (2009:321).
12. Cf. Andreasso and Jacobson (2005:221).
13. See, for instance, Church and Ware (2000:166).
14. Cf. Salvatore (2006).
15. Ibid.
16. See, for instance, Baye (2010: 416).
17. Cf. Hirschey (2009: 567) and Douglas (1992:469).
18. See, for example, Andreasso and Jacobson (2005:218).
19. See, for instance, Salvatore (2006).
20. Very few countries were not under SAPs, Botswana being an example.
21. See, first degree price discrimination
22. See, Baah-Nuakoh (1997:161).
23. Cf. Regent Business School (2007:74).

6

Non-Price Strategies

Learning Objectives

The main objectives of this chapter are:

- To identify the main non-price strategies which are made by firms for the sake of non-price competition;
- To elaborate on the non-price strategies; and
- To outline their applicability and relevance in Africa with special reference to regional integration.

Introductory Note

Firms with market power sometimes prefer non-price competition to price competition to outwit their rivals. As has been stated by Douglas,[1] "Any fool can cut prices, but it takes genius to conduct a successful promotional campaign." Indeed, advertising and promotional campaigns and other non-price strategies are difficult to conduct successfully.

Furthermore, non-price strategies may be more suitable than price strategies in some cases. For instance, newly introduced goods, goods whose attributes are fully unknown before purchasing (*experience goods*), and those goods whose attributes are partially unknown (*credence goods*) need more advertising and promotional approaches.[2]

This chapter identifies and examines various non-price strategies. It finally outlines their applicability and relevance in Africa, with special reference to regional integration.

Identification of the Main Non-Price Strategies

The main non-price strategies cited in various literature sources are advertising, research and development, and protection for intellectual property, integration and mergers and diversification.[3] These fall under conduct in the S-C-P model. They are examined in detail hereunder.

Advertising

Basic Definitions and Concepts

Advertising is a method employed by producers to inform and persuade consumers to buy their products so that they promote sales. It is therefore part of promotional strategies. Advertising may be done directly or indirectly. *Direct advertising* is a straightforward method of advertising. It includes advertising directly in newspapers, on radio, on television or by displaying the product. *Indirect advertising* is practiced somewhat latently; for instance, by establishing a *brand name* (special name or label) and establishing positive reputation.

Advertising may also be informative or persuasive. *Informative advertising* is a way of providing consumers with factual information about a product's attributes such as price and physical appearance. *Persuasive advertising is directly* convincing consumers to change their perceptions of a product by making subjective claims or statements which may not be easy to prove, e.g. 'consuming brand X of peanut butter will make you younger and sexually powerful'.

In general, advertising, whether informative or persuasive is one of the main strategies used by firms to compete. There are, however, specific reasons why firms invest in advertising. The main ones are outlined in the next section.

Main Specific Rationales for Advertising

Increasing Revenue or Sales and Profit

Advertising expenditure is expected to increase revenue or sales and profit. Consider Figure 6.1 as an illustration. Advertising will shift the demand curve to the right from D_0 to D_1. In this case, quantity demanded will increase from Q_0 to Q_1, thereby increasing revenue from P_0Q_0 to P_0Q_1 and profit from $\pi_0 = P_0Q_0 - C$ to $P_0Q_1 - C$ (assume price (P_0) and cost (C) remain constant).

The shift will depend on advertising sensitivity or *advertising elasticity of demand*. For an empirical example, see Appendix 6.1.

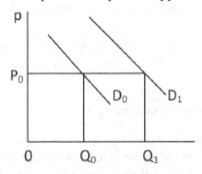

Figure 6.1: Shift of the Demand Curve to the Right at Constant Price

Strategic Rationale

Established firms with market power may advertise for strategic reasons. If advertising shifts the demand curve in a manner similar to that explained above, it may discourage rivals, new and potential entrants. This is especially pronounced when rivals or new entrants who use the same strategy find advertising to be less effective or more costly than in the case of established firms which enjoy economies of scale, consumer loyalty and relatively large market shares.[5]

Increasing Price

A monopolistic firm may easily advertise its products and simultaneously raise the price.[6] In so doing, the firm will be increasing revenue and profit based on the shift of the demand curve.

In Figure 6.2, for example, price may be increased from P_0 to P^*, thereby increasing the revenue from P_0Q_0 to P^*Q^* and profit from $\pi_0 = P_0Q_0 - C^*$ to $\pi^* = P^*Q^* - C^*$ (assume the cost C^* remains constant).

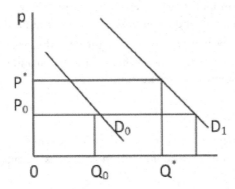

Figure 6.2: Shift of the Demand Curve to the Right and Price Increase

Launching and Popularising New Products, Special Products and Brands

For new and special products and brands, advertising is ideal to provide early consumers and potential consumers with information about them.

For special products (experience and credence products) advertising is ideal because their attributes have to be known after purchasing them, contrary to search products.

Advertising also establishes and magnifies the images of new and special products and brands, thereby strengthening consumer loyalty to the products.[7]

Advertising under Different Markets

Introductory Note

Despite the above-mentioned generalised rationales for advertising, the importance or intensity of advertising varies according to market structure or types of market. The scope for advertising under perfect competition is theoretical zero while it is relatively limited under monopoly as elaborated hereunder.

Advertising under Perfect Competition

Theoretically, there is no role of advertising under perfect competition essentially because information is assumed to be perfectly known to all participants in the market.

Advertising under Monopoly

Under the other extreme case of monopoly, the scope of advertising is relatively limited as, in theory, monopolists have no competitors. However, they have potential entrants. Monopolists can use strategic advertising to bar them. They may also advertise to launch and popularise new or special products and brands.

As monopolists, they have the power to increase the price as price makers simultaneously with advertising. The ultimate aim, in general, is to increase total industry demand and maximise revenue and profit.

Advertising under Oligopoly

Oligopolistic firms may attempt to avoid price competition by advertising and practicing other non-price competition strategies because of their close independence since they are few.

Under oligopoly the incentive to advertise is strong in order to increase total industry demand and to attract consumers away from their rivals.[8]

Monopolistic Competition

Under monopolistic competition the intensity to advertise will depend on the number of firms in industry or market concentration. In general, however, the incentive to advertise, as was the case with monopoly and oligopoly, is to increase total industry demand.

Relationship between Advertising Intensity and Market Structure

In general, the relationship between profit-maximising *advertising intensity* (measured by advertising-to-sales ratio[9]) to market structure (measured by market concentration ratio) is as shown in Figure 6.3.

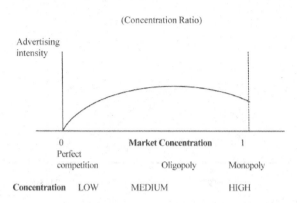

Figure 6.3: Relationship between Advertising Intensity and Market Structure
Source: Modified from Clarke 2000:127

Note that the advertising intensity is low at the two extremes (perfect competition and monopoly). In fact, for perfect competition both the advertising intensity and concentration ratio are equal to zero: underscoring the proposition that there is no need to advertise under perfect competition. For monopoly, however, the advertising intensity is lower than that under oligopoly, but the concentration ratio is maximum (1).

The quadratic form has been supported empirically (Sutton 1974) as shown in detail in Appendix 6.2. Other authors who subsequently supported the model include Weiss et al (1963), Buxton *et al.* (1984) and Uri (1987).

Regarding causations between advertising intensity and concentration, some authors maintain the reverse or two-way causations implied in the S-C-P model. Fruitful advertising campaigns affect market shares and hence concentration; so that, not only may concentration affect ad vertising intensity in an industry, but a reverse effect is also possible.[10]

Optimal Advertising

Optimal advertising is the profit-maximising level of advertising expenditure. It is also assumed to be the sales or revenue-maximising advertising. For the expected case of quadratic form, it is easy to visualise that a firm cannot continue advertising indefinitely due to diminishing returns. It will eventually reach a point where further advertisement will lead to lower profit as shown in Figure 6.4.

In this illustration, profit (π) is assumed to be a function of advertisement expenditure, i.e. $\pi = f(A)$. In a specified form:

$$\pi = \alpha_0 + \alpha_1 A + \alpha_2 A, \ ^2\alpha_2 < 0$$

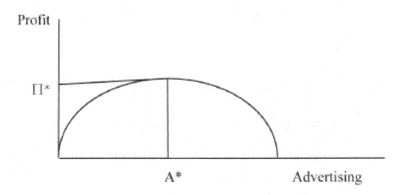

Figure 6.4: Optimal Advertising Level and Optimal Profit

The optimal advertising level is A* when profit is at its maximum level (π*). Further expenditure or *investment in advertising* after A* leads to lower returns.

The use of the economic optimisation example is in order:

Using the profit function for the New Millennium Company in Namibia specified in 2011 as follows:

π = 10000 + 200A – A²;

we can find the optimal levels of advertising and profit as follows: Applying the economic optimisation rule (fist order condition):

dπ/dA = 200 – 2A = 0

Therefore A* = 100

Putting this value in the profit function

π* = 10000 + 200(100) – (100)²

i.e. π* = 20000.

Therefore the company advertised profitably up to the level A* = N$100; thereafter the company got lower than the maximum N$20000 profit.

Note that in the absence of advertising (A = 0) the company still made profit of N$10000. By advertising, it doubled its profit.

The more used approach is employing the neo-classical general rule: MR = MC for profit maximisation.

In this case:

MR_A = MC_A   (6.2)

where MRA = marginal revenue from advertising

    MCA = marginal cost of advertising

It pays to increase advertising expenditure when MR_A> MC_A; otherwise reduce advertising expenditure (see Figure 6.5).

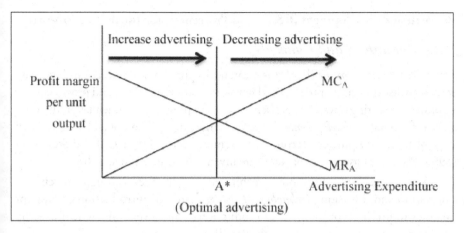

Figure 6.5: Optimal Advertising at MRA = MCA
Source: Hirschey (2009)

Note that first order condition, the marginal profit from advertising is zero.

i.e. $M\pi_A = 0$ (6.3)

where $M\pi_A = MR_A - MC_A$ (6.4)

Collusive Advertising

A similar approach to oligopolistic collusive pricing explained in the previous chapter may be made to illustrate *collusive advertising*. Replacing 'low price' by advertise and 'high price' by 'do not advertise' the following payoff matrix is in order:

Table 6.1: Payoff Matrix for an Advertising Game

		Firm Y	
Strategy		Advertise	**Do not advertise**
Firm X	Advertise	(20, 20)	(50, 10)
	Do not advertise	(10, 50)	(30, 30)

In this case, if firm Y advertises, the payoff for firm X will be $20 if it also advertises, and $10 if it does not advertise. If, however, firm Y does not advertise, firm X will get a profit of $50 if it advertises and $30 if it does not advertise. The dominant strategy for firm X is to advertise.

Similarly, if firm X advertises, firm Y's payoff will be $20 if it also advertises; otherwise it gets $10. If firm X does not advertise, firm Y will get a profit of $50 if it advertises and $30 if does not advertise. Advertising is also the dominant strategy for firm Y.

If both do not advertise as collusively agreed, each firm will get a profit of $30.

Research and Development (R&D) and Protections for Intellectual Pro-perty

Basic Definitions and Concepts

Research and Development (R&D) is a careful inquiry-study (*research*) in industries and other institutions that tries to find new information, products and processes or to improve the existing ones; the goal being technical progress, commercial production, and profit making *(development)*. *Diffusion* is more often than not added as the final stage of the R&D process. According to Schumpeter (1928, 1950) and Stoneman (1995) the three basic stages of R&D are invention, innovation and diffusion.

R&D, therefore, promotes technological change through invention, innovation and diffusion. *Technological change* being the introduction of superior qualities to products or methods of production, which eventually render existing products or production processes obsolete.[11]

While *invention* may be regarded as development of new ideas, *innovation* is considered the successful application of the new ideas.[12]

Diffusion is the spread of the new ideas or research output to other firms apart from the original innovator.[13]

Rationale for R&D

R&D, like advertisement, is a business strategy under the conduct (C) in the S-C-P paradigm. It is assumed that the higher the expenditure or investment in R&D, the more profit the firm can make, and the better the performance (P) of the firm. The reverse is also possible.

R&D, through technological change, has a positive impact on output, product quality, employment, wages and profits, and leads to growth of the economy and development in general.[14] R&D may, therefore, be regarded as the engine of technological change which is crucial to growth and development.[15]

R&D, like advertisement, provides an outlet for non-price competition between rival firms. Investment in R&D and the pace of diffusion determine the pace of technological progress.[16]

The strategic importance of R&D is closely related to its strategies: offensive, defensive, imitative, and dependent strategies. These are explained below:

An *offensive strategy* is a way used by a firm to dominate its market through introduction on of new technology which is normally controlled through legal property rights and patents. The strategy is the basic rationale for monopolistic and other firms with substantial market power to invest in *strategic R&D* aimed basically at preventing entry and imitation.

A *defensive strategy* is essentially a strategy for survival. In order to survive, some firms invest in R&D. They attempt to improve on the innovations of offensive firms.

An *imitative strategy* is basically a copying strategy. Normally, it is legalised by acquiring a license in the short run and exploring free knowledge in the long run. An imitative strategy is usually less expensive as it can use relatively cheap labour substitutes and less expensive means of copying than being innovative.

Some countries like China have used imitative strategies in order to exploit technologies that have been developed elsewhere. They have done this through imitating, then adopting and finally creating own technologies. African countries may wish to learn from such countries.

A *dependent strategy* is a strategy whereby firms do not initiate R&D and technologies but adopt them when handed to the firms mostly as a condition of relationship preservation. The practice is common in Japanese electronics and motor industries. The relationship may sometimes develop into vertical integration.[17]

R&D Investment under Various Markets

Background Information

In order to understand the root explanation of R&D under different markets or market structure, a retrospective approach is in order.

The work of Schumpeter (1950) is basic in this case. Many authors[18] support the Schumpeterian view that there is a positive relationship between innovation and market power, and large firms are more innovative than small firms. Investment in R&D will thus vary across various markets and will be relatively easy in large firms owing to economies of scale.

There are also two connections between market structure and innovation. First, patents allow a firm to gain market power by innovating. Second, a firm with market power may be able to prevent entry and imitation through defensive patents or maintain its power through the introduction of new products.[19]

R&D Investment under Monopoly

Many authors[20] also still support the Schumpeterian hypothesis that there is a position association between innovation and monopoly. Monopolists may invest in R&D and advertising to prevent entry and imitation. However, unlike competitive firms, monopolistic firms tend to be relatively bureaucratic, technically inefficient in production and too complacent to allow further technological progress since they may be earning abnormal profit. The need to invest more in R&D to increase the abnormal profit may not be given top priority.

R&D Investment under Generally Competitive Firms

Unlike the case of monopolistic firms, competition pressure under competition markets forces firms to be relatively cost-conscious, allowing no technical inefficiency (X-efficiency).

As Arrow (1962) argues, the incentive to innovate may be greater under competitive markets than it is under monopoly. A competitive firm earns profit from its new R & D process over more units than does a monopolist.

R&D Investment under Oligopoly

It is commonly argued that oligopoly is the most conducive market structure to fast pace of technological change.[21] This is basically because oligopolists are relatively interdependent, and have ability to collude and to form co-operative joint ventures which enjoy economies of scale.

The oligopolistic firms, therefore, have greater means and incentive to invest in R & D than firms operating under other market structure.

R&D and Intellectual Property Protection

Firms which engage in R&D are expected to gain technological advantage, thereafter obtain patents and other types of intellectual property protection. There are four main types of intellectual property protection: patents, copyrights, trademarks and trade secrets. They are defined and explained below.

Patents are (intellectual) property rights that confer monopoly rights to an innovation; they are forms of prizes for firms to compete.[22] Patents empower investors with exclusive rights to new products, processes, substances and new designs. Examples of new products are new machines and manufactured parts or tools; processes include chemical and electrical processes in manufacturing; substances include chemical compounds and mixtures; and examples of new designs are new shapes of product.[23] Many governments and private organisations in advanced countries promote patents and rewards to inventors, innovators and discoverers. The US government has even relaxed antitrust prohibitions to allow firms to coordinate R & D through joint ventures.[24] Africa should learn lessons from these governments.

Copyrights are intellectual property rights which give their creators exclusive production, publication or sales rights. They include artistic, dramatic, literacy, and musical works. Specific examples include articles, books, computer-based material, drawings, maps, musical compositions and photographs.[25]

Trademarks are symbols, words or other marks used to distinguish a good provided by one firm from those provided by others.[26]

Trade secrets are forms of (intellectual) property protection which use hidden information. A commonly quoted example is the formula for Coca-Cola which is hidden or protected through secret keeping.[27]

R&D Intensity as a Measure of Technology

R&D intensity may be defined in a similar way we defined advertising intensity, i.e. R&D spending is a ratio of sales or revenue for a given firm, or R&D spending as a ratio of turnover. The latter was used by OECD (1994) to categorise high and low technology. The detailed categorisation is shown in Table 6.2.

Table 6.2: Technology Categorisation of Industries Based on R&D

Serial No.	Category	R & D Turnover (%)
1	High-tech industries	>5.0
2	Medium high-tech industries	3.0 – 5.0
3	Medium low-tech industries Low-	0.9 – 2.9
4	tech industries	0 – 2.8

Source: OECD (1994) and Andreasso & Jacobson (2005: 297)

Examples of high-tech industries are pharmaceuticals, aerospace, machinery and computers and electronics. Industries like rubber and plastics, food, soap, and food are normally in lower categories.[28]

Product Differentiation

Basic Definitions and Concepts

Despite the existence of many definitions of product differentiation, the main difference stems from the emphasis on who is differentiating – the producers or the consumers. In theory, however, both are expected to 'differentiate' the products. Consider the following definition:

Products differentiation can be viewed as the ability of producers to create distinctions (in a physical or in a psychological sense) between goods that are close substitutes, so that consumers no longer regard them as identical or near-identical. (Lipczynski *et al.* 2009: 383).

The emphasis here is on the producers although the consumers are brought in the definition at the end.

Historically, however, the consumers or buyers have been emphasized. According to Bain (1968: 223): 'Product differentiation refers to the extent to which buyers differentiate, distinguish, or have specific preferences among the competing outputs of the various sellers."

This is in line with Chamberlin's (1933) view that much of the product differentiation is perceived rather than real.

In this textbook, a balanced working definition is suggested as follows:

Product differentiation is real or perceived distinction of products which were formerly regarded as identical by both producers and consumers.

Real distinction is based on physical attributes like shape and other differences arising from R&D application. Quality is also easily recognised through reliability, efficiency and performance.

Perceived distinction is subjective or psychological as the judgment of the quality or distinction may be influenced by effective advertising, promotion and other factors.

Product differentiation may also be regarded theoretically as horizontal or vertical.

Horizontal product differentiation is product distinction based on individual preferences, and not on consumers' general agreement.

Vertical product differentiation is product distinction based on commonly agreed quality or attributes. If all or most of the consumers prefer milk chocolate to non-milk chocolate, they are practicing vertical product differentiation.[29]

More often than not, products are differentiated horizontally and vertically in practice. Product differentiation may also be classified into natural or strategic type.

Natural product differentiation is product distinction based on natural attributes rather than imposed attributes by producers or suppliers. Examples are consumers' preferences, community or national sources, e.g. Italian shoes or Swiss watches which are assumed to be of high quality.

Strategic product differentiation is product distinction done deliberately by producers or suppliers, e.g. creation of new brands. Strategic product differentiation can also be used to discourage new entrants into the market.[30]

Rationales for Product Differentiation

Like the cases of advertising and R & D strategies, the overall rationale for product differentiation strategy is a weapon for non-price competition. Specific reasons for product differentiation are:

Increasing revenue or sales and profit

Like advertising, product differentiation is expected to increase revenue or sales and profit as implied in the S-C-P paradigm. This is done by increasing demand as is the case in advertisement.

Establishing Brand Loyalty

Another reason for product differentiation, like the case of advertising, is to establish brand loyalty to consumers.

Strategic Rationale

Product differentiation may be adopted by incumbent firms which enjoy economies of scale to raise barriers to entry.

In this case, the incumbent firms practice *strategic product differentiation* as explained earlier.

Product Differentiation under Various Markets

Production Differentiation under Perfect Competition

Like the case of advertising, the role of product differentiation under perfect competition is negligible as the products are assumed to be homogeneous and have no substitutes. Under the perfect competition model, there is no incentive for any individual firm to expand special effort in increasing sales, given the assumption that each firm can sell as much as it wants without such extra effort.[30]

Product Differentiation under Imperfect Market

Whereas under perfect competition firms can adjust only the quantity supplied once price is in equilibrium, those under imperfect competition can adjust their advertising and promotional efforts, product design or differentiation, and distributional channels. This includes the case of monopolistic firms. However, as argued in the case of R & D, monopolistic firms may be satisfied by the existence of abnormal profit and unique products, thus they may not give product design or differentiation top priority.

Most literature sources discuss product differentiation under monopolistic competition where very similar product exist.[31]

Normally, firms in monopolistically competitive industries use two strategies to persuade customers to buy their differentiated products. First, they use *comparative advertising*, defined as a form of advertising where firms endeavour to increase the demand for their brands by differentiating them from those of their rivals. Second, they introduce new products and advertise them to all. These new products may also be meant for *niche markets* (markets tailored to meet the needs of a particular segment of the market) or *green market* (a form of niche market where firms target products useful to consumers who are concerned about environmental issues).[32]

Like the case of monopolistic competition, firms under oligopoly may also be employed so as to increase sales. They also involve advertising and R & D as explained earlier.

Under oligopoly, *collusive product differentiation* is also possible. A payoff matrix for product differentiation can be constructed as the case of the payoff matrix for advertising as shown in Table 6.1. In this case, the words advertise and *do not advertise* should be replaced by *differentiate and do not differentiate* the product respectively.

Measures of Product Differentiation

Background Information

The simple commonly employed measures of product differentiation are cross-price elasticity of demand and advertising intensity.[33]

Cross-price Elasticity of Demand

Cross-price elasticity of demand measures the sensitivity of quantity demanded to change in the price of another product; the higher the difference between the products the lower the cross-price elasticity of demand.

Advertising Intensity

As noted earlier, advertising intensity is normally estimated by advertising-to-sales ratio. Advertising intensity is, in fact, a proxy for product differentiation. The higher the amount spent by a firm on advertising, the more its product is differentiated. This is expected because of the existence of a positive relationship between advertising and product differentiation.

Integration and Mergers

Basic Concepts and Definitions

In its simple form, *integration* or *consolidation* occurs by merging two or more firms into a single firm.[34] A merger is the joining together of two or more firms into a single firm; usually one retains its identity. In practice, *acquisitions* and *takeovers* are forms of mergers; however, none of the firms legally retains its identity.[35]

Integration is usually viewed broadly in two ways: first, as an existing or organisational structure; and second, as a strategic component in the conduct and behaviour element in the S-C-P paradigm.

In the first sense, *integration* is defined as the extent to which a firm carries successive stages in designing R & D, processing (production), marketing and distribution of a product. In this case, the firm is *vertically integrated*. To emphasise the organisational structure, this type of integration is also called *corporate integration*. If the different stages are undertaken by separate firms in a particular industry (instead of a single firm), the integration is called *industrial integration*.36

There are three main types of corporate integration:

(i)   Horizontal corporate integration. This is the combination of two or more firms, plants or processes that are at the same stage of transformation process;

(ii) Vertical corporate integration: The combination of two or more firms, plants or processes that are at separate stages of the same transformation process.

(iii) Conglomerate corporate integration. This combination of two or more firms, plants or processes that are in different product areas.[37]

The second sense of integration is reflected in the conduct item of the S-C-P paradigm. Integration is viewed synonymously as a merger.[38] This line of analysis leads to three of mergers or integration.

Horizontal integration or horizontal merger. This involves firms producing the same or similar and substitutable product (e.g. brands of soap).

Vertical integration or vertical merger involves firms operating at different stages of the same production process.

Conglomerate integration or merger is the combination of firms producing different products (product lines) into a single firm.

It should, however, be noted that, viewed comprehensively but somewhat differently, *vertical integration* occurs when a firm moves into another production or distribution either via vertical merger or by introducing new production or distribution means. In this case, *backward integration* or *upstream integration* takes place when the firm moves into production of raw materials and inputs; but when the move is on final production and distribution, *forward integration or downstream integration* takes place. When a motor car firm, for example, merges with a machine tools firm, the integration is backward or upstream; but when the motor car firm acquires a distribution firm the integration is forward or downstream.[39]

Incentives for Integration and Mergers

Background Information

The incentives for integration and mergers are more pronounced in the case of vertical integration/vertical merger.[40] They include the following:

Transaction Economies

As shall be explained below, most of the reasons for firms to merge or integrate vertically are centred on transaction economies: benefit from reduced costs and market externalities. Normally, integration leads to economies of scale which include transaction economies. Former transaction costs like cost of searching for suppliers of inputs and distributors of output are practically eliminated.

Technological Economies

With vertical merging or integration, firms are likely to realise reduction in technological cost (technological economies) through combined R&D and technological progress or through combining technologically interdependent firms, e.g. iron and steel producing firms; pulping and newsprint production; barley/wheat and beer production. In so doing, the implied transaction costs are reduced.

Increased Efficiency and Welfare

Transaction economies are positively related to increased efficiency and welfare. In this case, efficiency is viewed in terms of minimisation of transaction costs. This is also in line with the S-C-P paradigm in which mergers are viewed as one of the business strategies of increasing efficiency, profitability and growth which are elements of performance. Growth may also lead to increase in welfare.[41]

Circumventing Government Regulations

Another reason related to reducing transaction costs for vertical merging or integration is circumventing or bypassing regulations related to taxes, prices and related aspects. This is basically done by firms which practice vertical integration and aim at overcoming or exploiting differences in tax and price control regulation in different countries, regions or between upstream and downstream.

If corporate tax rates are higher in South Africa than they are in Botswana, for instance, establishing a subsidiary in Botswana through vertical integration with the main firm in South Africa would be the right decision in order to circumvent higher taxes. This may also be done when one location or part of the production process (e.g. upstream) has lower or controlled prices. The move would be towards the lower price location or part of the production process.

In general, the resultant pricing is called *profit-switching transfer pricing*.[42]

Reducing Uncertainty and Assurance of Inputs Availability and Output Markets

Since transactions between firms at different process stages are mostly uncertain, vertical mergers and integration reduce such uncertainty. They also assume availability of inputs and reliable distribution of final output to the market.

Increasing Market Power

When firms merge or integrate, their market power increases. Firms which integrate vertically with an input firm and a distributing firm, for instance, generally enjoy transaction economies or economies of scale or scope, thereby enjoying higher profits. Such firms may also acquire monopolistic behaviour like practicing price discrimination and barring entry.

Eliminating Market Power

This may happen in the case of victims of another firm's market power. The commonly cited example[43] is that of dairy farmers who face a single processor, who buys their milk at a low, monopsonic price. If farmers unite vertically by forming their own processing firm, they may eliminate the market power of their rival and simultaneously increase their market power.

Correcting Market Failure

Vertical integration may be useful in correcting market failure due, for instance, to externalities. By internalising the externalities through new ownership and use of the same trademark or logo arising from integration, market failure is corrected and consumers will perceive the same quality of the firms' product regardless of the firms' location.[44]

Diversification Basic Concepts and Definitions

Diversification is firms' involvement into the production of new, related or unrelated products (*product extension diversification or multi-product diversification*) or into a different geographical market (*geographical diversification or market extension diversification*).

Diversification may occur through internal expansion into different product lines or through mergers or acquisitions (*conglomerate   diversification   or pure diversification*). Conglomerate diversification or merger may also be regarded as a form of horizontal corporate integration.

Incentives for Diversification

Cost Savings

Cost savings may be realized through economies of scope, transaction economies, reduction of risk and uncertainty and reduction of tax exposure.[45]

Economies of scope are benefits for multi-product diversification. In general, however, cost savings are realised through economies of scale. While *economies of scale* are realised when the firm reduces its long-run average cost by increasing its *scale of production, economies of scope* are realised when long-run average cost savings are achieved by spreading costs of the *production of several products.*[46]

Transaction economies arising from the reduction of transaction costs also form the basis of the incentives for diversification in a similar way with mergers and corporate integration. Diversified firms which supply both goods and services may reduce transaction costs related to, for instance, service delivery. Another source of reduction of transaction costs is the case where diversified firms are regarded as conglomerates which are also internal capital market or are vehicles for the exploitation of specific assets.[47]

Regarding reduction of risk and uncertainty diversification, mergers and integration may be regarded as means of reducing transaction costs arising from risk and uncertainty. This is likely to raise finance at lower costs.

Regarding the tax exposure reduction front, if the tax system allows tax deduction of interest payment, a diversified firm may practice debt (external) financing rather than equity (internal) financing in some activities or subsidiaries. This may lead to an overall reduction in the firm's taxable profit.[48]

Enhancing Market Power and Diversifying Competition Strategies

A diversified firm which operates in a number of geographical and product market is likely to have enough competition resources to fight rivals.

Diversification can also lead to a variety of competition strategies such as cross- subsidisation and predatory pricing, tying and reciprocity. All these, except reciprocity, have been explained in the previous chapter. *Reciprocity* is an agreement strategy that firm A purchases inputs from firm B on the understanding that firm B also purchases inputs (or something else) from firm A.[49] Diversification may even involve global diversification strategies such as international predatory pricing strategy.

Managerial Incentives

As argued earlier, unlike owners (shareholders) whose principal objective is profit maximisation, salaried managers who control firms' operation may be interested in other objectives such as prestigious cars and other assets, growth of the firm, and large employment. Since diversification is likely to meet these objectives, they may be regarded as managerial motives for diversification, which may also be in line with owners' objective of maximising profit.[50]

Measures of Diversification

Background Information

Measures of diversification are comparable to the measures of concentration as will be noted in the subsequent explanation.

Number of Activities

The simplest case is the number of activities involved by the diversified firm preferably using 3 – 4 digit International Standard Industrial Classification (ISIC). This is analogous to the reciprocal of number of firms as an index of concentration. However, this measure is regarded as too simple for analysis.

Diversification Ratio

Diversification ratio, also called *Specialisation ratio,* is the ratio of non-primary activities to all activities:

$$DR = \frac{Y}{X+Y}$$

where   DR = diversification ratio

          X = firm's primary activity

          Y = non-primary activities

X and Y are usually measured in terms of employees, sales or output.

Clearly, when Y = 0, DR = 0, it implies the firm is not diversified but specialised. The greater the Y, the more the degree of diversification. The maximum value of DR is 1. This measure is comparable to the concentration ratio. Its limitation is that it does not indicate the relative importance of each of the Y-activities.[51]

Herfindahl Index of Specialisation

The *Herfindahl index of specialisation,* H(S) is centred on a weighted sum of the share of each activity in the total activities. If a firm has n activities

$$H(S) = \sum_{i=1}^{n} S_i^2$$

where s_i = the share of sales, output or employment in activity i to the total. The more specialised the firm, the greater the H(S).

This index is comparable to the Hirschman-Herfindahl Index (H) of concentration.

A variant of the index was suggested by Berry (1975). Berry's index (B) is:

$$B = 1 - \sum_{i=1}^{n} s_i$$

If the firm is completely specialised B = 0.

Other Measures

There are other relatively less common indices comparable to concentration indices such as the entropy index explained in Appendix 4.2.[52] Some authors[53] have also suggested a comparability between mergers and acquisitions (M & As) and internal expansion. Since both of them apply to one firm the two strategies are not necessarily alternatives. Furthermore, recent empirical evidence has shown that M & As, internal expansion and *joint ventures* (joint ownership or co-operation of firms) are the main means of diversification. They should not be regarded as alternative strategies of diversification.

Applicability and Relevance of Non-Price Strategies in Africa

Applicability

Most of the explained non-price strategies are applicable and can be applied in Africa. Advertising and promotional strategies in general; R&D and protection of intellectual property; product differentiation; and diversification through mergers; joint ventures and acquisitions are common in Africa.

Advertising and promotional activities are indeed very common in Africa. In Tanzania, for instance, every year on 7th July (*Saba-Saba*) they hold a trade fair in Dar-es-Salaam for business people to exhibit their products. Neighbouring countries, SADC members and the international community in general also participate in the fair.

Promotional activities are also common in Tanzania. Promotional campaigns are normally done in shops, restaurants and bars where certain brands of beer, non-alcoholic drinks and other products are sold at lower promotional prices. In this case, other pricing strategies are employed. Examples include "buy two and get one free", "buy three and get a free T-shirt".

Advertising to boost revenue and profit is also common in Africa. An illustration is in order: Using the demand function and cost function before introducing advertising for the Wacha-wivu Company in Kenya estimated in 2013, i.e.

$Q = 8000 - 100P$ and $C = 5000 + 50Q$

where

Q = quantity demanded

P = own price

C = Total cost

the profit may be obtained as follows: Before Advertising

From the estimated equation

$P = 80 - 0.01Q$

Therefore, revenue, $R = PQ = (80 - 0.01Q)Q$

$$R = 80Q - 0.01Q^2$$

Thus marginal revenue = $MR = 80 - 0.02Q$

But marginal cost (MC) = 50

Since MR = MC

Thus $80 - 0.02Q = 50$

$$Q = 1500$$

and $P = 80 - 0.01 (1500)$

i.e. $P = 65$

But profit, $\pi = R - C$

$= (80Q - 0.01Q2) - (5000 + 50Q)$

$= 30Q - 0.01Q2 - 5000$

$= 30(1500) - 0.01(1500)2 - 5000$

$= 17500$

Therefore, before introducing advertising the Company made a profit of Ksh17,500.

After Introducing Advertising

It was estimated that the demand doubled due to the positive impact of advertising. The profit function after advertising π_A can be found (when MRA $= MC_A$) as follows:

$QA = 2(8000 - 100P)$

$= 16000 - 200P$

Thus $P = 80 - 0.005QA$ Therefore revenue R will be PQA

$R = (80 - 0.005Q_A)Q_A$ or $80Q_A - 0.005Q^2$

Therefore $MRA = 80 - 0.01Q_A$

But $MR_A = MC_A$

Assuming the cost function remained the same.

$80 - 0.01Q_A = 50$

$Q_A = 3000$

and $P = 80 - 0.005 (3000)$

$= 65$

Profit $\pi_A = R_A - C$

$= 80Q_A - 0.005Q^2 - (5000 - 50Q_A)$

$= 30Q_A - 0.005Q_A^2 - 5000$

$= 30(3000) - 0.005(3000)2 - 5000$

$\pi_A = 40,000$

As a conclusion the Wacha-wivu Company enjoyed a higher profit of Ksh 40,000 because of advertising than the profit of Ksh 17,500 before introducing advertising. It more than doubled the profit while the sales doubled from 1,500 to 3,000 at the price Ksh 65.

Another non-price strategy used in Africa is Research and Development (R&D). Nevertheless, African experience in R&D is generally gloomy. There are, however, some institutions earmarked for R&D. Examples from Tanzania include the Tanzania Industrial Research and Development Organisation (TIRDO), the Centre for Agricultural Mechanisation and Rural Technology (CAMERTEC), the Institute for Production Innovation (IPI) and the overall Commission for Science and

Technology (CST). Despite the establishment of such institutions, few innovations have been promoted.[54] Hindering problems include lack of enough finance and low allocation of funds for R&D, and misallocation of engineers and other scientists to administrative and political tasks. Government spending on R&D had been around only one per cent of total government expenditure and misallocations of scientists even in the technology institutions is common in Tanzania.[55]

By the mid 1990s, however, there were few industrial firms in Tanzania engaged in R&D activities. A comprehensive survey in 1994 revealed that firms engaged in R&D were mainly large. Sixteen per cent of the large firms were involved in R&D, while 12 per cent of medium-scale firms and only 3 per cent of small-scale firms were engaged in R&D.[56]

Regarding R&D and intellectual property (IP) rights, the World Intellectual Property Organisation (WIPO) has attempted to promote them in Africa. In 2006, IP audits were conducted in 20 African countries, whereby Ethiopia, Kenya, Mozambique, Nigeria and Uganda were assisted in developing IP strategies and Tanzania and Ethiopia were assisted in establishing IP Advisory Services and Information Centres.[57] Copyright Acts have also been in order. In Tanzania, for instance, the Copyrights and Neighbouring Act No. 7 of 1999 established the Copyright Society of Tanzania (COSATA) in 2001 with the responsibility of promoting the protection of the rights of authors, artists, musicians and publishers.[58]

Hitherto, some African countries like Botswana, Ethiopia, Mozambique, Nigeria, Tanzania and Uganda have been having national IP strategies and are an encouraging stage of promoting IP policies. However, much has to be learnt from more developed countries, and even other less developed countries such as those in Asia and Latin America.

Regarding merging and acquisition, case study 6.1 below, for instance, provides an example of the 2011 acquisition made by South Africa's Pretoria Portland Cement (PPC) in Botswana and potentially elsewhere in Africa.

Case Study 6.1: Pretoria Portland Cement's Acquisitions in Botswana as it Expands Across Africa (2011)

As part of its Southern Africa expansion strategy, Pretoria Portland Cement (PPC) has acquired three aggregate quarries from Quarries of Botswana.

The P50 million (US$6.8 million) acquisition is part of the cement giant's expanding footprint and will make PPC's aggregates division the largest aggregate producer in Botswana.

New quarries in Gaborone, Francistown and Selebi-Phikwe, will expand PPC's existing portfolio in Botswana to meet the local market demand for aggregates, which is a complementary product to cement.

> The investment will see PPC's aggregates division increase its total capacity from 3 million to about 4 million tons per annum and employ approximately 100 employees.
>
> PPC is also pursuing expansion opportunities in other parts of Africa.

Source: The Botswana Sunday Standard, October 9 – 15, 2011: 14

Another example of international geographical diversification effort is the Mlimani Holdings Limited joint venture – a multi-activity company owned jointly by Botswana-based Turnstar Holdings and the University of Dar-es-Salaam (Tanzania), later to be regarded as an acquisition.[59]

Competition Authorities/Commissions in Africa adjudicate applications for mergers, including acquisitions and in some cases joint ventures, among other activities. Most of these institutions have been established recently with the increasing intensity of competition. In Botswana, for instance, the Competition Authority became operational in 2011. The authority authorizes mergers (when one company buys a stake or completely buys another company). During January and February 2013, for instance, the Botswana Competition Authority authorized 6 mergers after it determined that they would not result in substantial lessening of competition and have no significant negative effect on public interest. Their merger/acquisition included:

(1)   Acquisition of 25 per cent equity capital in Cathay Fortune Investments Limited by China-Africa Liantuo Mining;

(2)   Acquisition of Pinnock Holdings (PTY) LTD and Sachet Investments (PTY) LTD contracts by Yalda Limited;

(3)   Acquisition of 100 per cent interest in Reinforcing Steel Contractors Botswana by CA Steel (PTY) LTD;

(4)   Acquisition of all the Outstanding issued share capital in Hana Mining Limited by Cupric Canyon Capital LP;

(5)   Acquisition of 100 per cent issued Share Capital in Camp Management Services Botswana (PTY) LTD; and

(6)   Acquisition of Intellectual Property Rights of Over the Counter Products of Glaxosmithkline PLC by Aspen Pharmacare Holdings Limited.[60]

Policy Issues and Regional Integration

There are several areas where regional integration policies need intensification and effective implementation.

- The current policy on trade fairs in the Southern African Development Community (SADC), for instance, should include more promotional and advertising activities and should also be used as means of strengthening co-operation and co-ordination within the region. The ultimate goal should be shifting the focus from existing traditional business links to new opportunities.61

- There is also a need to deepen various regional integrations through developing better trade-industry-infrastructure linkages while promoting industrial production and regional trade.

- Geographical/market extension diversification is quite important in the regions and Africa as a whole. Traditional textile and cloth manufacturers in Tanzania, for instance, may wish to venture into marketing the product elsewhere in SADC or even outside the region.

- Mergers, acquisitions and joint ventures (MAJVs) should be enhanced as a means of diversification. Particular attention should be paid to R&D joint ventures and co-ordination in SADC, COMESA (Common Market for Eastern and Southern Africa), EAC (East African Community), and other regional communities.

- In addition to MAJVs, firms in the regions can also adopt alliance strategies that involve less commitment such as licensing co-ordination, sub-contracting and regional workshops relevant to further diversification in regions.

Lessons from Outside Africa

- Some countries, especially from the East, have managed to create technology through imitation and adoption. Africa should also learn from such countries.

- The United States and Europe promote significantly intellectual property rights including patents and rewards to scientists and innovators. This is an important policy lesson to Africa.

- As noted earlier the US government has allowed firms to co- ordinate R&D through joint venture despite the anti-trust resistance. Such approach should be considered positively by African governments.

Conclusion

This chapter has identified and examined the main non-price strategies which are made by firms as weapons for non-price competition. They include advertising as a promotional strategy; R&D and protections of intellectual property; product differentiation; integration, mergers and diversification. The chapter has concluded by examining the applicability and relevance of the strategies to Africa. Policy issues and regional integration and lessons from outside Africa have also been spelt out.

Review Questions

1. (a) Differentiate between informative advertising and persuasive advertising. Give examples from your own country.

   (b) What is meant by advertising intensity?

   (c) Discuss the relationship between advertising intensity and market structure.

2. (a) What is meant by optimal advertising?

   (b) The demand function and cost function before introducing advertisement for the Chapakazi Company are

   $Q = 25,000 - 100P$

   $TC = 250,000 + 50Q$

   respectively

   where Q = quantity demanded

   P = price

   TC = Total cost

   Calculate and comment on the impact of advertising on sales and profits if after advertising the demand doubles.

3. Differentiate between the following giving examples from your own country, if applicable.

   (a) Vertical and horizontal product differentiation

   (b) Vertical and horizontal integration.

4. (a) Define the following concepts:

   (i) Advertising

   (ii) R & D

   (iii) Product differentiation

   (b) Explain how the three concepts are related.

5. (a) Differentiate between integration and diversification.

   (b) Why is the Herfindahl Index of Specialisation considered superior to the Diversification Ratio?

   (c) Are the incentives for integration and diversification the same? Elaborate.

6. Discuss the applicability and relevance of non-price strategies to Africa.

Appendix 6.1: Empirical Example of Advertising Elasticity of De- mand

Consider a consultant of Achimota Firm who estimated the following demand function for special peanut butter (X) from annual data between 1980 – 2012:

$$LnQ_x = 5.1 + 0.9lnM - 0.7lnP_x - 0.2P_y + \mathbf{0.6lnA_x}$$
$$\quad\quad (3.1)\ (0.1)\quad (0.2)\quad\quad (0.1)\quad (0.2)$$
$$\quad R^2 = 0.85$$

where Q_x = quantity demand for the special peanut butter.

      M = Money income

      P_x = price of peanut butter.

      P_y = price of related product

      A_x = advertising expenditure

(Numbers in brackets are standard errors).

Focusing on the advertising expenditure variable A_x and quantity demanded (Qx) it is noted that there is a positive relationship between the two variables: if advertising expenditure increases by 1 percent quantity demanded will increase by 0.6 percent, *ceteris paribus*. This will cause the demand curve to shift positively (to the right). The coefficient 0.6 is the *advertising elasticity of demand* for the special peanut butter and is statistically significant: indicating the importance of advertising in determining the quantity demanded of the special peanut butter.

Interesting questions to the reader are:

(1) Which other variable will shift the demand curve to the right?

(2) Will advertisement of the related product Y also shift the demand curve to the right?

(3) Why is the coefficient 0.6 the advertising elasticity of demand?

Appendix 6.2: Relationship between Advertising and Concentration

Sulton (1974) tested the quadratic relationship between advertising intensity and concentration using a sample of 25 industries in the UK.

As opposed to a linear relationship, the non-linear (quadratic) model was superior in some aspects such as degree of fit (measured by R^2) and levels of significance as shown below:

$$A = 0.99 + 0.013C_5 \quad\quad\quad\quad\quad R^2 = 0.01$$
$$\quad (1.29)\quad (1.13)$$

$$A = -3.15 + 0.19C_5 - 0.0015C_5^2 \quad\quad R2 = 0.34$$
$$\quad (2.36)\ (3.71)\quad (3.51)$$

where

A = advertising expenditure to gross sales

C_5 = five firm sales concentration

      (t ratios in brackets)

The quadratic model indicates that advertising intensity increases from low to medium concentration industries, reaching a maximum of $C_5 = 0.64$ percent and then falls for more concentrated industries.

Source: Clarke (2000: 128)

Notes

1. Douglas (1992: 527).
2. Nelson (1970) categorised goods into two types: (i) *search goods* (those with 'search attributes', such as size and weights, which can easily be evaluated before purchasing the goods. Examples include food items, clothes, radio and others). (ii) *Experience goods* (those with 'experience attributes' which can only be known after purchasing them). Examples are newly introduced goods, particularly wine and quality of paint and others.
   Darby and Karni (1973) adds a third category – *credence goods* (those goods whose attributes may not be fully evaluated even after repeated purchases, e.g. 'brand names' goods and professional services like those of doctors and lawyers). See, also, Douglas (1992: 447).
3. See, for instance, Andreasso and Jacobson (2005, ch.10); Besanko et al (2010, part 2); Clarke (2000, ch. 6 – 9); Lipczynski (2009, ch.14-20); Peppal et al (2009, part vi) and Pappal et al (2011, part II), and Waldam and Jensen (2007, ch. 12 – 14, 16).
4. Cf. Martin (1993: 162) and Douglas (1992: 530).
5. For details, see, for instance Martin (1993: 141, 162) and Douglas (1992: 542.
6. Cf. Martin (1993: 162).
7. See, for instance, Lipczynski et al 2009: 421).
8. For details see Lipczynski et al (2009: 418).
9. Equivalently: *advertising expenditure*, sales or revenue.
10. For details see Clarke (2000: 4, 130).
11. See Lipczynski et al (2009: 455).
12. Ibid.
13. Ibid.
14. Ibid.
15. For details see Church and Ware (2000: 576).
16. Cf. Lipczynski et al (2009): 9).
17. For more details see, especially, Lipczynski et al (2009: 471 & 472).
18. Examples include Galbraith (1952), Nelson and Winter (1982), Kamien and Schwatz (1982), Geroski (1991), Church and Ware (2000), Carlton and Perloff (2005), and Lipczynski (2009).
19. See also Carlton and Perloff (2005: 560).
20. Examples include Galbraith (1952), Nelson and Winter (1982), Kamien and Schwatz (1982), Geroski (1991), Church and Ware (2000), Carlton and Perloff (2005), and Lipczynski (2009).
21. For details see Lipczynski et al (2009: 456 – 468).
22. Cf. Church and Ware (2000: 577).
23. For further details see, especially Carlton and Perloff (2005: 526).
24. Ibid, p.539.
25. Ibid, p.528.

26. Ibid, p.529.
27. Ibid, p.526.
28. Cf. Andreasso and Jacobson (2005: 297) and Baye (2010: 251).
29. For details see Lipczynski et al (2009: 385).
30. See Andreasso and Jacobson (2005: 245).
31. See more examples from Carlton and Perloff (2005: 2000), Lipczynski *et al* 2009: 388), Waldman and Jensen 2007: 416).
32. Baye (2010:299).
33. For details and other measurements (entropy index and hedonic prices) see, for instance, Andreasso and Jacobson (2005: 249).
34. A company may also be used instead of a firm especially in managerial economics.
35. For details see, for instance, Clarke (2006: 299), Lipczynski et al (2009: 499).
36. For details see Andreasso and Jacobson (2005: 266), Clarke (2000: 172).
37. Cf. Andreasso and Jacobson (2005: 266).
38. See, for instance, Lipczynski et al (2009: 5000), Church and Ware (2000: 684).
39. For details see, for instance, Andreasso and Jacobson (2005: 267), Clarke (2000: 173). 40. Horizontal and conglomerate merger and integration tie neatly in diversification as will be noted in the subsequent section. For motives for horizontal mergers see for instance, Lipczynski et al (2009: 501).
41. See especially Andreasso and Jacobson (2005:269), and Waldman and Jensen (2007: 562).
42. For details see especially Andreasso and Jacobson (2005: 271).
43. For further details see, for instance, Carlton and Perloff (2005:399).
44. Ibid.
45. Cf. Lipczynski et al (2009:573) and Andreasso and Jacobson (2005:275).
46. For details see Lipczynski et al (2009:573).
47. Ibid.
48. Ibid, p.574.
49. Ibid, pp.570 – 573.
50. See also Marris' (1966) managerial theory of the firm.
51. Cf. Lipczynski et al 2009:583).
52. See also Clarke (2000:200).
53. For details see especially Andreasso and Jacobson (2005:276).
54. See Bongenaar and Szirmai (2001:172).
55. Cf. Semboja and Kweka (2001:162).
56. Ibid.
57. See WIPO: 2007:20-21.
58. United Republic of Tanzania 2003a.
59. *Tanzania Sunday News*, March 17, 2013: 1 and Botswana *Weekend Post* 12-18 October 2013a: 22.
60. See Botswana Competition Authority (2013), *Botswana Competition Bulletin*, Vol. I, 1-2.
61. Cf. Chipeta and Schade (2007:30).

III

Industrial Location and Finance:
Theory and Practice

7

Industrial Location: Theory and Practice

Learning Objectives

The main objectives of this chapter are:
- To briefly explain the link among parts I – III.
- To provide basic concepts and measures of industrial concentration.
- To present retrospectively an overview of theories of industrial location.
- To identify and outline the determinants of industrial location.
- To examine and give examples of practice from Africa.

Introductory Note: The Link Among Parts I, II and III

It should be recalled from the preface that the traditional industrial economics (Part I and II) is an input to industrialisation and development analysis.

The main relationship among parts I to III hinges squarely on the need of profit maximisation and cost minimisation in promoting industrial performance. The first part underlined the relationship through (i) the basic conditions and performance in the S-C-P model, (ii) theory of the firm, and (iii) market structure analysis. The second part underscored the need for minimisation of marginal cost in pricing theory before adding profit margins. This part also underlines the need for minimising costs and maximising profit through industrial location and finance.

A manufacturer who wants to set up a factory will normally consider simultaneously three aspects: first, the scale of operation; second, the production techniques; and finally the location of the factory. While the first two aspects are fully covered in conventional economic theory, industrial location is based on both economic and geographical theories.

This chapter provides basic concepts and measures of industrial location, and presents both economic and geographical or geo-economic theories of industrial location. Determinants of industrial location are thereafter outlined. The chapter finally examines, by giving examples, the practice of industrial location in Africa.

Basic Concepts and Measures of Industrial Location

Industries are not normally spread evenly over a country but tend to concentrate or be located at some sites (localisation). *Industrial localisation*, therefore, may be viewed as concentration of industries in general or specific industries in a given area or location. Industrial location is thus analogous to market concentration examined in Chapter Four.

Industrial localisation is normally attributed to where the raw materials and markets are available. Industries that are, for economic reason, located where heavy or bulky materials are available are *rooted industries*. Textile industries are usually 'rooted' to sources of raw material (cotton). Similarly, mines are 'rooted' where minerals are available.

Industries located where the markets are may be referred to as *tied industries*. Beverage industries are normally 'tied' to markets in urban centres. Industries which are neither 'rooted' to the sources of raw materials nor 'tied' to the markets are *footloose industries*. They can economically and conveniently be located elsewhere.[1]

In order to gauge the degree of concentration in a given location, the location quotient is usually applied, to which we now turn.

Location quotient[2] is calculated as follows:

$$L_q = \frac{WP_{ij}}{WP_{ic}}$$

where Lq = location quotient

WPij= percentage of the working population in industry i in location j

WPic = percentage of the working population in industry i in the whole country.

If the location quotient is more than 1, the location is said to have more than its fair share of the industry under consideration. Where the location quotient is less than 1, the location is said to have less than its 'fair share' of the industry in question. An example is in order:

Example

The interpretation is as follows: Area X in country Y had 30 per cent of its working population in the food processing industry while 40 per cent of the working population in the industry in the country was so employed. The location quotient can be calculated as follows:

$L_q = WP_{ij}/WP_{ic} = 30/40 = 0.75$

Area X has less than its 'fair share' in the Food Processing Industry.

A similar measure is the *localisation coefficient*. It is calculated by the following formula: when workers are partitioned off regionally, the coefficient is the sum, divided by 100 of the plus deviations of the regional percentage of workers in the particular industry from the corresponding regional percentage of workers in all industry.[3] It measures the local concentration of a particular industry compared with the distribution of the industry as a whole. The localisation coefficient ranges between zero and one. When it is zero it means that the distribution of workers in that particular industry coincides completely with the distribution of industrial workers in general. When the location coefficient is 1, workers in the particular industry are all concentrated in one region or location in general.

An Overview of Theories of Industrial Location

A Retrospective Note

The theory of industrial location became clear after the works of Marshall (1898, 1899). Marshall identified six main factors in the location or *localisation* of industries: physical conditions, demand conditions, political/cultural influences, hereditary skills, the growth of subsidiary trades and labour market for special skills.[4] Most of the subsequent authors, as will be elaborated shortly, based their theories mainly on the work of Marshall.

Economic Theories of Industrial Location

Marshall Theory of Industrial Location

Marshall theory of industrial location identified both causes and advantages of localisation.[5]

Causes of localisation included physical conditions, demand conditions and political/cultural influences.

Physical conditions were mostly geographical, covering raw materials that are expensive to transport, climate, the soil and the topography of an area. These were assumed to be the basic causes of localisation.

Demand conditions referred essentially to the market of the product produced.

Political/cultural influences focused on the political beliefs and culture of the people, and their social and political institutions. These were also regarded by Marshall as causes of localisation.

Advantages of localisation included hereditary skills, growth of subsidiary trades, and local market for special skills.

Hereditary skills included cases of people living and working together in traditional communities using similar and specialised skills which were passed over to new generations. Such skills were advantages to industrial localisation.

Growth of subsidiary trades: Industrial localisation also took advantage of subsidiary trades, i.e. intermediate good firms which were attracted by the local industries. Intermediate goods included equipment. Such localisation also promoted specialisation in the sense that subsidiary industries devoting themselves to one small branch of the process of production could employ specialised machinery and keep it constantly busy if they were supplying a large number of firms in the main industry.[6]

Local Market for Special Skills: Marshall argued that a localised industry gains great advantage from a constant market for skills. Special industries also tend to localise where special or specialised skills are available.

In general, Marshall argued that the firm should aim at maximisation of economies of scale including *external economies*, i.e. advantages accruing to one firm from agglomerating or locating close to others (*agglomeration economies*) and/or locating where there are public facilities such as *public utilities* (electricity, water and gas) and infrastructure. Examples of agglomeration economies include benefits from common pool of input such as labour, equipment or capital in general. Marshall considered agglomeration economies the essence of the growth of subsidiary trade.

Least Cost Theory

The least cost theory school, though implied in Marshall's external economies, was popularised by Alfred Weber in 1909.[7] Like Marshall, Weber's main interest was to construct a theory of localisation or location which could be applicable to all industries. The cost theory is a generalised theoretical school of thought which classifies the factors of location into two: those influencing inter-regional location of industries (*regional factors of industrial location*) and those influencing intra- regional location (*agglomerating factors of industrial location*). In the first group, it identifies three factors which vary regionally: raw material costs, transport costs, and labour costs. In the second group, it defines agglomeration as concentration of production for a commodity at one place. Like in the case of Marshall, agglomeration economies are the benefits of such concentration.[8] Where location was a function of transport cost, Weber used a *location triangle* in his simplified analysis. The three points of the triangle were the main two sources or supply of raw material and energy (M1 and M2) and the centre of consumption or source of market or demand for the produced product (C) as illustrated in Figure 7.1.

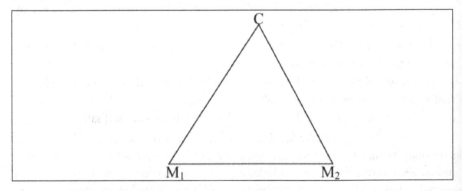

Figure 7.1: Weber's Location Triangle

In this case, the location or least cost point (P) would be within the triangle. The exact position of the point would depend on the magnitude or weight attached to C, M_1 and M2. In other words, the balance of weights or *pull forces* would determine the exact position of P.

Where location was dominantly a function of labour costs, a firm could vacate its least transport cost site and relocate to cheap labour.

Similarly, where location was dominantly a function of agglomeration, the location decision would be in favour of the agglomeration centre. Weber also argued that the agglomeration might also attract a firm through expansion and merger which would lead to transaction economies and other related advantages of mergers.[9]

Other than Marshall's and Weber's relatively general theories of industrial location, there are other theories which focus on one or less general aspects such as the transport cost theory and the market area theory of industrial location, to which we now turn.

Transport Cost Theory

Transport cost theory focuses on costs of transport, although it marginally includes other costs like production costs. It is essentially a sub-theory of Marshall's and Weber's theories of industrial location. It classifies transport into two categories: terminal costs and haul costs. *Terminal costs* are regarded as fixed costs of warehouses, docks, offices and maintenance, while *haul costs* include fuel costs and wages for drivers and crew.

The eminent works of Hoover (1937, 1948), maintained that road transport and rail transport had low terminal costs but high running costs (line and haul costs), while water transport had high terminal costs but low running costs. Therefore, assuming terminal costs were fixed, regardless of the length of the haul, an entrepreneur would settle for a long-distance location from sources of raw material provided there was water transport, and would do otherwise in the case of road and rail transport.

Like Weber's theory, Hoover's transport cost theory was criticised on the ground that it did not take into account government intervention. When the government runs the rail transport, for example, that form of transport could be the cheapest.[10]

Robinson (1958) acknowledged Weber's theory, rather than Hoover's theory, as transport costs depended mostly on the weights of raw materials and finished products. The raw material and market were regarded to be crucial in transport cost analysis.

Market Area Theory

Market area theory is another school which diverged from generation like the cases of Marshall's and Weber's theories. It focused on the demand conditions as Marshall would call the focus or on Weber's consumption centre.

One of the early works was by Fetter (1924). Fetter maintained that most entrepreneurs would locate their firms near the market in order to maximise revenue, hence profit. Since the success of a firm is directly related to the volume of sales, a firm would try to set prices lower than those of rivals, thereby increasing the size of the market area, revenue and profit.

Losch (1940) advanced the theory further by maintaining that manufacturers tended to give preferences to locating their firms near areas with large market in order to maximise profit. Labour, transport and other costs were considered neutral in the analysis. Although Losch's approach is essentially based on demand analysis, some authors refer to it as the central place theory of Losch.[11]

Other Economic Theories

In addition to the afore-examined economic theories, there are several others. As examples, some are explained briefly hereunder:

Locational inter-dependence Theory

Locational inter-dependence theory is a theoretical school of thought which examines the impact of demand on location and also confines to the factors which determine the attraction of producers to one another. Its roots may be traced back to the Marshall theory of industrial location.

Hoteling (1929) and Smithies (1941) are two leading members of this school.[13]

Locational Substitution Theory

Locational Substitution Theory is another theoretical school of thought which links the approaches of Weber and Losch. It is based on the principle of substitution which specifies the conditions for substitution of one location for another just as substitution of labour for capital and vice-versa in the neo-classical theory of the firm. One of the important proponents of this theory is Israd (1960).[14]

Apart from the afore-examined dominant economic theories of industrial location, there are other technical factors which tend to strike a balance between geographical and socio-economic aspects. Examples are in order:

Geo-economic Theories of Location

The Central Place Theory

The central place theory maintains that large cities would be central to production and consumption while relatively small towns with the lowest levels of specialisation would be equally spaced and surrounded by hexagonally shaped hinterlands. Production, therefore, tends to be centralised, so is the market. The central places or cities become the centres of attraction of more factories.[15]

The theory was the first systematic, geographical or geo-economic theory of location. It was significantly developed by Christaller (1933) and is comparable to the approach of Losch (1940) who maintained that firms tend to be located near areas with large market in order to maximise profit.

Renner's Theory of Industrial Location

Renner's theory of industrial location postulates that location of industries tends to obey *the law of location for manufacturing* which states that manufacturing tends to locate at a point which provides optimum access to its ingredients. Renner (1947, 1950) identified six geo-economic ingredients: raw materials, market, labour and management, power, capital, and transportation.

Furthermore, Renner provided a scheme of three *industrial symbioses*: (i) *disjunctive symbiosis*, where unrelated industries (having no organic i.e. economic or technical connections) gain advantage by existing together at a particular place; (ii) *conjunctive symbiosis*, where related industries (with organic connection) exist together; and (iii) *conindustrialisation*, which is an advanced stage of conjunctive symbiosis characterised by a huge industrial belt of interconnected industries.[16]

Renner's theory seems to be comprehensive like the Marshall theory of industrial location except its analysis tends to have more geographical than economic aspects.

Rawstron's Theory of Industrial Location

Rawstron's theory of industrial location is a theoretical school of thought based on three geo-economic principles or restriction: physical, economic and technical restriction. The theory was developed by Rawstron (1958).

The *physical principle* or *restriction* is based on the ability of a firm to produce or procure natural resources at the site. Therefore the location of the site will depend on that ability as a restriction.

The *economic principle or restriction* embodies *spartial margins to profitability* based on variations of costs of production (location costs) i.e. costs of material, land, labour, marketing, and capital. Although transport cost was not explicitly included, it is embodied in the costs of transporting material and marketing. The summation of the costs will determine where a firm should be located.

The *technical principle or restriction* examines the effect of the level of technology on location. There should be stable technology of production. Stable labour-intensive technology, for instance, will point to reliable supply of cheap labour as a location site.[17]

Thompson's Theory of Industrial Location

Thompson's theory of industrial location is a general geo-economic theoretical approach to industrial location based on a set of sub-theories. Examples of the sub-theories included in Thompson's theory (1966) are:

(i) the *cycle sub-theory*, which underscores an established manufacturing area which goes through a predictable sequence of change; (ii) the *concentration sub-theory*, which underlines the trend that strong locational activities cause industries to cluster and eventually to form a hierarchy of concentration; (iii) the *agglomeration sub-theory*, which stipulates that the benefits which large urban centres offer to industry increase as economic development increases; (iv) the *changing role sub-theory*, which maintains that the importance of manufacturing industry to the overall economy of an area changes as economic development advances; and (v) the *differential growth sub-theory*, which states that different growth rates of industries in an area are caused by demand conditions.

Most of these sub-theories are implied either explicitly or implicitly in Marshall and subsequent theories of industrial location[18]; but are synthetically analysed by Thompson.

Behaviour (Marginal Location) Theory

The behaviour (marginal location) theory is a theoretical school of thought which underscores behavioural and psychological factors rather than the classical approach based on maximisation of profit and perfect information. Entrepreneurs may not necessarily aim at maximising profit but satisfaction or utility, even if profits were marginal.

Pred (1967), for instance, argued that setting a factory was very much influenced by geographical, psychological, experience and other factors. A good post experience based on entrepreneur's satisfaction might influence the location of a factory (*pull factor*), but a bad experience may discourage such location (*push factor*).[19]

Other Geo-economic Theories of Industrial Location

Despite the afore-explained geo-economic theories, there are several others. Two[20] are explained below as examples:

Urban Centre Size and Industrial Structure Theory

The urban centre size and industrial structure underscores the relationship between town size and industrial structure which could indicate the patterns and factors of industrial location in urban areas of various sizes.

Alexander (1954) and Murphy (1966) made substantial contribution to this geo-economic base theory of industrial location.[21]

Krugman's Theory of Industrial Location

Krugman's theory of industrial location is basically a critique of Marshall's theory and of the mainstream economics for overstressing the neo-classical theory of industrial economics at the expense of geographical theory.

Despite the rigorous models, the economic analysis should not understate important geographical aspects such as spatial distribution related to path dependence, circular causation and discontinuous change. Furthermore, increasing return and economic geography analysis need great attention, just as international aspects also require special attention.[22]

Determinants of Industrial Location

Background Information

From the afore-presented background and theories of industrial location, despite the interrelationship of factors, we may deduce two main categories which influence industrial location: economic factors and geo-economic (technical) factors. We may add 'other factors' as a third category. All categories are outlined hereunder.

Economic Factors

Economic factors include:

- Heavy and bulky raw materials which are expensive to transport. These essentially throw light on the causes of rooted industries.
- Costs of land, buildings and infrastructural facilities such as transport charges and infrastructural facilities such as transport charges and public utilities (electricity, water and gas).
- Demand conditions. They imply proximity to local markets, urban centres
- and export ports. Availability and costs of skilled and unskilled labour.
- External economies of scale including agglomeration economies.

Geo-economic (technical) factors

Geo-economic or technical factors include the following:
- Nature and quality of raw material from land, e.g. forest products, minerals and agricultural inputs.
- Energy sources such as coal and electricity.
- Availability of good land, soil, and topography of the area under consideration.
- Availability of water for industrial uses and drinking.
- Good climate.
- Geographic conditions of firm location in relation to transport facilities by rail, road, water and air.
- Urban centres and population structure involving quantity and quality of human resources; demographic composition such as age, sex, literacy.
- Scale and technique of production or technology in general.

Other factors

Examples of other factors are:
- Political and cultural influences.
- Government policy and intervention, e.g., freedom to choose investment location, subsidies/taxes.
- Nature of industries, e.g., footloose industries which can be located economically far or near raw materials and markets.
- Historical factors such as colonial-based export enclaves.
- Behavioural, personal and physiological factors based on experience, age, or satisfaction of the entrepreneur, e.g., locating a factory in one's birthplace.

Practice of Industrial Location in Africa

Retrospective Approach

It has been shown empirically that many modern industries of ex-colonial economies in Africa are located in export enclaves because of historical reasons.[23]

In 1966, five years after Tanzania's independence, for example, Dar-es-Salaam had more than its 'fair share' in most of industries as indicated by industries with location quotient of more than 1. They include beverages, tobacco, footwear, furniture, paper, printing, leather, rubber and metals. For details, see Table 7.1.

Table 7.1: Location Quotient of Tanzania's Manufacturing Industries*

Industry	Dar-es-Salaam	Tanga-Arusha-Moshi	Other
Food	0.74	0.93	1.39
Beverage	1.32	1.48	0.13
Tobacco	1.42	0	1.48
Textiles	0.95	0.22	1.84
Footwear	1.42	1.32	0.16
Wood	0.39	1.97	0.77
Furniture	1.95	0.35	0.48
Paper	2.63	0	0
Printing	1.95	0.39	0.45
Leather	1.18	0.58	1.19
Rubber	2.63	0	0
Chemicals	0.92	1.03	1.06
Non-metals	1.97	0.32	0.48
Metals	2.37	0.03	0.29
Non-electrical	1.26	1.55	0.10
Electricals	0	1.64	1.58
Transport	2.42	0.26	0
Miscellaneous	1.13	1.55	0.29

* Based on 1966 Industrial Survey
Source: Rweyemamu (1973: 161)

Dar-es-Salaam, being the major city and port, was ideal for exporting raw materials and industrial output by water and air mainly to the colonisers. With time, the urban centre was expanded and other factors like availability of market and skills, availability of water for industrial use, availability of skilled and unskilled labour, and external economies including agglomeration economies attracted more industries.

A similar argument may be advanced in the case of other large port-cities in Africa like Accra (Ghana), Dakar (Senegal), Lagos (Nigeria), Maputo (Mozambique) and Mombasa (Kenya).

Factors affecting Industrial Location Revisited

In section 7.5 we identified economic, geo-economic (technical) and other factors in- fluencing industrial location. Let us revisit them with reference to examples in Africa.

As noted in the previous section, economic factors based essentially on demand conditions, availability of skilled labour, and external economies are easily explained with reference to large urban centres in Africa, as may be the case elsewhere. Examples include Accra (Ghana), Blantyre (Malawi), Gaborone (Botswana), Harare (Zimbabwe), Johannesburg (South Africa), Kampala (Uganda), Kinshasa (Democratic Republic of Congo), Nairobi (Kenya) and Windhoek (Namibia).

Regarding rooted industries located in areas where the materials are available, examples are many in Africa. In Tanzania, for instance, the textile industry is located near cotton-growing regions, especially Mwanza and Musoma. This explains the lower location quotient (0.95) for Dar-es-Salaam and higher (1.84) for other upcountry areas.[24]

Mining activities in Botswana and Tanzania are also located where minerals are available like Orapa and Shinyanga respectively.

Fish, dairy and fruit canning plants are also located where products and possibly markets are available. Examples are the fish and dairy plants in Mwanza and fruit cunning plants in Iringa (Tanzania).

Regarding availability of labour, the following examples are in order. The Maskom and Orange Communication firms in Botswana, for example, are mostly found in Gaborone where skilled labour involving electronic technology is readily available. The market is also a factor of the location.

Conclusion

This chapter has examined industrial location guided by the cost-minimization and profit-maximisation motive.

Guided by the same motive, industrial finance is analysed in the next chapter.

Review Questions

1. Discuss critically the Marshallian factors influencing industrial location in your country.
2. Dar-es-Salaam (Tanzania) had 35 per cent of its working population in the textile industry, while the percentage of the working population in the textile industry in Tanzania was 37. Calculate the location quotient and comment on your answer. (Hint: see endnote 24)

Notes

1. These terms were popularised by Florence (1948). See also Sutcliffe (1971: 114).
2. Cf. Isard (1960) and Florence (1948).
3. For details, see Rweyemamu (1973: 161).
4. See, especially, Chapter X of Marshall's (1989) book.
5. For details, see Andreasso and Jacobson (2005: 188 – 91).

6. Ibid, p.189.
7. Alfred Weber was a German economist. His origin work was *Uber den Standort der Industrien* (1909). The English translation was titled, *Theory of the Location of Industries*, published in 1929 by the University of Chicago Press.
8. For details, see Barthwal (1985: 368).
9. Cf. Mabe (2001). Revisit also the advantages of integration and mergers in section 6.7.2.
10. See, for instance, Mabe (2001: 16).
11. See also, for instance, Barthwal (1985: 375).
12. For more examples, see for instance, Barthwal (1985).
13. Ibid, 376.
14. Ibid.
15. For details, see Barthwal (1985: 364).
16. Ibid.
17. See also, Barthwal (1985: 365).
18. Ibid, 367.
19. Ibid. Pred (1967) is quoted by Barthwal (1985:366).
20. For more factors see, for instance, Barthwal (1985: 366 – 77).
21. Ibid, 366.
22. For details, see Andreasso and Jacobson (2005: 21 – 26, 187 – 91).
23. For details, see Rweyemamu (1973: 159).
24. It will be recalled that the location quotient is calculated as a ratio of percentage of the working population in industry i in location j to a similar percentage in the industry for the whole country. In 1966, for example, Dar-es-Salaam (Tanzania) had 35 per cent of its working population in the textile industry, while the percentage of the working population in the textile industry in Tanzania was 37. Thus the location quotient = 35/37 = 0.95.

8

Industrial Finance: Theory and Practice

Learning Objectives

The main objectives of this chapter are:
- To provide an overview of theories of industrial investment;
- To examine the main sources of industrial finance;
- To present, with examples, quantitative approaches to industrial finance; and
- To examine the practice of industrial finance in Africa.

Introduction

As will be underscored in the next section, industrial finance emphasises internal funds theory of industrial investment which states that investment depends on the level of retained profit. This is in line with the emphasis on industrial performance in terms of profitability in the S-C-P analysis, explained in chapter 2 of this book.

Industrial finance, like any other sectorial finance, depends basically on the ability of firms to invest. Thus relevant theories of investment are underscored in this chapter. Financial implications of the theories are then illustrated quantitatively.

The chapter finally examines the industrial financial practice in Africa.

Overview of Theories of Industrial Investment

Basic Concepts and Definitions

Industrial finance is important for the promotion of firms' investment and growth. The main factors which form the basis of industrial investment theories are output and profits. Profits form the core of the *internal fund theory of industrial investment*.

However, it should be underlined that it is not gross profits or net profits which are crucial for investment, but *retained profits or retained earnings*. These are net profits less dividends (shareholders' portion of net profits). Net profit is hereby defined as gross profit – interest – corporate income taxes. Gross profit – interest is profit before taxes or operating profit.[1]

Note that the difference between *total value of production and other incomes and total expenditure is called gross profit;* and the distribution of gross profit into interest, taxes, dividend and retained earnings is called appropriation of income.[2]

External fund theory of industrial investment encompasses all forms of borrowing and grants.

Theories of Industrial Investment

Introductory Note

There are two main theories of (industrial) investment: the internal fund theory of investment and the external fund theory of investment, to which we now turn.

Internal Fund Theory of Investment

The internal fund theory of investment maintains that the desired capital stock, and hence investment depends on the level of retained profits. Formally:

$I = f(\pi)$,

where I = investment

π = retained profits

It should be underscored that investment may lead to more retained profits and further investment, i.e.

$\pi = f(I)$

This implies the essence of growth of firms resulting from profit and increase in investment.[3]

It should also be noted that retained earnings and depreciation expense (funds set aside as plant, equipment, and other items depreciate) are the main sources of funds internal to the firm.[4]

Proponents of internal funds theory maintain that internal funds are an important determinant of investment, particularly during recession.[5]

External Fund Theory of Investment

The external fund theory of investment maintains that external sources of finance are also crucial for investment, given the usually insufficient funds from internal sources. They include, for instance, grants and all types of borrowing, including sales of bonds.

External sources of funds, however, have some limitations. Grants are normally discouraged during trade liberalisation and free trade era. Borrowing commits a firm to a series of fixed payments; should a recession occur, it may be impossible to meet the commitments of the firm, given high interest rates. The firm may be forced to borrow or sell stocks on unfavourable terms or even be declared bankrupt. Similarly, firms may be reluctant to raise funds by issuing new stock.[6] These adverse results strengthen the arguments of proponents of the internal funds theory of investment.

Source of Finance for Industrial Investment

From the above-presented theories, the main sources of finance may be categorised as follows:

1. *Internal or Self-finances*

    These comprise retained earnings a firm makes and provision for depreciation, allowances, taxation and other reserves or provisions.[7]

2. *External sources*

    These may be categorised as:

    (i)   Short and medium-term external funds comprising of mainly bank credit, hire-purchase debt, trade credits and fixed deposits.

    (ii) Long-term external funds, i.e., the sale of shares and loan capital.[8]

    (iii) Grants, mainly from governments.

Quantitative Approaches to Industrial Finance

Basic Quantitative Approach

In this section the basic quantitative approach is presented in detail. It involves the application of quantitative, especially mathematical, tools to financial analysis and problem-solving in industrial economics.

Reference is essentially made to internal and external funds for investment explained in the previous section. Specific applications and examples such as those related to rates of depreciation, rates of interest and annuities are provided.

Depreciation

Basic Concepts and Definitions

It should be noted that, depreciation expense is regarded as funds set aside as industrial plant, equipment, and other items lose value (depreciate) over time.

There are mainly two types of depreciation. *Linear or straight-line depreciation and non-linear* or *compound depreciation*. The former involves depreciating industrial property by the same percentage of the original cost. The latter deals with depreciating property at a 'faster' rate than when using a linear depreciation.[9] Relatively many industrial firms use linear depreciation mainly for its simplicity and convenience.

Linear Depreciation

Consider the original cost (c) of an industrial property which depreciates linearly over T years. After t years its value (*undepreciated value or book value*), Vt, will be:

$$V_t = c - \left(\frac{c}{T}\right) t \qquad\qquad (8.1)$$

or by factorisation

$$V_t = \left(1 - \frac{t}{T}\right) c \qquad\qquad (8.2)$$

The derivation of the formula can be shown immediately as follows: After 1 year, the value is:

$$V_1 = c - \frac{c}{T}$$

Or

$$V_1 = c - \frac{c}{T} \times 1$$

After 2 years, the value is:

$$V_2 = c - \frac{c}{T} \times 2$$

After 3 years, the value is:

$$V_3 = c - \frac{c}{T} \times 3$$

After t years, the value is:

$$V_t = c - \frac{c}{T} \times t$$

or

$$V_t = \left(1 - \frac{t}{T}\right) c$$

as is the case in equation (8.2).

Example: 8.1

An industrial equipment of the Tanzania Breweries Co. Ltd is depreciated linearly over 10 years. Deduce the book value after 3 years if its original cost is Tsh60,000 million.

Solution

Applying equation 8.2, i.e.

$$V_t = \left(1 - \frac{t}{T}\right) c$$

Its book value V after 3 years will be

$$V_3 = Tsh \left(1 - \frac{3}{10}\right) 60,000 \text{ million}$$

i.e. V_3 = Tsh42, 000 million

Compound Depreciation

Compound depreciation is non-linear. Consider the simple case (*the double-declining-balance*) where an industrial property valued at c is depreciated over a period of T years. In this case, it is depreciated each year by 2/T. One hundred per cent of its value at the beginning of that year.[10]

Therefore, the book value is multiplied by $\left(1 - \frac{2}{T}\right)$ each, so that

$$V = c \left(1 - \frac{2}{T}\right) t \qquad\qquad (8.3)$$

If the industrial equipment worth Tsh60,000 million (as was the case of linear depreciation) is depreciated by the double-declining-balance method over 10 years, the book value after t years is given by:

$$V_t = 60,000 \left(1 - \frac{2}{10}\right) t$$

Therefore, after year 1, the value will be $V_1 = $ Tsh60,000 $\left(1 - \frac{2}{10}\right)^t$ million = 48,000 million.

At the end of year 2,

$$V_2 = \text{Tsh60,000} \left(1 - \frac{2}{10}\right)^2 \text{million} = 38,400 \text{ million.}$$

and so on. Therefore,

$$V_t = \text{Tsh60,000} \left(1 - \frac{2}{10}\right)^t \text{million.}$$

Example 8.2: Re-do the question in example 8.1 by using the double-declining-balance method and compare your answer when linear method is used in example 8.1.

Solution:

$$V_3 = \text{Tsh60,000} \left(1 - \frac{3}{10}\right)^3 \text{million.}$$
$$= \text{Tsh20,580 million.}$$

The value in the case of the double-declining-balance method is about Tsh21,000 million, almost a half of that obtained in the case of linear method, indicating that 'faster' depreciation takes place when double-declining-balance (compound) method is used.

Interest and Value of Money over time (Future Value)

Basic Concepts and Definitions

Interest is a charge for money use over time expressed in terms of amount paid or received. It is the extra money that is paid back when money is borrowed or received when money is saved or invested. This extra money expressed as a percentage of the amount borrowed or saved or invested (*the principal*) is called the *rate of interest or interest rate*.

There are two main types of interest: simple interest and compound interest. *Simple interest* is the interest determined when the interest does not itself earn interest but the interest rate applies only to the amount borrowed or saved for investment purpose. *Compound interest*, on the other hand, is the interest determined when interest is added to the principal at regular intervals of time and thereafter the interest itself earns interest. These definitions will be illustrated in the subsequent sub-sections.

Simple Interest

Simple interest rate is easy to calculate since it does not involve compounding. If, for example, a firm borrows $100million from a commercial bank at the simple interest rate of 10 per cent, at the end of year 1 the simple interest will be $100(0.1) million i.e. $10 million. The amount to be paid back will therefore be $(100 + 10) million, i.e. $110 million. At the end of year 2 the simple interest will be $(10 + 10) million or $2(10) million, i.e. $20 million. The amount to be paid back will, therefore, be $120 million, i.e. $(100 + 100 (0.1) 2) million. It may be deduced that at the end of year t the simple interest will be $10 t million and the amount to be paid back will be $100 + 100(0.1)t]. In general

$F_t = P + Prt$

where

F_t = Future value or amount to be paid back

P = principal

r = interest rate

t = time

By factorisation:

$F_t = P(1 + rt)$ (8.4)

Example 8.3: An industrial company has borrowed Kenyan shillings (Ksh) 10million at 10 per cent simple interest rate from Kenya Commercial Bank. What will be the amount to be paid back after 2 years?

Solution

Applying the formula 8.4, i.e. F = P(1 + rt)

the amount to be paid back (F_t) will be

F_t = Ksh [10 (1 + 0.1 x 2)] million

= Ksh [10 (1.2)]million

= Ksh 12million

Compound Interest

Annual Discrete Compounding

In practice, simple interest is used only for short-term transactions; for long-term transactions compound interest is applied. Reconsider example 8.3 where an industrial company in Kenya had borrowed Ksh 10million. If 10 per cent interest rate were to be compounded annually the amount to be paid back at the end of year one would be Ksh(10+ 10x 0.1)million or Ksh(10+ 1)million i.e. Ksh 11million. Note that Ksh1millionis the interest.

At the end of year 1 the new principal will be Ksh11million and not Ksh10million as in the case of simple interest. The amount to be paid be paid back will be the new principal Ksh11million plus the total interest, Ksh1.1million i.e. Ksh12.1million. This is more than Ksh12million in the case of simple interest in example 8.3.

The general formula which involves interest compounding is, therefore:

$$F_t = P(1 + r)^t$$

where

F_t = the future value or new principal

P = the original principal

r = compound interest rate

t = time

It is derived generally as follows:

At the end of year one amount to be paid back will be, will be

$$F_1 = P + Pr = P(1 + r) \text{ or } P(1 + r)^1.$$

At the end of year two, the amount to be paid

$$F_2 = P(1 + r) + P(1 + r)r$$
$$= P(1 + r)(1 + r)$$
$$= P(1 + r)^2$$

At the end of year 3 the amount to be paid back, F3, will be

$$F_3 = P(1 + r)^2 + P(1 + r)2r$$
$$= P(1 + r)^2(1 + r)$$
$$= P(1 + r)^3$$

and so on such that at the end of year t the amount to be paid back will be

$$F_t = P(1+r)^t \qquad\qquad 8.5)$$

Since we are considering interest payments over distinct separate time periods, this type of compounding is called *discrete compounding*. When compound interest is made over a continuous time period, it is called *continuous compounding*. This will be explained shortly.

Example 8.4: Find the future value or the amount to be paid back to the Kenyan Commercial Bank if the original principal is Ksh10million, compound interest rate is 10 per cent and duration is 2 years.

Solution: Applying the formula 8.5 i.e.

$$F_t = P(1 + r)^t$$

$$Ft = Ksh10 (1 + 0.1)^2 \text{ million}$$
$$= Ksh10 (1.1)^2 \text{ million}$$
$$= Ksh12.1 \text{ million}$$

This is as expected from the previous explanation.

Example 8.5

(a) An industrial enterprise has borrowed $10 million to buy an important input at 10 per cent interest compounded annually for 2 years. Find the future value of money to be paid back.

(b) Re do the problem if interest rate is increased to 12 per cent.

(c) If the duration were 5 years, how much would the enterprise pay? (All other information in (a) remains constant)

(d) Comment on your answers.

(e) Deduce from your answers why managers of enterprises in general may hesitate borrowing in order to finance their enterprises and suggest an

(f) alternative.

Solution

(a) Since

$F_t = P(1 + r)$ in general

In this case:

$F = \$10(1 + 0.1)^2$ million.

$= \$12.1$ million

(b) If $r = 12\%$

$F_2 = \$10(1.12)^2$ million

$= \$12.5$ million

(c) If $t = 5$

$Ft = \$10(1 + 0.1)^5$ million

$= \$16.1$ million

(d) The answers indicate that the higher the interest rate the higher the amount to be paid back. A similar trend applies in the case of time or duration.

(e) Managers may hesitate to borrow because of the trends explained in (d). They would like to abstain from paying back more money than they borrow. An alternative to this is promotion of internal funds (retained profit) to finance their purchases and investment.

Discrete Multiple Compounding

Although more often than not interest rates are expressed on annual basis, some interest is compounded monthly, weekly or even daily. If, for instance, a bank charges 6 per cent interest on a loan, if it is compounded monthly, it does not imply that the bank charges 6 per cent every month, but it charges a twelfth of 6 per cent, i.e. $\frac{6}{12}$ or $\frac{1}{2}$ of 1 per cent each month.

The formula which is normally used when interest is compounded m times a year is:

$$F_t = P \left(1 + \frac{r}{m}\right)^m \qquad (8.6)$$

where m is the number of times (frequency) interest is compounded in a year. It can be deduced that when m = 1, the annual compounding formula:

$$F_t = P(1 + r)^t$$

appears.

When interest rate is compounded more than once a year, the process is called *multiple compounding*. In the case of non-continuous frequency, it is called discrete *multiple compounding*. This is illustrated in the subsequent example.

Example 8.6

(a) Re-do Example 8.5(a) when compounding is done semi-annually.

(b) Should managers be sensitive to frequency of compounding when seeking a loan? Explain.

Solution

(a) Applying the formula:

$$Ft = P \left(1 + \frac{r}{m}\right)^{tm}$$

when P = \$10 million, r = 0.1, t = 2 and m = 2

$$F2 = \$10 \left(1 + \frac{0.1}{2}\right)^{2 \times 2} \text{ million}$$

$$= \$10(1.05)^4 \text{ million}$$

$$= \$12.2 \text{ million}$$

(b) Managers should be sensitive to frequency of compounding when seeking a loan because the higher the frequency the larger the amount to be paid back as illustrated in the case when m = 1, and m = 2, in the previous examples.

(c) Continuous Interest Compounding

Although interest rates are, in practice, done on discrete basis, it is also worth noting that compounding can be made over a continuous time period. In this case, it is referred to as *continuous compounding*. The future value Ft, with continuous compounding, is:

$$F_t = P e^{rt} \qquad 8.7$$

where e = 2.71828 (an exponential constant)

other notations remain as stated before.

Example 8.7

Re-do example 8.5(a) and compare your answer with that in the example dealing with discrete compounding.

Solution

Applying the formula

$F_t = Pe^{rt}$

under continuous compounding

$F_2 = \$10_e^{0.1\times2}$ million

$= \$10(2.71828^{0.2})$ million

$= \$10(1.221)$ million

$= \$12.2$ million

The answer ($12.2 million) is greater than that in the case of discrete compounding ($12.1 million), underscoring the proposition that the higher the frequency, the more the amount to be paid back.

Discounting and Present Value

Basic Concepts and Definitions

Discounting is the process of finding the present value of future investment flows at appropriate interest rate popularly called *discount rate*.

Present value is the amount received by discounting future investment flows at a given discount rate.

Discrete Discounting

Discrete Discounting is the process of finding the present value when the discount rate is compounded at non-continuous time periods.

Since

$F_t = P(1 + r)^t$

the basic formula when P is the subject is:

$$P = \frac{F_t}{(1+r)^t} \qquad (8.8)$$

or

$$P = F_t (1 + r)^{-t} \qquad (8.9)$$

In this case P may be regarded as the present value PV so that the formulae (8.8) and (8.9) may be written as

$$PV = \frac{F_t}{(1+r)^t} \qquad (8.10)$$

or

$$PV = F_t (1 + r)^{-t} \qquad (8.11)$$

The following example will illustrate the use of the basic formula.

$$PV = \frac{F_t}{(1+r)^t}$$

Example 8.8

A firm in Namibia wants to buy machines worth Namibian dollar (N$) 10 million five years from now. It is known from a reliable bank source that the discount rate is 7 per cent. How much should the firm invest today to raise the required amount in five years time?

Solution

Since the basic formula is

$$PV = \frac{F_t}{(1+r)^t}$$

In this case

$$PV = N\$ \left[\frac{10,000,000}{(1+0.07)^5}\right]$$

or $PV = N\$ \left[\frac{10,000,000}{1.4025517}\right]$

i.e. PV = N$7,129,862

The reader may check if this present value will lead to N$10,000,000 in five years' time if it is treated as the principal using the formula

$$P = F_t (1 + r)^t$$

Discrete Multiple Discounting and Continuous Discounting

In a similar way to annual discounting the formulae for present value in the case of multiple and continuous discounting can be deduced as follows:

(i) As noted earlier for discrete multiple discounting

$$Ft = P\left(1 + \frac{r}{m}\right)^{tm}$$

Thus

$$PV = F_t / \left(1 + \frac{r}{m}\right)^{tm} \qquad (8.12)$$

or

$$PV = F_t \left(1 + \frac{r}{m}\right)^{-tm} \qquad (8.13)$$

(ii) Since for continuous discounting

$$F_t = P_e$$

Therefore

$$PV = F_t / e^{rt} \qquad (8.14)$$

or $PV = F_t e^{-rt} \qquad (8.15)$

Example 8.9

Re-do example 8.8 if discounting is done (i) quarterly (ii) continuously.

Solution

(i) Given $PV = F_t / \left(1 + \frac{r}{m}\right)^{tm}$

and F = N\$10,000,000, r = 7%, and m = 4, t = 5

$$PV = N\$10,000,000 \Big/ \Big[1 + \frac{0.07}{4}\Big]^{5 \times 4}$$

$$PV = N\$10,000,000/(1.02)^{20}$$

=N\$10,000,000/1.5

= N\$6,666,667

(ii) When discounting is done continuously

$$PV = F_t/e$$

$$= N\$10,000,000/2.71828^{0.07 \times 5}$$

=N\$10,000,000/2.71828^{0.35}

= N\$10,000,000/1.419067

= N\$7,046,884

Annuities

Basic Concepts and Definitions

An *annuity* is a stream of constant flows or equal payments that occur at the end of each period of time for a given number of periods.11 A loan for an industrial equipment, for instance, may involve an annuity in the sense that the firm which is borrowing will make a sequence of equal payments for some length of time. Similarly, a firm which deposits money in a saving account under annuity conditions may be interested to know whether the money available after a given period should be able to purchase some industrial equipment or not.

Problems involving *annuity* make use of geometric progression as a tool of analysis. Geometric progression or geometric series may be expressed as:

a, ar*, ar*^{2}, ..., ar*^{n}. Its sum, S_n, is:

$$S_n = a + ar* + ar*2 + ... + ar*^{n-1} \tag{8.16}$$

where a = a number

r*= the common ratio (r* is different from interest rate r).

It can be shown formally that:

$$S_n = a \frac{(1 - r*^n)}{(1 - r*)} \tag{8.17}$$

For the actual proof see Appendix 8.1.

It should be noted that the derivation of the compound interest rate formula (equation 8.5).

i.e. $F_t = P(1 + r)^t$

reflects the concepts of geometric progression. In that case, the current principal P is borrowed at compound interest, r. The principal P, and the amount owed at the end of the first year, second year, third year etc., i.e. P, P(1 + r), P(1 + r)^2, P(1 + r)^3... form a geometric series, with common ratio (1 + r).

This is not the case with simple interest rate where the principal (P), and the amount owed at the end of first year, second year, third year etc, (P + Pr, P + 2Pr, and P + 3Pr...) form an *arithmetic progression* with a common difference, Pr.

Future Value of an Annuity

The future value of an annuity is calculated similarly to the future value of a normal principal whose interest rate is compounded annually. The formula

$$F_t = P(1 + r)^t$$

is usually used frequently to arrive at the formula for the future value of an annuity (FA):

$$FA = A\left[\frac{1-(1+r)^t}{1-(1+r)}\right]$$

This is explained systematically in the subsequent example.

Example 8.10

If an industrial company deposits $1 million in a saving account at the end of each year for 5 successive years, and the interest rate, 10 per cent, is compounded annually. Will the money available in the account at the end of 4 years be able to purchase a machine worth $4 million?

Solution

It should be noted that reference is made to the current time as t = 0; 1 year later as t = 1; 2 years later as t = 2 etc. Furthermore, the common practice in finance which assumes that the first deposit occurs at t = 1, the second at t = 2 and so on is adhered to for a *regular annuity*.[12] It is thus assumed that the initial deposit of $1 million will earn interest for 4 years, and the last deposit will be just $1 million with no interest on it.

Using the standard compound interest rate equation

$$F_t = P(1 + r)^t$$

The amount of money to which $1 million will grow when 10 per cent interest rate is compounded annually may be computed as follows:

For the first deposit, $F_t = \$1(1 + 0.1)^4$ million, i.e. $1,464,100; since the initial deposit will earn interest for 4 years.

Similarly for the second deposit $Ft = \$1(1 + 0.1)^3$ i.e. $1.331,000. For the third deposit, $F_t = \$1(1 + 0.1)^2$ i.e. $1,210,000. For the fourth deposit, $F_t = \$1(1 + 0.1)^1 = \$1,100,000$. Finally, the future value for the last deposit will be just $1 million with no interest on it.

The total future value or future value of the annuity will be $(1,464,100 + 1,331,000 + 1,210,000 + 1,100,000 + 1,000,000) or $6,105,100 i.e. $F_t = \$[1(1$

+ 0.1)⁴ + 1(1 + 0.1)³ + 1(1 + 0.1)² + 1(1 + 0.1) + 1] million, i.e. $F_t = [1 + 1(1 + 0.1)^1 + 1(1 + 0.1)^2 + 1(1 + 0.1)^3 + 1(1 + 0.1)^4]$ million. The total future value or the *future value of the annuity* F_A will be \$(1,464,100 + 1,331,00 + 1,210,000 + 1,100,000 + 1000,000) i.e. \$6,105,100, which is enough to purchase the machine worth \$4 million.

Note that the flow or future value of the annuity, F_A, may be written as:

F_A = \$[1(1 + 0.1)⁴ + 1(1 + 0.1)³ + 1(1 + 0.1)² + 1(1 + 0.1)¹ + 1] million

or F_A = \$[1 + 1(1 + 0.1)¹ + 1(1 + 0.1)² + 1(1 + 0.1)³ + 1 (1 + 0.1⁴] million. This is clearly a geometric progression with (1 + 0.1) or (1 + r) as a common ratio, r*.

Thus $F_A = \$1 \left[\dfrac{1-(1+0.1)^5}{1-(1+0.1)} \right]$ million = \$6,105,100

By analogy, the general formula is:

$$F_A = A \left[\frac{1-(1+r)^t}{1-(1+r)} \right] \qquad (8.18)$$

where F_A = future value of an annuity

A = an annuity where a constant amount A is deposited at the end of each year.[13]

r = rate of interest

t = time or year

Note that as was the case of multiple compounding in equation 8.6, the future value of an annuity can be obtained by a similar approach by dividing the interest rate by frequency of compounding and multiply the time by the frequency.

Present Value of an Annuity

A similar numerical approach to a future value is used hereunder for derivation of a general formula for the present value of an annuity when interest rate is compounded annually.

The standard formula expressed as equation 8.10, i.e.

$$PV = \frac{F_t}{(1+r)^t}$$

is used frequently to arrive at the formula for the present value of an annuity

$$PVA = A \left[(1 - \frac{1}{(1+r)^t})/r \right]$$

This is explained systematically in the next example.

Example 8.11

A firm would like to begin withdrawing \$1 million each year from a saving account in order to enhance its financing obligations. If the withdrawing is done for a period of four years at an interest rate of 10 per cent compounded annually, how much money would have to be in the account initially so that no money is left in the account after the last withdrawal.

Solution

This problem requires computation of the present value for each withdrawal. Let this be PVA. Using equation (8.8), i.e. the formula

$$PVA = \frac{F_t}{(1+r)^t}$$

The following results are obtained:

Withdrawal	PV	Amount
4	$\frac{\$1\ million}{(1+0.1)^4}$	$683,013
3	$\frac{\$1\ million}{(1+0.1)^3}$	$751,315
2	$\frac{\$1\ million}{(1+0.1)^2}$	$826,446
1	$\frac{\$1\ million}{(1+0.1)^1}$	$909,091

Therefore, present value of the annuity = $3,169,865

It should be noted that the present value is a geometric progression whose common ratio is $1/(1 + 0.1)$ or $1/(1 + r)$, r being the interest rate. In other words:

$$PVA = \frac{\$1}{(1+0.1)} + \frac{\$1}{(1+0.1)^2} + \frac{\$1}{(1+0.1)^3} + \frac{\$1}{(1+0.1)^4}$$

Applying equation 8.17 (sum of geometric progression) can be expressed as:

$$PVA = \frac{\$1}{(1+0.1)}\left[1 - \left(\frac{1}{1+0.1}\right)^4\right] / \left[1 - \frac{1}{(1+0.1)}\right]$$

$$= \frac{\$1}{(1+0.1)}\left[1 - \frac{1}{(1+0.1)^4}\right] / \left[1 - \frac{1}{(1+0.1)}\right]$$

$$= \$1 \left[1 - \frac{1}{(1+0.1)^4}\right] / [(1+0.1) - 1]$$

$$= \$1 \left[1 - \frac{1}{(1+0.1)^4}\right] / 0.1 \qquad = \$3,169,85$$

By analogy, the general formula is:

$$PV_A = A \left[1 - \frac{1}{(1+r)^t}\right] / r \qquad (8.19)$$

$$\text{or simply } PV_A = \frac{A}{r}\left[1 - \frac{1}{(1+t)^t}\right] \qquad (8.20)$$

where PV_A = present value of the annuity (annual compounding)

A = annuity

r = rate of interest

t = time

Note that as was the case with future value of annuity, multiple compounding can also be calculated in a similar way.

Loan Amortisation

Loan amortisation is a process of paying off a debt usually by making small regular payments over time. The small payment may involve reduction on the principal. It is in fact the inverse of a problem of finding the present value of an annuity as shown hereunder:

i.e. $A =$

From equation (8.20):

$$rPV_A = A \left[1 - \frac{1}{(1+r)^t} \right]$$

Thus

$$A = rPV_A \; / \left[1 - \frac{1}{(1+r)^t} \right]$$

i.e. $A = \left[PV_A \dfrac{r}{1 - \frac{1}{(1+r)^t}} \right]$ (21)

$$A = \left[L \dfrac{r}{1 - \frac{1}{(1+r)^t}} \right]$$ (22)

where PV_A = present value of annuity of the principal or, in this case, amount of loan, L.

Other notations remain as explained in equation 8.20.

Example 8.12

The Kwacha Industrial Company Ltd has taken a loan from a bank in Zambia worth Kwacha 100 million. The loan has to be paid in 5 instalments. If the interest rate is 12 per cent and is compounded annually, find the annual payment.

Solution

Applying equation 22.

Payment per period = Amount of loan $\left[\dfrac{0.12}{1 - \frac{1}{(1+0.12)^5}} \right]$

$$= \text{Kwacha } 100 \left[\dfrac{0.12}{1 - \frac{1}{(1.12)^5}} \right] \text{ million}$$

$$= \text{Kwacha } 27.74 \text{ million}$$

Annual Percentage Rate of Interest and Effective Rate of Interest

Annual percentage rate of interest (APR) is the rate of interest per period multiplied by the number of periods in a year. If, for instance, a bank is charging 1 per cent per month on an industrial equipment loan, the APR will be 1 x 12 per cent or 12 per cent.

Effective rate of interest (R) is the *nominal rate of interest or quoted interest rate*, r, compounded m times a year. It is also regarded as the difference between future value and the principal. It is given by the formula

$$R = F - P = \left(1 + \frac{r}{m}\right)^{m} - 1 \qquad (23)$$

where

R = effective rate of interest

F = future value of a \$, or any other currency, compounded m times in one period at

a rate of r per cent per period.

P = the unit principal

Applying the formula with reference to APR,

$$R = \left(1 + \frac{APR}{m}\right)^{m} - 1 \qquad (24)$$

Example 8.13

A bank charges 1.2 per cent rate of interest per month on an industrial hardware loan.

(a) Find the APR

(b) Find the effective annual rate of interest

Solution

(a) APR = 1.2 x 12 per cent = 14.4 per cent

(b) Applying equation 24

Thus $R = = \left(1 + \frac{0.144}{12}\right)^{12} - 1 = 15.4$

The effective annual rate of interest is 15.4 per cent.

Practice and Sources of Industrial Finance in Africa

Hitherto, general, theoretical and quantitative aspects of industrial finance have been examined. This section focuses on the practice and sources of industrial finance in Africa.

Like elsewhere, both internal and external sources of funding are applicable in Africa. Findings by Mabe (2001), for instance, in the main city (Gaborone) and small town (Maun) in Botswana indicate that both sources of finance were used. However, the main source was internal finance, forming 65 per cent. Loans and grants from the government, took the smaller share (35 per cent). For details, see Table 8.1.

Table 8.1: Sources of Funds in Gaborone and Maun (Botswana) 2000/2001 (Percentages)

Location	Internal (Own) finance	Bank loans	Government grants
Gaborone	73	13	14
Maun	57	21	22
Simple Average of both location	65	17	18

Source: Mabe (2001: 31)

Note that (1) most of the firms in Maun were new, small and owned mostly by citizens. These were given more grants by the government. (2) The ratio of internal: external sources, i.e. 65: 35 is comparable to even more developed economies. A study by Fazzan *et al.,* (1988)[14], for instance, showed that retained earnings in USA were increasingly dominant in the 1970s and 1980s. The ratio of internal sources (mainly retained earnings) to external sources was 71: 29. In India, however, the proportion of internal sources to external sources was 40: 60 as indicated in a study by Industrial Credit and Investment Corporation of India (ICICI, 1980).[15]

Regarding start-up capital for small and medium industrial investment in Botswana, Kapunda *et al.* (2008) found that about 84 per cent used personal savings, 8 per cent obtained loans from family members, 5 per cent took loans from commercial banks, while 2 per cent got subsidized loans from the Citizens Entrepreneurial Development Agency (CEDA). The remaining percentage was for others. In this case the proportion of internal sources: external sources was 84:16.

Regarding quantitative approach the application, use of linear and compound depreciation, and simple and compound interest in African institutions is quite common. Proxy examples in the cases of Kenya, Zambia and other African countries have been provided throughout the discussion examples and exercises in this chapter.

Conclusion

This chapter has provided an overview of theories of investment with reference to main sources of finance. Internal and external sources of funding have been examined qualitatively and quantitatively. Finally, the chapter has presented practice and sources of industrial finance in Africa.

Review Questions

1. (a) What is meant by internal funds theory of investment?
    (b) With reference to a named African country, differentiate between internal and external sources of finance.

2. If the original cost of an industrial equipment is C and it is depreciated linearly over N years:
   (a) Show that its book value V at the end of n years is given by

   $$V = C \left(1 - \frac{n}{N}\right)$$

   (b) Deduce the book value of the equipment after 3 years if its original cost is P60,000 and is depreciated linearly over 10 years.
   (c) The enterprise had borrowed the P60,000 from a private financing agency at 12 percent interest rate and then decides to sell the equipment after 3 years at the book value. How much extra funding will be required to pay the loan if the interest rate is compounded quarterly?
   (d) Deduce from your answers why managers may hesitate to borrow in order to finance their firms and suggest an alternative.
3. The terms of a short-term loan require that a firm make a lumpsum payment of Ugandan shilling (Ush) 25 million at the end of 2 years. Find the present value if the interest rate is 18 per cent compounded
   (a) annually
   (b) monthly
   (c) continuously.
4. A firm in South Africa has borrowed rand 50,000 to be paid in 10 annual instalments. What annual interest rate must be made if the interest rate is 14 per cent compounded annually?
5. A bank charges 1.1 per cent rate of interest on an industrial equipment loan.
   (a) What is the corresponding annual percentage rate of interest?
   (b) Considering the annual percentage rate of interest, find the effective annual rate of interest.

Appendix 8.1: Derivation of the Sum of Geometric Progression

Given the sum of geometric progression as:

$$S_n = a + ar^* + ar^{*2} + ar^{*3} + \ldots + ar^{*n-1} \quad \ldots \ldots \tag{i}$$

If r^* is multiplied throughout the equation.

$$r^*S_n = ar^* + ar^{*2} + ar^{*3} + ar^{*4} + \ldots ar^{*n-1} + ar^{*n} \tag{ii}$$

Subtract (ii) from (i):

$$S_n - r^*S_n = a - ar^* \tag{iii}$$

This can be expressed as:

$$(1 - r^*)S_n = a(1 - r^*) \tag{iv}$$

$$\text{Therefore } S_n = a \frac{(1-r^*)}{(1-r^*)} \tag{v}$$

This is the formula for the sum of geometric progression.

The reader may wish to explain why r* should not be allowed to be equal to 1.

Notes

1. Cf. Barthwal (1985: 245).
2. Cf. Barthwal (1985) *Accounting Procedure: Value of Production and Other income* include:
    (a) Sales net of excise duty and similar items;
    (b) Change of the value of the stock of finished goods and work-in-progress;
    (c) Other income such as dividends, interest, rent, by product sales, work done for others; and
    (d) Non-operating surplus or deficit.
    Total expenditure includes:
    (a) Material, stores, and other manufacturing expenses; (b) Current repairs;
    (c) Salaries and wages;
    (d) Managerial remunerations; (e) Welfare expenses;
    (f) Selling expenses;
    (g) Depreciation;
    (h) Other provisions like rent, provident fund, local taxes, bad debts, and royalties;
    (i) Insurance charges; and
    (j) Other miscellaneous expenses such as R & D expenses.
3. For details of profit-growth models such as those of Marris and Radice see, for instance, Devine *et al.* (1985: 151).
4. For details, see Edgmand, (Third edition) (1987: 110).
5. Ibid, p.11.
6. Ibid.
7. Compare with the provisions under total expenditure in note 2.
8. For details see, for instance, Barthwal 1985: 230 – 234).
9. See, for instance, Freund and Williams (1983: 144).
10. Ibid, p.145.
11. Cf. Mukras 2004: 297.
12. All annuities in this text are regular. They are assumed to involve constant or equal payment at the end of each year. Payments made at the beginning of each year are shifted back 1 year. This is consistent with the approach of most introductory textbooks in finance (Freund and Williams 1983: 135).
13. If the deposits are made at the beginning of each year, the formula would be
$$F_A = A(1 + r) \left[\frac{1 - (1+r)^t}{1 - (1+r)} \right]$$
14. For details, see Dornbusch *et al* (2001: 339).
15. Quoted by Barthwal (1985: 235).

IV

Public Policy and Industrial Development in Africa

9

Public Policy for Industrial Development in Africa

Learning Objectives

The main objectives of this chapter are:
- To explain the rationale for public policy with reference to industrial development in Africa;
- To review national industrial policies in selected African countries;
- To explain and assess the effort made towards a public industrial policy in Africa;
- To explain public competition policy and its role in enhancing industrial development with reference to African economies;
- To explain and assess the effort made towards a competition policy in Africa;
- To examine generic policies underscoring those related to protection of industries and privatisation in African countries.

Introductory Note

Public policy may be included explicitly in the S-C-P paradigm as shown in Appendix 2.2. This may lead to direct implications in the structure-conduct-performance paradigm. Public policy or government intervention in monopoly firms, for instance, may lead to lower profitability and hence to decrease in performance. Indeed, traditional industrial economics is an input to public policy and industrial development.

Although public policy, government intervention and government regulations are sometimes used interchangeably, in this chapter *public policy* refers to guidelines to a purposive course of action adopted or proposed mainly by governments for public interest.

With reference to industrial development in Africa, the rationale for public policy is explained in this chapter. An overview of national industrial development policies in some African countries is also provided; followed by an explanation of public industrial policy harmonization and potential regional industrial policies and a potential African industrial policy. Public competition policy and its role in promoting industrial development in theory and practice is explained with reference to examples from African countries. Regional competition policies and a potential public competition policy for Africa are also explained thereafter. Finally, *generic policies* are examined. These correct both market failure and government failure. Protection of industries and privatisation are underscored.

Rationale for Public Policy in Africa

Directrationale for Public Policy with Reference to Industrial Development

Market failure

The direct rationale for public policy on industrial development has been attributed mainly to market failure which leads to inefficiency. This justification is sometimes classified as *efficiency-oriented government intervention*.[1] In the case of industrialisation, it includes economies of scale, unfair or imperfect competition and market power. National security and self-reliance may also be included. This type of justification is explained hereunder.

Economies of Scale

Established firms that have achieved economies of scale and learning-by-doing try to bar new entrants. This has led to the argument of protecting new or infant industries and even small scale industries. This rationale was very common after most of African countries got independence, especially those that followed a socialist roadmap like Tanzania, Zambia and Ghana.[2] Although the current trade liberalisation era is discouraging protection of new or infant and small industries, many African countries are still protecting and subsidising them. Others are supporting them within a given framework of time. In the Southern African Custom Union (SACU), for example, the provision in Article 26 of the SACU Agreement calls for infant industry protection of the less developed members: Botswana, Lesotho, Namibia and Swaziland (BLNS) against the more developed South Africa. However, specific time framework is set and reviewed whenever there is need to do so.[3]

Monopoly and Market Power

If economies of scale leading to natural monopoly government intervention may be justified to regulate market power, the government will try to keep prices as close as possible to marginal costs for consumers' benefits.[4] This is because monopoly prices tend to be a burden to poor consumers especially when natural monopolies are those dealing with *public utilities* like water and electricity which are essential to life. This explains further why water and electricity companies have been partially (as parastatals) or wholly owned by governments in Africa as illustrated in chapter[4].

National Security and Self-reliance

Governments may wish to develop or maintain a particular industry for reasons of national security and self-reliance.[5] The industries may include those which are dealing with defence, citizen empowerment, or self-reliance and economic independence. Governments may subsidise, protect or run such industries. Industries dealing with defence (weapons and military hardware) are common in advanced countries. In Africa, some governments like Botswana and Tanzania try to promote citizen-owned and rural industries, especially small and medium enterprises (SMEs), for citizen empowerment and self-reliance, rural industrialisation, employment creation and national security. Large intermediate and capital goods industries (investment industries) may also be important for national security as they ensure sustainability, self-reliance, and economic independence, since they are rich in backward and forward linkages.[6] Since 1975 Tanzania has attempted to embark on such industries, basically for the afore-mentioned reasons. The Basic Industry Strategy (BIS) in Tanzania (1975 – 1995) was an attempt to build such industries. They were essentially to change gradually the structure of the industrial sector from producing mostly consumer goods to more intermediate and capital goods. This was followed by another long-term industrialisation policy – the Sustainable Industrial Development Policy – SIDP (1996 – 2020) which aims at self-sustainability and economic independence.[7]

Investment goods industries are normally very expensive and their pay-back periods are usually very long. No wonder, private investors tend to shy away from such investment. Government intervention, therefore, becomes inevitable when such investments are considered important for national security and self-reliance. The investment may be done through public-private joint venture where private investments are given enough incentives such as long tax holidays and relatively small tax rates.

Another approach is to involve co-operation within Africa especially through regional blocs like the East Africa Community (EAC) and the Southern African Development Community (SADC). Both the BIS and SIDP, actually, encouraged the regional or African approach as will be elaborated later in this chapter.

Indirect Rationale for Public Policy with Reference to Industrial Development

General Proposition

Almost all other arguments[8] for public policy can be explained indirectly in favour of industrial development. Three examples are sufficient to explain the proposition. These are presented hereunder:

Public Goods

Public goods or collective goods in their pure form, are basically non-rival (use by one does not preclude use of another) and non-exclusive (use cannot be rationed). This makes it impossible for a private entrepreneur to supply these goods, and government is called into being the supplier because of its ability to recover costs through taxation or user fees.[9]

Public goods may be pro-industrial development. Universal education, for example, which can efficiently be funded by government is an input to tertiary education provided by industrial or technical colleges. In many countries, including Botswana and Tanzania, many such colleges are fully or partially owned by government.

Infrastructure too is an example of public good. Roads, railways, large-scale water projects, and provision of new technologies that cannot be patented are examples of infrastructure. These are crucial for industrial development as they are the source of agglomeration economies in Africa and elsewhere, as explained in chapter seven.

Externalities

An *externality* is any positive or negative valued impact from any production or consumption action that affects someone but whose benefits and costs are not fully reflected in the benefits received by someone or cost paid by that individual. Normally, positive externalities are underprovided and negative externalities are overprovided unless public policy is implemented to regulate the situation. Public health (which is essential for industrial workers) and industrial/technical education, for instance, are normally underprovided. Hence government is justified in providing them.

Overprovision is common in the case of pollution. Government intervention through regulation and laws as is done in many African countries becomes important. Chemical pollution, for instance, by an industrial activity which harms nearby industrial fishing and canning in cities near lakes or oceans like Mwanza and Dar-es-Salaam in Tanzania and elsewhere calls for public policy.

Welfare

Public policy may be motivated by government goals other than mere efficiency. Even if markets work in improving people's welfare, they may not do it the way government wants. Government may aim at, for instance, distributing land, through land reform, in specified ratio of land area for private (industrial) investors to land area for small farmers (peasants) or redistributing earning through specified pay-as-you-earn system. This is unlikely to be done by markets, however efficient they may appear to be. The examples given illustrate *non- efficiency-oriented government intervention.*[10]

Another example is in order. Government may aim at supporting small-industrial enterprise in order to empower citizens, promote rural industrialisation and eventually reduce poverty as the case in Botswana, Tanzania and possibly elsewhere in Africa. Even if markets were to work in this aspect, it would not lead to the targeted rates of poverty reduction.

Public Industrial Policies for Development in Africa

Conceptual and Definitional Background

Most of the definitions of industrial policy have elements of public policy or government intervention. Johnson (1984: 8),[11] for example, defines industrial policy as 'the initiation and co-ordination of government activities[12] to leverage upward the productivity and competitiveness of the whole economy and of particular industries in it'. Dietrich (1992) defines industrial policy as directed public interventions at the sectorial or firm level, aimed at stimulating lines of economic endeavour by restructuring or promoting the activities of a particular firm or sector. Andreasso and Jacobson (2005:446) refer to industrial policy as 'all activities of public authorities that affect, directly or indirectly, the performance (for example, productivity, profitability, international competitiveness) of the manufacturing and service sectors'. Makoa (2008:64) reproduces a *Google Dictionary* definition of industrial policy as 'any government regulation or law that encourages the ongoing operation of, or investment in industry'. The study also reproduces[13] the World Bank definition: 'government efforts to alter industrial structure to promote productivity-based growth'. Vickers (2008:7) cites[14] industrial policy as 'a process of strategic collaboration between the private sector and public authorities with the aim of uncovering where the most significant obstacles to restructuring lie and what type of interventions are most likely to remove them (and promote industrialisation). In this textbook, industrial policy is defined as guidelines to a purposive course of action adopted or proposed mainly by government to promote industrial development.

This is in conformity with the case of the East Asian newly industrialising countries (NICs) where the visible hands of the governments guided industrialisation especially during the early period of industrial development.[15]

National Industrial Policies in Africa

Major Trends and Aspects of National Industrial Policies

After independence many African countries embarked on industrialisation guided by the implied policy statement: industry is the leading sector; agriculture is the base. With time, some countries came up with clear and comprehensive documented industrial policies.

Most of the early industrial policies were based on *import-substitution strategies* (producing for domestic market and substituting for imports). This was a very common approach not only in Africa but among most less developed countries (LDCs) in the 1960s. The basic argument was to save foreign exchange for importing less but producing more goods in LDCs.[16] However, increasing competition and globalisation since the early 1990s has led to outward-oriented (export – oriented) strategies.

The major contents of a typical documented industrial policy in Africa encompasses background information, objectives, policy issues and strategies to guide the implementation of the policy. Furthermore, it normally includes aspects of small and medium enterprises (SMEs). With time, as the case with Botswana and Tanzania, separate policies on SMEs are formulated.

In the next sub-section, an overview of selected national policies is presented to illustrate some of the aspects in this sub-section.

Industrial Policy in Botswana

Botswana's first documented industrial development policy was introduced in 1984. This was the time when the mining share to gross domestic product (GDP) was the highest (close to 50 per cent). The government, therefore, had to consider seriously diversifying the economy away from mining, taking into account the risk of overdependence on the sector. Industry was considered central in the diversification process. The main objective of the policy, therefore, was to diversify the economy. Other objectives were promotion of the private sector, and creation of employment opportunities for the growing population of Botswana.[17]

The 1984 industrial development plan was led mainly by an import-substitution strategy. This was appropriate for the then closed economies of the Southern African region. It became an underlying premise of Botswana's industrial policy and the subsequent national development plans.[18]

In the mid-1990s a review was undertaken, necessitated mainly by the increasing competition and globalisation forces. Following this, a revised policy was published in 1998 (*Government Paper No. 1*). While the objectives remained essentially the same, there was considerable change in the main strategy.[19]

The strategy was export-oriented. It addressed several issues which also essentially necessitated it: (i) globalisation and the emphasis on open and free trade stressed by the World Trade Organisation (WHO) which came into being on 1 January 1995 as a successor to the General Agreement on Tariffs and Trade (GATT) and as a result of the Uruguay Round of multilateral trade negotiations, which lasted from 1986 to 1994;[20] (ii) the need to promote rapid growth in productivity and efficiency as critical elements of competitiveness in global trade in goods and services; (iii) Botswana's accession to the SADC protocol on trade and co-operation, and SACU agreements on trade and industrial development, which provide for increased competition for investment and trade opportunities within the region; and (iv) the limited scope for development based on Botswana's small market.[21]

In order to meet the challenges of the changing regional and global environment, the industrial policy aimed at developing an efficient and competitive outward-oriented industrial and service sector. In this regard, the government was to provide an environment conducive to the development of the private sector through bilateral and multilateral negotiation with the aim of maximising access to export markets. Furthermore, the government was to encourage investors and entrepreneurs to improve labour productivity, competitive unit labour costs, cost of public utilities, and support on small-scale rural entrepreneurs. For details on the supporting principles for the industrial policy and relevant policy thrusts, see Appendices 9.1 and 9.2.

The emphasis on service industries which directly or indirectly support the manufacturing industry was the major improvement on the previous strategy as development of the manufacturing sector alone cannot be regarded as a panacea for Botswana's unemployment and lack of economic diversification problems.[22]

As part of the process of implementation, the government established a high-level national committee to implement the industrial development plan. Additional measures included institutional support such as the Botswana Export Development and Investment Agency (BEDIA), Botswana Development Corporation (BDC), Financial Assistance Policy (FAP) which in 2001 evolved into Citizen Entrepreneurial Development Agency (CEDA) to support small, medium and micro enterprises (SMMEs financially.

The 1998 Industrial Development Policy was applicable in Botswana up to 2013 so was the separate SMMEs Policy which evolved from the 1998 Industrial Policy in 1999. The objectives of the SMMEs policy include, among others: fostering citizen entrepreneurship and empowerment; achieving economic diversification and creating employment thereby reducing poverty. For details, see Appendix 9.3.

In 2014 a new Industrial Development Policy (2014-2028) was launched. This regarded the industrial sector as the engine of growth. Its main theme was placing Botswana among the industrialised economies of the 21st century. Its vision was to have diversified sustainable and globally competitive industries (Republic of Botswana 2014:6).

As noted in Kapunda (2016) while the policy strategy will remain based on export-led growth, meeting both domestic and export market as was the case of the previous industrial development policy the current one strengthens the various aspects of the policy such as development of industry shills, small medium and micro-economics and others as shown in Table 9.1.

Table 9.1: Summary of Botswana Industrial Policy Path

IDP I:1984-1998	IDP II: 1998-2012	IDP II: 2014-2028
Import Substitution Domestic Markets Private Sector Development	Export-Led Growth Both Exports and Domestic Markets Private Sector Development Creation of Institutional Structure for Privatization Competitive Manufacturing and Services Industries Creation of Industrial Development Institutions Human Resource Development and Training (Institutions) Policy for Technology and Industrial Development Institutional support for SMMEs Participation in Industrial Development	Export-Led Growth Both Exports and Domestic Markets Creation of Opportunities for Private Sector Development Strategic use of Privatization Development of High-Priority High Impact Sectors/Initiatives (Big Bangs) Strengthening Implementation of Industrial development Initiatives Strengthening development of relevant industry skills Effective use of Technology for Industrial Development and Global Competitiveness Strengthening SMMEs Participation in Industrial Development Initiatives

Source: Republic of Botswana (2014) *Industrial Development Policy for Botswana*

Industrial Policy in Lesotho

Despite lack of early comprehensive documents on industrial policy in Lesotho, the policy may be traced to the mid-1960s, the period beginning barely one year after independence in 1966. Furthermore, Lesotho's industrial policy, like that of Botswana, has been shifting strategies over time. The first period (1966 – 1985) was basically guided centrally by government despite some degree of free market mechanism. Like in the case of Botswana, national institutions were to lead the implementation of the policy. Examples include the Lesotho National Development Corporation (LNDC) established in 1967 with a broad industrial development mandate; the Basotho Enterprises Development Corporation (BEDICO) established in 1977 to assist local or Basotho entrepreneurs and to support SMEs; and the Lesotho Bank charged with provision of loans to industrial enterprises and other financial services.[23]

The objectives of the policy included creation of jobs; achieving industrial efficiency high productivity, and high growth rates; increasing national income; producing and availing industrial products at low costs and prices; and stimulating demand for industrial production both domestically and export-wise.[24]

The 1980 – 1985 Year Plan made the industrial objectives and strategies more holistic than before as it underscored a multi-focused approach. The strategies included improved management; skills training; creation of industrial estates; mobilisation of capital; localisation; export-oriented production and foreign trade promotion; improved marketing arrangements; pricing policies with control; tourism; a labour-intensive construction unit; mineral resource exploration. Although some of these strategies were not directly relevant to industrial development, they affected the implementation of the industrial policy.

The second period of the industrial policy was from 1986 to the time of writing this book. This period was influenced by the adoption of reform or structural adjustment programmes (SAPs) towards the end of the 1980s and the ascendancy of globalisation and free-market ideology. This replaced the centrally-guided regime (*developmentalism*). The framework and strategy for industrial policy and development were hinged squarely on free-market mechanism. An export-oriented industrial strategy was also underscored.

Lesotho's liberal industrial development policy weakened the LNDCs role and influence, so that up to the time of writing this book, the organisation was an advisory body only, rather than an active participant in the actual industrial production process. Foreign direct investment (FDI) assumed importance as an alternative to state-supplied capital. The country adopted a *laissez faire* industrial development policy.[25]

Industrial Policy in Namibia

In 1992 Namibia adopted a White Paper on industrial development. The paper underscored the industrial policy of Namibia. It outlined a pattern of industrialisation comparable to that pursued by Taiwan in the 1960s, where export processing zones (EPZs) and support of small and medium enterprises were advocated in a small economy. Its objectives were: to increase value added in manufacturing and service industries; to promote forward and backward linkages in the industrial sector; to increase the share of manufactured products in total exports; to enhance product and export-market diversification; and to encourage competitiveness through increased productivity and quality.[26]

As was the case with the previous outlined industrial policies, the White Paper had to be reviewed. It was reviewed in 1998 to address the shortcoming noted over time.[27] However, more review inputs were called for. One visible attempt to conduct a review was embarked on in 2003 by the Namibian Economic Policy Research Unit (NEPRU), which resulted in a document entitled: 'Second Industrial Policy and Strategies'.[28] This was a great input to the Ministry of Trade and Industry. However, by the time of writing this textbook, the country was mostly applying the policies in the 1992 White Paper. It should be noted, however, the industrial policy in Namibia has been and is still outward-oriented, with established links to export markets such as South Africa, the European Union (EU), and North America. This is expected since it was formalised in the 1990s when outward-oriented policies were the result of the increased global competition unlike the case of 1980s' industrial policies in Botswana, Tanzania and many other African countries that got independence and formulated their policies earlier than Namibia. *Industrial Policy in South Africa*

For some time, the main objective of the industrial policy in South Africa has been to enhance productivity and efficiency of firms.[29] However, by 2005 the industrial policy had also to contribute greatly to raising South Africa's growth rate as per the Accelerated and Shared Growth Initiative for South Africa (ASGISA). In 2007, South Africa adopted the National Industrial Policy Framework (NIPF) aimed at diversifying the production and export structure, promoting labour-intensive industrialisation, moving towards a knowledge economy, and contributing to the industrial development of the region. Industrial Policy Action Plans (IPAP) were also adopted in the same year to implement the framework. The first IPAP was for the period 2007/08 while the second IPAP covered the period 2010/11 – 2012/13.[30]

Although South African industrial policy remains multi-focused, it has only two explicitly targeted sub-sectors – clothing and textiles, and autos and auto- components. The main strategy is export-oriented. However, the restrictions imposed on industrial policy by international agreements remain a challenge.

The two sub-sectors mentioned above, for example, are open to successful challenge in the WTO as, in both sub-sectors, exporters receive support through earning rebates on imports that are proportional to their export – the Import Rebate Credit Certificates (IRCCs) in respect of autos and auto components, and the Duty Credit Certificate Scheme (DCCS) in respect of clothing and textiles. Furthermore, the disciplining and monitoring standard that linked support to successful engagement in the export market, for instance, has been removed, rendering the policy both less effective and much more difficult to monitor and control.[31]

By the time of writing this textbook, there were recommendations to review the industrial policy to involve improved professionalism, collaboration between capable government and bureaucracy and business.[32]

Industrial Policy in Tanzania

From independence in 1961 to 1974, Tanzania's industrial policy, although not comprehensively documented but implied in the five-year plans, was based essentially on import-substitution strategy. The objective was to produce mainly for the domestic market and substitute for imports, thereby saving foreign exchange. Most of the industries were guided and partially owned by the National Development Corporation (NDC).[33]

Several studies,[34] however, had criticised the import-substitution strategy for its overdependence on imported inputs; its low backward and forward linkages and its concentration on consumer goods like food and drinks, cigarettes and textiles at the expense of producer goods like iron and steel and chemicals.

In 1975 a long-term industrial policy centred on *basic industry strategy* (BIS) was launched. It was to cover the period up to 1995. The strategy was basically a reaction to the import-substitution strategy which was criticised basically in line with the argument stated earlier and that it could not be met because of increasingly high cost of imported inputs for the production of mostly consumer goods. Consequently, the expected foreign exchange saving and related advantages were not realised.

The BIS (1975 – 1995) aimed at great structural change, leading to significant growth of the economy and self-reliance. The strategy sought to restructure the economy by:[35]

- Establishing and strengthening greater inter-industry linkages;
- Orientating industry towards increased production of producer goods;
- Orientating the economy towards greater national autonomy through (i) reduced reliance on foreign markets for domestic production; and (ii) reduced dependence on essential imports for consumption; and
- Increasing the share of manufacturing in total GDP.

The long term priorities of BIS were:

- To establish basic industries particularly those producing iron and steel, coal, chemicals and construction materials;

- To establish engineering and metal working industries, workshops for manufacturing spare parts, tools and machine parts in order to enhance self-reliance and expand the local market for iron and steel;
- To produce products for the basic needs of Tanzanians. The basic needs include food, water, clothing, construction materials, health services, and education;
- To establish small and medium industries in the regions, districts and in the villages with a view to producing basic necessities where most consumers reside and spread industries in the regions and zones;
- To expand agricultural processing industries and produce exportable products so as to increase the country's foreign exchange earnings;
- To increase scientific, technical and technological knowledge by expanding training of working in industries and by establishing centres for industrial services and technology; and
- To make efforts to utilise local raw materials available in the country in order to implement the above mentioned targets and objectives.

Note that the strategy underscored meeting both domestic demand (basic needs) and exports.

In general the target was to increase significantly the percentage of value added of producer or *investment goods* or *capital goods* like iron and steel, metal and engineering products and reduce the percentage of value added of consumer goods like food processing, beverages and tobacco. Table 9.1 shows essentially the planned36 and projected percentage of value added for 1980 and 1995 respectively, the base year being 1974.

Table 9.2: Planned and Projected Industrial Structural Change 1980 and 1995 (Percentage of value added)

Sub-sector	1974 (Actual)	1980 (Planned) (Actual)		1995 (Projected)
Iron and steel, metal and engineering products Chemical and chemical products	(15.30)	14.80	(19.39)	30.30
Wood products, Paper and Printing	(16.20)	18.00	(13.25)	16.30
Non-metallic products	(11.50)	10.60	(6.92)	9.90
Food processing, Beverage and tobacco	(4.00)	6.00	(4.23)	3.60
Textile, leather and sisal products	(32.00)	29.10	(34.06)	21.20
	(21.00)	21.50 (22.15)		18.70
Total	100.00	100.00100.00		100.00

Source: United Republic of Tanzania (1982), The First Five Year Union Plan (1981/82 – 1985/86), Vol. 1, p.63

Five years after the launch of the BIS (1980) the planned situation was somewhat not on track in general. However, the basic sub-sector, iron and steel, metal and engineering product showed the expected trend. The actual percentage of value added (19.39) was greater than the planned figure (14.80 per cent). This was an achievement towards the projected 30 per cent for 1995.

The increasing intensity of competitiveness and globalisation in the mid-1990s, however, shifted the industrial policy towards export-orientation. This trend, among other reasons, led to a new long-term policy: the Sustainable Industrial Development Policy (SIDP) in 1996 with a time horizon of 25 years, up to 2020, to which we now turn.

SIDP aimed at self-sustainability and economic independence while maintaining competitive capacity. Its implementation was to be done in phases: Phase 1 was devoted to privatisation and rehabilitation with the objective of improving their competitive capacity under the current era of competitive market economies and globalisation.

Phase 2 aimed at attracting and drawing investors towards agro-processing activities.

Phase 3 aimed at establishing Export Processing Zones (EPZ) under the supervision of the National Development Corporation (NDC). This was to promote the export-oriented strategy. In May 2003, the first industry to produce goods for export under the EPZ arrangement, NIDA Textile Mills Ltd, was inaugurated. Furthermore, by then the NDC had identified areas for EPZ development in the border regions (provinces): Tanga, Kilimanyaro, Kagera, Kigoma, Mtwara and Mbeya targeting the export market, especially in neighbouring countries: Kenya, Uganda, Burundi/Rwanda, Zaire, Malawi and Zambia.

Like, the BIS, SIDP promoted co-operation within Africa especially through regional blocs like the East African Community (EAC) and the Southern African Development Community (SADC). Both also promote small and medium industries.

Actually in 2002, Tanzania became the first country in Africa to organise a regional conference of African ministers of industry from EAC (Burundi, Kenya, Rwanda, Tanzania and Uganda). Sudan was invited as a potential member and Nigeria attended as an observer. The conference aimed at formulating joint programmes to promote and develop industrial production of textile and clothing, leather and leather products, agro-processing, and various intermediate and capital goods. These were incorporated in SIDP. The conference reached concensus on joint approach for the public and private sectors to strengthen such industries.[37]

SIDP also placed specific emphasis on the promotion of small and medium industries. It did so through the following measures: supporting existing and new promotion institutions, simplification of taxation, licence and registration of SMEs and improvement of access to financial services. In addition, SIDP encouraged informal sector business to grow and be formalised. Furthermore, the policy identifies measures to enable indigenous entrepreneurs, women, youth and people with disabilities to take part in economic activities.[38]

In 2003 a separate policy on small and medium enterprises was launched. Its vision, mission, overall objective and scope are outlined in Appendix 9.4.

Regional Industrial Policy Harmonisation and Potential Regional Industrial Policies

Theoretical Background

As regional blocs in Africa move towards full integration, industrial policy harmonisation becomes theoretically and practically an important agenda.

Industrial harmonisation can take several forms such as co-ordination of national industrial policies, harmonisation of national standards and regulations; and recognition of foreign regulatory regimes and conformity assessment procedures.[39]

Co-ordination may be based on formal agreements on, for example, the use of the principles of positive comity in the application of competition law, or may even be ad-hoc, as in co-operation on infrastructure and other projects promoting industrial development. Other agreements may be on co-ordination and harmonisation of tax policies and anti-dumping policies and protection of infant industries.40

Recognition of foreign regulatory regimes and conformity assessment procedures may also involve the adoption of international norms or the standards of a trading partner. Botswana, for instance, may consider positively professional qualifications of managers, industrialists, doctors etc. trained in a trading partner or member of SACU such as South Africa or Namibia. Such qualifications may be regarded sufficient to allow them practice, for instance, in Botswana.41

There are, however, a range of political, economic, size, and institutional variables that complicate harmonisation and achieving a common policy.42 These may dictate the level or nature of the common policy in a region.

Towards Harmonisation and Common Industrial Policies in Regional Blocs in Africa

Background Proposition

Hitherto, some visible efforts have been shown by regional blocs in Africa which promote common policies, including industrial policies. Examples are in order:

Southern African Customs Union (SACU)

The Southern African Customs Union (SACU) is regarded as the oldest functioning customs union in the world, formed in 1910.[43] Its members are Botswana, Lesotho, Namibia, South Africa and Swaziland.

SACU may also be regarded as a good example of a regional bloc which has visible efforts towards harmonisation and common industrial policy. Despite having different levels of development – South Africa being more developed than the others – SACU has managed to form several common agreements relevant to industrial development since its formation. The early agreements include those on common external tariffs, common revenue-sharing formula, and free trade within the customs.[44]

The 2002 New SACU Agreements included specific agreements and articles of industrial policy and development, especially article 38.2. In summary, the agreements underscored the following, among others:

- To facilitate the development of common policies and strategies including industrial policy and strategy;
- To promote fair competition, substantially increase investment and facilitate economic development;
- To facilitate the cross-border movement of industrial and other goods between the members, Tariffs were regarded as an instrument of industrial development policy.[45]

Furthermore the agreement was expected to:

- To harmonise policies in industry, agriculture and trade;
- To permit national protection for infant industries in the BLNS (Botswana, Lesotho, Namibia and Swaziland) for eight years; and
- To harmonise industrial product standards and technical regulation within the common customs area.[46]

In 2006 an international workshop involving participants from SACU countries and elsewhere was held in Pretoria, South Africa, to investigate the potential for harmonising industrial policies within SACU to ensure 'development integration' and to develop a more comprehensive perspective on the various challenges and opportunities in this regard.[47] The output of the workshop was proceedings on harmonising industrial policy in SACU.[48]

By the time of writing this textbook, the SACU nations as members of SADC were involved in negotiating around a Protocol on Industrial Policy Cooperation.

Southern African Development Community (SADC)

Since its establishment in 1980, the SADC, which was originally known as SADCC[49] and had 9 members,[50] has been emphasising coordination and cooperation among state members in several projects including industrial projects.

Since then, as it expanded[51] and became SADC in 1992, it started showing more visible efforts than before towards common market and harmonised policies including industrial policies. In 1996, for example, the SADC member countries signed a Trade Protocol which included:

- Promoting common policies on industrialisation to lead economic diversification and development in general in the region; and

- Establishing a free trade area in the SADC region and harmonising tariffs and non-trade barriers for industrial and other goods.

In 1998, SADC underscored the need to focus, in future, on policy formulation, co-ordination, and harmonisation of the policies including industrial policies as stated in the 1997 SADC Programme of Action (SPA). Based on similar emphasis, the SADC review report was approved by organisation's summit in 2001.[52]

In 2008, SADC agreed to establish a free trade zone with the East African Community (EAC) and the Common Market for Eastern and Southern Africa (COMESA).

The recent significant effort of harmonisation of industrial policies within SACU is likely to have a significant positive impact on industrial policy harmonisation within SADC, given that the SACU states are also members of SADC.

The current (2015-2063) SADC Industrialisation Strategy and Road Map requires policy harmonization effort in its implementation. (SADC 2015)

Currently, SADC has 14 members: Angola, Botswana, Democratic Republic of Congo – DRC (1997),[53] Lesotho, Malawi, Mauritius (1995), Mozambique, Namibia (1990), Seychelles (1997), South Africa (1994), Swaziland, Tanzania, Zambia, and Zimbabwe (the founder members of SADCC (1980) being in italics. Madagascar's (2005) membership, however, has been suspended after a coup d'état occurred there.

East Africa Community (EAC)

The East African Community (EAC) founder members are Kenya, Uganda and a SADC member, Tanzania. The first two are also members of COMESA.

The history of co-operation among the three states stretches back more than a century. Under British colonialism, the three countries were linked under the East African Common Services Organisation (EACSO), which included railways, harbours, posts and telecoms, airways, highjer education, medical and scientific research, single currency etc. It is this organization which was upgraded into the East Africa Community when the countries became independent. However, the early version of EAC was dissolved in 1977.[54]

In 1999, however, an EAC treaty became the basis of the re-launching of the community aiming at the establishment of a customs union, common market, monetary union, political federation, and harmonisation of various policies including industrial policies.

In 2005 the EAC customs union came into effect. It underscored harmonisation of tariffs, industrial policies and other policies. In general, the union formalised the 2004 EAC Customs Union protocol, where members were to eliminate all internal tariffs and other similar charges.[55]

Hitherto, the EAC has expanded to include Burundi and Rwanda in addition to founder members: Kenya, Tanzania and Uganda, and is giving priority to sectoral policy harmonisation including industrial policy harmonisation.

Common Market for Eastern and Southern Africa (COMESA)

The Common Market for Eastern and Southern Africa (COMESA) formally succeeded the Preferential Trade Area (PTA) for East and Southern Africa[56] when the 1993 COMESA treaty entered into force in 1994.

COMESA's objectives include the promotion of joint macroeconomic and sectoral policies including joint and harmonised industrial policies and establishment of customs union.[57] The long-term objective is to form a common market.

COMESA is a good example of regional bloc which also aims at unifying Africa. Since its establishment it has aimed at contributing to the objective of African Economic Community (AEC). Even the former PTA aimed at unifying the continent.[58]

By 1997, COMESA had 22 members: Angola, Burundi, Comoro, DRC, Djibouti, Eritrea, Ethiopia, Kenya, Lesotho, Madagascar, Malawi, Mauritius, Mozambique, Namibia, Rwanda, Seychelles, Somalia, Swaziland, Tanzania, Uganda, Zambia and Zimbabwe.[59]

By the late 1990s, four SADC members – Mozambique, Lesotho, Namibia and Tanzania withdrew from COMESA. The reasons cited included the high costs of membership of regional organisations, pressure from South Africa, the fast pace at which COMESA moved towards a customs union; in which case the three countries preferring participation in the SADC EU economic partnership agreement (SADC EPA) group.[60] However, hitherto, it continues with its objectives: unifying Africa and harmonising its policies including industrial policies.

Current members are Burundi (1981), Comoros (1981), DRC (1981), Djibouti (1981), Egypt (1999), Eritrea (1994), Ethiopia (1981), Libya (2005), Madagascar (1981), Malawi (1981), Mauritius (1981), Rwanda (1981), Seychelles (2001), South Sudan (2011), Sudan (1981), Swaziland (1981), Uganda (1981), Zambia (1981) and Zimbabwe (1981).[61]

Economic Community of West African States (ECOWAS)

The Economic Community of West African States (ECOWAS) was established in 1975. Since its establishment, ECOWAS's main aims have been to liberalise domestic trade, establish customs union, create an economic union, promote economic integration in industry and others. To implement these aims, coordination and harmonisation of policies including industrial policies were required.[62]

The 1991 Abuja Treaty and the subsequent revised ECOWAS treaty and other agreements underscore coordination and harmonisation of policies including industrial and trade policies.[63]

Currently, within ECOWAS framework, there exists a mechanism for reconsidering harmonising policies including industrial and trade policies.[64]

ECOWAS has 15 member countries ECOWAS, namely: Benin, Cape Verde, Burkina Faso, Cote d'Ivoire, Gambia, Ghana, Guinea, Guinea-Bissau, Mali, Niger, Nigeria, Liberia, Senegal, Sierra Leone and Togo.[65]

Towards Industrial Policy in Africa

Positive Background

The New Partnership for Africa's Development (NEPAD) adopted in 2001 identified economic transformation through industrialisation as a critical vehicle for growth and poverty reduction in the continent. This was followed by a Plan of Action for the Accelerated Industrial Development of Africa (AIDA) in 2008.[66]

Currently, efforts are being made to implement the AIDA.

Although, hitherto, there has been no common industrial policy in Africa, many countries, as we have noted, have comprehensive industrial policies. They commonly indicate strategies to promote economic development. There are also some efforts being made to harmonise industrial policies at regional level as has been explained in the previous section.

Harmonisation of industrial policies and developing a common policy for a region is not easy. It is even more difficult for a continent with complex differences. Europe almost reached a concensus on a common industrial policy during the period of the Renaissance. A divergence of views developed during the Industrial Revolution, and marked differences have persisted thereafter.[67]

However, Europe managed to form a Union, the European Union (EU), and is also in advanced stages of policy harmonisation, especially of industrial policy. This should be a lesson to Africa.

African Union (AU) and Industrial Policy Harmonisation

The African Union (AU) was established in 1999. It replaced the Organisation for African Unity (OAU) which was initially a political union and whose root may be traced back to the 1958 All African People's Conference in Accra, Ghana. This conference marked the adoption of regionalism as a strategy of rescuing the continent from colonial domination.

In 1980, the OAU endorsed the Lagos Plan of Action which underscored both political and economic independence. The plan underscored the importance of regional economic blocs (RECs) to establish free trade areas (FTAs), then common markets, and finally economic unions. The plan was also regarded as a unifying framework that would facilitate industrial and other policy harmonisation, leading to converging integration efforts in the three sub-regions: ECOWAS in West Africa, PTA in Eastern and Southern African countries and the Economic Community of Central African Countries.[68] The ultimate aim is African Union.

In 1991 the OAU endorsed the Abuja Treaty which led to the establishment of the African Economic Community (AEC) in 1994. The community became the focus of coordination and harmonisation of the RECs' policies including industrial policies.[69]

The AU aimed at accelerating the implementation of the Abuja Treaty and subsequent agreements and strengthening the RECs as the building blocs of the AU and AEC. Industrial policy harmonisation and other policies were underscored. For details of the regional blocs as pillars of the AEC, see Appendix 9.5.

In 2002, the AU held an inaugural meeting with the objective of accelerating Africa's political and socio-economic integration; coordinating and harmonising industrial and other policies of the existing and future RECs; and others.[70]

Some RECs are showing visible efforts towards African Union objectives. An example is the tripartite meeting of SADC, COMESA and EAC Heads of State and senior government officials in October 2008 in Kampala, Uganda. The meeting aimed at strengthening the RECs' cooperation and harmonising industrial and other policies. The three RECs agreed to establish a Free Trade Area which would eventually pave a way to Customs Union and be a united pillar of the AU.[71] A similar subsequent meeting held by SADC, COMESA and EAC in 2010 in Nairobi, Kenya, also underscored policy harmonisation, including industrial policy.[72]

Comparative Industrial Policies: Africa, the Newly Industrialised Countries, Europe and USA.

The often cited successful industrial development in the East Asian newly industrialising countries (NICs) is hereunder compared with the case of industrial policies in Africa for the latter to draw lessons from the former.

Firstly, with the exception of the *laissez-faire* Hong Kong, the others (Malaysia, Philippines, Singapore, South Korea, Taiwan and Thailand) had their industrial policies under great control of the government at some stages of industrialisation. They were mostly led by the 'visible hand' of the government. The South Korean government, for instance, gave enough support to semi-conductor manufacturers, who, by 1990, became major players in the field of information technology.[73]

The Taiwanese government also played an important role in promoting heavy or capital and technology-intensive industries in the 1970s.[74] In Singapore, the state heavily invested in construction, iron and steel and ship repair industries and silicon smelting.[75] Actually, even in Hong Kong, the state played a 'facilitative role' compared to 'directive intervention role' in other NICs.[76]

This is comparable with the first stages of industrialisation in Africa after independence with the exception of concentration of consumer goods industries in the case of Africa up to now.

Secondly, the NICs' industrial policies targeted selectively specified industries at different times. In the mid-1960s, for example, the 'strategic' industries of South Korea were identified as textiles and consumer electronics. The policy of selecting priority industrial activities was repeated again in the early part of the 1970s. Capital-intensive activities, such as steel, non-ferrous metals, chemicals, machinery, ship-building and subsequently electronic industrial equipment, became the priority.[77]

In Singapore, the Economic Development Board (EDB) 'laid down its priorities for industrial activities in anticipation of changes in Singapore's comparative advantage'.[78]

A similar policy would be important to Africa as most of the countries have very limited resources. Prioritisation is very important in this case.

Thirdly, the NICs were flexible in their industrial philosophy. They, for instance, changed their industrial strategy from import-substitution to export-led growth and eventually established intermediate and capital goods manufacturing industries, with aggressive export drive of the locally manufactured commodities into the global market.[79] Many African countries have also followed this philosophy despite the problem related to stable exporting and economic diversification in some countries like Botswana.

They also changed production techniques from labour-intensive to capital-intensive techniques and to R & D (or high skills)-intensive technique. This was expressed in shifts from consumer goods and labour-intensive industrialisation to producer or capital-intensive industrialisation expressed in terms of steel, shipbuilding, petrochemicals, electronics, biotechnologies and new material sciences. In Taiwan, for example, the government promoted the expansion of capital-intensive industries in the 1970s, whereas the 1980s witnessed an expansion of high technology and skill-intensive activities (information technology – IT, electronics, machinery and biotechnology). In 1973, the Korean government emphasised the development of new priority sectors: steel and non-ferrous metals, chemicals and petrochemicals, machinery, shipbuilding and electronic industrial equipment. Before this, they started with labour-intensive consumer goods industrialisation.

This may be regarded as a lesson to Africa as the continent seems to be taking too long to switch from consumer goods to producer or capital goods.

The NICs also changed from sectorial objectives to horizontal measures, such as promotion of SMEs, and R &D.[80] Most African economies are promoting SMEs but lag behind in R & D development.

NICs also relaxed their public policy by introducing corrective measures (generic policies) such as privatisation where necessary. Most African countries included such measures especially during the structural adjustment era (1980 and 1990s).

Finally, the NICs followed common strategic guidelines to industrial development and general development in the 1960s, a period that is commonly referred to as the 'East Asian miracle era'. This led to industrialisation strategies whose common characteristics are summarised in Table 9.2. Such common strategic guidelines to industrial development seem to be lacking in Africa in general.

Table 9.3: Common Approach in NICs' Industrialisation

Common Issue	Explanation
The state as an Investor	Already explained in this Section.
Selected industries	Targeting industrial areas or priority industries and protecting industries selectively. (Mostly covered in this section).
Flexibility in the industrial philosophy	Already explained in this section.
Financial Policy Instrument	This included regulation of the financial sector, taking the form of investment funds channelled in favour of the target industries.
Education	Active training through R & D and Human resource development, expansion of technical/engineering education relevant to industrial development
Infrastructure	Heavy direct and early involvement of government in infrastructure.
Trade Policy	Export protection as a product of heavy promotion.
Agriculture	Provision of inputs, procurement and pricing, land reforms; significant levels of public investment; generalised subservience of agriculture to industry in early stages of industrialisation.
Housing and Health Care	Subsidies and expansion of basic health care and housing for industrial and other workers and the population as a whole.

Sources: Stein (1995), Adongo (2008) and Andreasso and Jacobson (2005). However, the 1997 Asian crisis shook the miracle and led to further liberalisation in the NICs.

At regional level, African countries are motivated to strengthen regional blocs from increasing integration among world economies. The success of various regional blocs outside Africa (especially Asia, Europe and the Americas) is the basic motivating factor behind African countries to reconsider the issue more seriously if they are to avoid further marginalisation.[81]

At the continental level, Africa can learn from various continents, especially the European Union (EU). The EU industrial policy graduated from having mainly a supervisory function in the 1960s, to adopting a defensive stance in the 1970s, and to becoming more positive in the 1980s, and research-driven in the 1990s and early 2000s. Such stages may be worth considering in the attempt to formulate an industrial policy in Africa.

It should be underscored that industrial policy also exists in most advanced united economies like the USA. The USA has an industrial policy based on antitrust laws and competition policy in general and on the Interstate Commerce Act of 1887 and Sherman Act of 1890. R & D programmes form another important component of the US industrial policy.[82] The two components – competition policy and R & D development – are still lagging behind in industrial policy in Africa. The next section focuses on public competition policies for industrial development in Africa.

Public Competition Policies for Industrial Development in Africa

Conceptual and Definitional Background

Public Competition policy (also known as anti-trust policy[83]*)* refers to government guidelines which provide a framework to create a friendly environment that encourages competition and efficient use of resources and to prevent and redress anti-competitive practices and ensure fair competition.[84] More briefly, competition policy is a set of government measures aiming at protecting consumers and producers against anti-competitive practices and abuse of monopoly or dominant power. These measures usually include regulation of dominant firms, control of mergers and control of anti-competitive acts.[85]

Competition policy leads to the promotion of investment and innovation, broad choices for consumers, reduction of monopoly rents and consumer prices, and high quality of goods and services.[86]

Competition in this case means a situation in which people, firms and other organisations try to be more successful than others in offering products and services in a manner that is consistent with acceptable business behaviour and conduct, disabuse of dominant power in the market places, and fair business practices.[87]

Anti-competitive practices are uses of means which are unfair and inconsistent with acceptable competition codes and business behaviour. Examples include collusive tendering, refusal to supply, exclusive dealing, dumping and predatory pricing. .

National Competition Policies in Africa

Main Aspects of National Competition Policies in Africa

The increasing intensity of competition and globalisation in the late 1990s up to the current period has positive and negative aspects. The competition policies in Africa aim at discouraging the negative aspects including unfair and anti- competitive practices which may lead to high prices and reduction of general welfare and increase in poverty. The positive aspects such as efficiency and production of high-quality products are encouraged. The ultimate goal is gains through international trade, foreign direct investment (FDI), and poverty reduction. Normally competition policies are enforced through competition laws.

The next sub-section examines selected competition policies in Africa to elaborate the afore-noted and other aspects.

Competition Policy for Botswana

The competition policy for Botswana was established in 2005 as a guide to drafting of a competition law (Competition Act 2009). The competition policy is one of the very limited comprehensive competition policies in Africa.

The competition policy was formulated as a strategy for enhancing Botswana's ability to promote free entry in the market place by investors, and all firms, irrespective of their size; the attraction of both domestic and foreign investment flows; innovation and transfer right-holders; unfettered competition; acceptable business behaviour and conduct; fair business practice; efficiency; competitiveness, and consumer welfare.[88]

The competition policy was necessary in Botswana because it provides, through competitive markets, the best means of ensuring that the economy's resources are put to their best use by encouraging enterprise efficiency and widening choice. It was also considered necessary because where markets work well they provide strong incentives for good performance, thus, encouraging firms to improve productivity, reduce prices and innovate whilst rewarding consumers with lower prices, and a wider choice of high quality of goods and services.

The objectives of the competition policy in Botswana are:
- To enhance economic efficiency, promote consumer welfare and support economic growth and diversification;
- To prevent and redress unfair practices adopted by firms against consumers and small businesses in Botswana;
- To prevent and redress anti-competitive practices in the Botswana economy and remove unnecessary constraints on the free play of competition in the market;

- To complement other government policies and laws;
- To enhance the attractiveness of the Botswana economy for foreign direct investment by providing a transparent, predictable and internationally acceptable regulatory mechanism for firms to engage in economic activities;
- To support other policy initiatives such as citizen economic empowerment and access to essential services without prejudice to the pursuit of the overall efficiency and competitiveness of the economy; and
- To achieve deregulation where regulation is no longer needed.[89]

In order to implement the policy a competition authority was officially launched in 2012. The 2009 Competition Act remained the legal guidance of the competition policy. For details on the strategic policy considerations, see Appendix 9.6.

Note that special treatment, exclusion and exemptions were given to strategic industries such as SMEs and other aspects such as public utilities, intellectual property rights, and collective bargaining as pointed out in Appendix 9.6.

Competition Policy for Tanzania

The current National Competition Policy (NCP) of Tanzania is embodied in the 2003 National Trade Policy (NTP) for a Competitive Economy and Export-led Growth. Earlier, the Competition Policy has been guided by three laws: the Fair Trade Practices Act of 1994; the Energy and Water Utilities Regulation Act (EWURA) of 2001; and the Surface and Marine Transport Regulatory Act (SUMATRA) of 2001. The SUMATRA also amends the Fair Trade Practices Act to establish the Fair Competition Commission (FCC) in place of the Fair Trade Practices Bureau.[90]

The objective of the NCP is to address the problem of concentration of economic power arising from market imperfections, monopolistic behaviour in economic activities and consequent restrictive business practices. Restrictive business practices affect the consumer either by higher prices and unacceptable quality standards or limitations on the availability of goods and services.[91]

The objectives of NTP, however, are wider. They include:

- Promotion of industrial, agricultural and other sectorial production thereafter stimulating a process of trade development as the means of triggering higher performances and capacity to withstand intensifying competition within the domestic market;
- Involving economic transformation towards an integrated, diversified, and competitive entity capable of participating effectively in the multilateral trading system;

- Stimulation of investment flows into export-oriented areas in which Tanzania has comparative advantages as a strategy for inducing the introduction of technology and innovation into production systems as the basis for economic competitiveness; and

- Attainment and maintenance of long-term current account balance and balance of payment through effective utilisation of complementarities in regional and international trading arrangements as means of increasing exports combined with initiatives for higher efficiency in the utilisation of imports.

The ultimate target is to enhance income generation and people's earning, power and poverty reduction as per Tanzania's Development Vision 2025.[92]

For details on key Competition Policy and Law and Regional Trade Policy Implementation Matrix, see Appendix 9.7.

Regional Competition Policy Harmonisation and Potential Regional Competition Policies

Theoretical and Practical Background

As was the case of regional industrial policy statement as regional blocs in Africa move towards full integration, competition policy harmonisation becomes theoretically and practically an important agenda. This stems from the proposition that regional integration expands the market and introduces greater competition. Since markets are mostly imperfect, regulation and harmonisation of competition policies, as well common enforcement thereof become important.

As was the case of regional industrial policy, harmonisation of competition policies can take several forms such as co-ordination of national competition policies, harmonisation of national standards and regulations, and reducing trade imbalances with regional partners as has been underscored in the competition policy and law and regional trade policy matrix of Tanzania (Appendix 9.7).

Harmonisation and common competition provisions are needed so that the benefits of trade and investment liberalisation are not compromised by cross-border anti-competitive practices. This is important in most of the regional trade agreements (RTAs).[93]

Towards Harmonisation and Common Competition Policies in African Regional Blocs

Background Statement

Hitherto, some visible efforts have been shown by some regional blocs in Africa which promote common policies, including competition policies. Examples are in order.

Southern African Customs Union (SACU)

The Southern African Customs Union (SACU) is a good example of a regional bloc which is trying to promote common competition policy in Africa.

The realisation of the need to foster competition to stimulate growth in SACU prompted the inclusion of competition policy (article 40), unfair trade practices (article 41) in the 2002 SACU Agreement. These articles reflect the agreement of member states to adopt individual competition policies and to co-operate in their enforcement activities.[94]

Competition issues in SACU, nevertheless, are influenced by several considerations such as (i) special and differential treatment provisions granted to the BNLS countries (Botswana, Namibia, Lesotho and Swaziland), (ii) the need for common industrial policy, and (iii) asymmetry of industries within SACU.95 Some elaboration is in order.

On special and differential treatment for BNLS, article 26, for instance, requires protection of infant industries. However, this is considered a temporary measure as it is not a common policy of all SACU members.

The need for common industrial policy (article 38) requires SACU to implement this article. At the time of writing this book, SACU had called for a study to develop its industrial policy (Tender No: SACU/001/2012/0).[96] The purpose of the study was to provide input for a detailed SACU-wide Industrial Development Policy and Strategy to achieve balanced and equitable industrial development in the region despite asymmetry of industries within SACU.

Southern African Development Community (SADC)

The Southern African Development Community (SADC) is another example of a regional bloc trying to promote policy harmonisation: industrial competition, trade and other forms of policy harmonisation.

In September 2000, SADC launched its trade protocol which incorporated some elements underscoring the need for competition policy within SADC. The protocol was based on a Free Trade Area (FTA) within SADC. Regional companies were to improve their capacities and quality of output in the region as competition became more pronounced. Over time, companies would concentrate on improving their technological base for competitive production. The implication of FTA to the region is the call for harmonisation of competition policies, among others.[97]

In 2004 the SADC Council of Ministers endorsed the Guidelines for SADC EPA98 Negotiations (SEPA Negotiations) whose joint roadmap elements included, among others, harmonisation of policies including competition policies.[99]

Towards Competition Policy in Africa: Positive Background Information

Although, hitherto, there has been no common public competition policy in Africa as was the case of industrial policy, regional blocs, illustrated by SACU and SADC, for example, give hope for the formulation of a harmonised common competition policy in the continent.

Furthermore, the competition policy in other places, especially the European Union (EU) encourages Africa to formulate a similar policy.

Potential Competition Policy in Africa

The formation of the African Union is an important foundation of various harmonised policies such as competition policy.

The competition policy in Africa can start by coordination and cooperation, for instance, among competition authorities with the aim of harmonisation of competition elements such as means of combating anti-competitive practices in the continent. The EU took a similar approach guided by their 2004 Modernisation Package Act.[100] The next section provides details of the EU competition policy and lessons for Africa.

Comparative Competition Policy: Africa and European Union

The 2004 EU modernisation package consisted of five elements: (i) a more explicit mandate to exchange information (including confidential information) between national competition authorities; (ii) a co-operation arrangement whereby national authorities are required at times to assist in investigations; (iii) various articles outlining when the Commission will control enforcement of EU law by national authorities; (iv) a revised definition of the relationship between the Commission and national courts; (v) a more explicit; and (vi) a re-allocation of cases shifting more competence to the national authorities.[101]

The 2004 Modernisation Package Act stemmed from the 2003 regulations that represented the most comprehensive competition policy reform of the EU. For details, see Appendix 9.8.

Africa's common policy is not as kinetic as that of the European Union. Thus Africa needs:

- Harmonisation of competition policy rules throughout the regions;
- Close coordination and cooperation of national competition authorities; and
- Common guidance on the implementation and enforcement of the anticipated competition policy.

Generic Policies and Industrial Development in Africa

Background Information

Generic policies are public interventions which correct both market failure and government failure.[102]

The rationale for public policy presented in earlier provides examples of correction of market failure. They include protection of infant industries and regulation of monopolies.

Government actions or policies may also fail to deliver. Great bureaucracy and inefficiency in some public enterprises may lead to correction of the government failure through privatisation.

Privatisation in Africa

Privatisation in Africa, as the case elsewhere, has been viewed differently. However, the common narrow definition of *privatisation* may be generalised as 'de-nationalisation or transferring the ownership of public enterprises to private buyers'. The transfer of ownership is usually through selling all or some of the assets of public enterprises or other public entities to the private sector. This particular form of privatisation is sometimes called *divestiture*, which may also be done by liquidation of assets, to distinguish it from other forms of privatisation.[103]

Some countries, especially those that are at the early stages of privatisation, tend to adhere to the broad definition of *privatisation*: all measures[104] and policies aimed at strengthening the role of the private sector in the economy. Botswana is an example that, since 2000, has adopted the broad definition.[105]

As noted in chapter 5, privatisation and price control measures have been common since the introduction of the structural adjustment programmes in the mid-1980s in Ghana, Kenya, Nigeria, Tanzania, Zambia and in many other African countries.

Even the non-African countries, like the newly-industrialising countries (NICs), as noted in this chapter, had to be flexible to correct the government failure through privatisation at a later stage of development. The wave of privatisation also did not spare the UK, France, Germany and other advanced countries in the twentieth century.[106]

Arguments for Privatisation Policy

Privatisation policy has been advocated globally as means to correct government failure by enforcing market discipline and promoting efficient allocation and use of economic resources. While the reasons for privatisation differ from one country to another, the policy objectives are similar. They include:[107]

- Promoting competition, improving efficiency and increasing productivity of enterprises;
- Accelerating the rate of economic growth by stimulating entrepreneurship and investment;
- Broadening and deepening the capital market;
- Increasing direct citizen participation in the ownership of national assets;
- Withdrawing from commercial activities which no longer need to be undertaken by the public sector;
- Reducing the size of the public sector; and
- Relieving the financial and administrative burden of governments.

Conclusion

In this chapter, public policy has first been defined before explaining its rationale. The focus, however, has been on public industrial policy and competition policy. Both of them have been examined with reference to African countries, and regions with a view of presenting potential industrial and competition policies in Africa.

Finally, as a caution, generic policies which correct both market and government failures have been outlined, underscoring protection and privatisation policies with reference to industrial development.

Review Questions

1. What is the difference between industrial policy and competition policy?
2. To what extent is government intervention justified in protecting infant industries and regulating monopolies?
3. Compare and contrast industrial policies of any two African countries.
4. Do regional industrial and competition policies exist in Africa? Explain.
5. (a) What can Africa learn from industrial policies of
    (i) the newly industrialising countries (NICs)?
    (ii) the European Union (EU)?
   (b) What can Africa learn from competition policies outside Africa? Specify your focus.
6. (a) Differentiate between generic policy and privatisation policy.
   (b) Discuss the advantages and disadvantages of privatisation policy.

Appendix 9.1: Principles for the 1998 Botswana Industrial Development Policy

In response to the above factors, the Government will follow an Industrial Development Policy based on the following principles:

(i)   Encouragement of highly productive and efficient export industries based, to the extent possible, on local natural resources and integrated with foreign markets and technology;

(ii)   Promotion and expansion of efficient supporting services and components manufacturers, many of which will be small and medium size businesses; and

(iii)   Assistance will continue to be provided to small-scale rural entrepreneurs and, where appropriate, local community and non-governmental organisations will be utilised to develop business activities and opportunities in rural villages.

Source: Republic of Botswana (1998: 5).

Appendix 9.2: Policy Thrusts – Competitive Manufacturing and Service Industries in Botswana

To achieve the goal of developing an efficient and competitive export-oriented industrial and service sector, the Government will adopt the following policies:

(i)   Trade negotiations, both bilateral and multilateral, will be vigorously pursued to ensure that such negotiations lead to maximum market access for Botswana exports and lowest possible prices for the inputs required by Botswana industry;

(ii)   The decisions regarding location and technology to be used within Botswana will be left to the investors in the trade competitive sectors and will not be influenced through subsidies or land allocation policy. Programmes to encourage competitive and high-technology investment will be directed to areas with high potential for industrial location;

(iii)   Investors and entrepreneurs will be encouraged to use incentive schemes to improve labour productivity and to achieve competitive unit labour costs; (iv) Investment protection and double taxation agreements will be negotiated urgently with countries that are the major sources of investment and of important input services;

(v)   The provision of serviced industrial and commercial land by the private sector will be facilitated, and the price of unserviced land should be minimal, taking into account its opportunity cost. Local Authorities will also be encouraged to make land and services available to investors within their areas of jurisdiction. Special emphasis will be placed on making unserviced and serviced land available in areas likely to be of high investor interest;

(vi)   The BDC will continue to provide factory shells to investors. The Botswana Export Development and Investment Authority, once operational, will also be responsible for the provision of factory shells to investors;

(vii)   Efforts to reduce the cost of utilities will be continued, compatible with covering the full cost of such services, and any remaining cross-subsidisation from the business sector to the urban and rural consumers will be eliminated where possible. Appropriate mechanisms will be established to develop utility rate policies for public monopolies, whether operated by public or private interests;

(viii)   The capacity to utilize international data banks to locate competitive inputs, identify export opportunities and make such information available to the private sector will be developed. A counterpart data bank on Botswana industrial and export capacities will also be developed, made available to the public, and kept up to date;

(ix)   In partnership with private sector organisations, the Ministry of Commerce and Industry will develop and support programmes to assist new and expanding exporters to develop the marketing, financial and administrative procedures necessary to increase their export activities;

(x)   The provision of exclusive licences for manufacturing will be eliminated by amending the Industrial Development Act of 1988;

(xi)   Local authorities, in cooperation with the local business community, will be encouraged to design investment promotion strategies for their communities and to assume responsibility for providing factory shells and other services;

(xii)   Additional support for the tourism industry will be provided through the development of a comprehensive tourism master plan which will cover training facilities and programmes, the improvement of the quality of accommodation and services, the diversification of tourism products, the promotion of Botswana as a tourist destination, the increased participation of Batswana in management, and the development of attractions outside the Wildlife and National Parks areas; and

(xiii)   The prospects for establishing a free zone or some other variant of a free trade zone, as a mechanism for facilitating and stimulating investment in the export sector, will be evaluated.

Source: Republic of Botswana (1998:12).

Appendix 9.3: Objectives of the SMME Policy in Botswana

(i) *Foster citizen entrepreneurship and empowerment*, and thereby increasing the proportion of economic activity under the control of citizens. The Task Force pointed out that while the numbers and types of citizen-owned businesses have increased dramatically since 1982, there remains concern over the competitiveness of many citizen-owned businesses, due to lack of an indigenous entrepreneurial culture, and a comparatively low level of entrepreneurial skills. Each of these issues must be addressed if Batswana are to participate more fully in the economy.

(ii) *Achieve economic diversification*. This is one of the fundamental objectives of the Industrial Development Policy (1998). It is also an important tenet of the National Development Plan 8 theme of sustainable economic diversification;

(iii) *Promote exports*. Although most micro enterprises do not have export potential, there are a significant number of small and medium enterprises which have export potential and could exploit opportunities abroad, given the right environment and appropriate Government support;

(iv) *Encourage the development of a competitive and sustainable SMME community*. Unless this objective is realized, the policy will fail. The Task Force has made a very important point by stating that, all too often, the promotion of micro and small enterprises is associated with calls for protectionism and the introduction of policies that encourage inefficient and unproductive enterprises. Such enterprises will not survive in a modern competitive economy, and the objective of the policy should be to reward competitiveness and to discourage inefficiency;

(v) *Create sustainable employment opportunities*. It is a proven fact that job creation is one of the most important contributions made by SMMEs. The challenge is to ensure that these employment opportunities are sustainable;

(vi) *Promote the development of vertical integration and horizontal linkages between SMMEs and primary industries in agriculture, mining and tourism*. The Task Force has pointed out that there are many small business opportunities associated with the exploitation of natural resources which have not been effectively pursued. There is also a need to develop linkages between SMMEs and larger firms operating in Botswana through sub-contracting for the provision of goods and services; and

(vii) *Improve efficiency in the delivery of services to businesses*. According to the Task Force, many small business support services in Botswana e.g., advisory and training, have been of inferior quality and poorly marketed. Such services must be delivered more effectively.

Source: Republic of Botswana (1999:3).

Appendix 9.4: Vision, Mission, Overall Objective and Scope of the SMEs Policy in Tanzania.

Vision

- The objective of the National Vision 2025 is to transform the predominantly agricultural economy to a semi-industrialised one. The SME sector has a significant role to contribute towards attaining this goal. It is on this basis that the Sustainable Industrial Development Policy identified specific strategies targeting at stimulating the SME sector to be able to play this crucial role.
- The vision of the SME Development Policy is to have a vibrant and dynamic SME sector that ensures effective utilisation of available resources to attain accelerated and sustainable growth.

Mission

The mission of this Policy is to stimulate development and growth of SME activities through improved infrastructure, enhanced service provision and creation of conducive legal and institutional framework so as to achieve competitiveness.

Overall Objective

The overall objective of this policy is to foster job creation and income generation through promoting the creation of new SMEs and improving the performance and competitiveness of the existing ones to increase their participation and contribution to the Tanzanian economy.

Scope of the Policy

The policy covers the following key areas:
- Reviewing and reconsidering public policies and regulations that discriminate against or hinder the start-up, survival, formalisation and growth of SMEs.
- Enhancing the growth of the sector.
- Identifying and assigning clear roles of key actors.
- Developing strategies that will facilitate provision of financial and non-financial services to SMEs.
- Developing and institutionalising public-private partnerships for SME sector development.

Source: United Republic of Tanzania (2003b:16).

Appendix 9.5: Main Regional Blocs (RECs) in Africa

	(2004)	
Pillars of AU/AEC (Regional Blocs – RECs)[a]	Per capita (PPP$US)	Member States
AEC	2,406	54
ECOWAS	1,361	15
ECCAS[b]	1,451	11
SADC	3,152	14
EAC	1,065	5
COMESA	1,811	19
IGAD[c]	1,197	7
Other African Blocs		
CEMAC[d]	2,435	6
SACU[e]	10,605	5
UEMOA[f]	1,257	8
UMA[g]	5,836	5
GAFTA[h]	3,822	5

Notes:

a. The Sahrawi Arab Democratic Republic (SADR) is only a signatory to the AEC, but not participating
b. ECCAS – Economics Community of Central African States
c. IGAD – Intergovernmental Authority on Development
d. Economic bloc inside a pillar (RECs)
    (Central African Economic and Monetary Community)
e. Economic bloc inside a pillar (RECs)
f. Economic bloc inside a pillar (RECs)
    (Economic and Monetary Union of West African States or Union économique et monétaire ouest-africaine)
g. Potential member (Arab Maghreb Union)
h. Greater Arab Free Trade Area

Source: IMF (2005), CIA World Fact book, IMF, WEO Database

Appendix 9.6: Strategic Policy Considerations for Botswana's Competition Policy Success

Government recognizes that the following strategic policy considerations are critical for the success of Botswana's Competition Policy:

a) **Establishment of a Competition Authority**

Government will establish a Competition Authority whose responsibility will be to implement the Competition Policy and its related legislation.

b) **Ensuring Consistency of the Competition Policy With Other Government Policies**

i) In order to strengthen Government's ongoing efforts to create and maintain a more conducive environment for stimulating and enabling the growth and diversification of the economy, the Competition Policy will be consistent with other policies such as the Policy on Small, Medium and Micro Enterprises, Industrial Development Policy and the Privatisation Policy.

ii) In addition, Government will maintain a non-interference and competitive environment whilst ensuring consistency between this Policy and other socio-economic development policy initiatives.

iii) Government will work in collaboration and harmony with other countries and organisations at the bilateral and multilateral levels to respond to existing and potential cross-border anti-competitive practices, including but not restricted to, various types of anti-competitive behaviour, abuse of dominant position in the market and various types of anti-competitive combinations.

iv) The principles of competition should be embedded in the process of policy making, legislation and enforcement, and applied at both local and central Government levels.

c) **Development of Public Awareness and Support for Competition Enforcement**

Implementation of the Competition Policy will be accompanied by the development and implementation of a strategy for educating the public and stakeholders on its important role in the economy and to the nation, in general. In this regard, Government will develop and implement educational and awareness campaigns aimed at ensuring that all stakeholders, including the general public, civil society organisations, politicians, public servants, the legal fraternity, the business community, sectorial regulators, academics, and the media clearly understand this Policy.

d) **Interfacing the Competition Authority With Other Sector Specific Regulatory Bodies**

i) Government recognises the important role and advantages of having sector or industry specific regulators such as the Bank of Botswana and the Botswana Telecommunications Authority.

However, Government will ensure that all sector-specific regulatory bodies fall under the ambit of the Competition Law.

    ii)   Legislation related to this Policy and other existing pieces of legislation, which have a direct or indirect bearing on the Competition Policy, will be harmonised and interfaced in order to ensure consistency and fairness in their application.

    iii) In sectors characterised by economic/commercial activities, complex science, engineering and technology or having natural monopoly or other special elements, the Competition Authority and Sector Specific Regulators collaborate and complement each other.

e) **Structural Reform of Public Monopolies**

    i)   Government remains fully committed to restructuring public enterprises within the broader framework for increasing the role of the private sector in the economy. Government will, therefore, continue to look into ways of structurally reforming public monopolies operating in sectors such as telecommunications, water, electricity and meat export with a view to opening up some of the services they provide to competition.

    ii)   Government will, however, retain monopoly powers, where necessary, to provide major infrastructure facilities whilst at the same time opening up activities like connection and distribution services to competition.

    iii) In keeping with the objectives of the Privatisation Policy and this Policy, Government will, prior to introducing competition in a market traditionally supplied by public enterprise or monopoly, undertake a review of the entity or entities concerned. Such a review will take into consideration the commercial objectives of the business as well as the merits and demerits of separating any natural monopoly elements from potentially competitive elements of the public monopoly.

f) **Mergers and Acquisitions**

In order to safeguard competition in the market place, Government will, if and when necessary, review mergers and acquisitions, including joint ventures and other forms of business alliances.

g) **Professional Services**

In order to ensure that laws such as those which regulate professional associations and any other laws that have a direct or indirect bearing on competition do not inhibit the effective working of competitive markets, Government will include all professional associations, whether enacted by law or not, within the ambit of both this Policy and its related legislation.

h) **Consumer Protection**

Through this Policy and its related legislation, consumers will be protected from any deceptive and fraudulent behaviour of sellers. In this regard, the formulation of a Competition Law will take into account the provisions of the Consumer Protection Act [CAP 42:07] that deal with unfair business practices. In addition, administration of the Consumer Protection Act will be placed under the Competition Authority. The thrust of Consumer Protection under this Policy will include:

- Maintaining an institutional emphasis on consumer welfare objectives;
- Reducing the opportunity for business to deny consumers the benefits of competitive markets in the short-term by engaging in unfair business practices;
- Promoting dialogue between consumers and their stakeholders;
- Providing market-driven inducements to domestically traded goods and services to meet basic standards of fair trading; and
- Cooperating and networking regional and international competition authorities and sector specific regulators to exchange and share information and ideas on principles of competition administration.

i) **Small Scale Firms**

This Policy seeks to promote the efficiency and competitiveness of small scale firms which form a large proportion of the industrial base in Botswana. In this regard, small scale firms will be included within the ambit of this Policy in order to challenge and encourage them to think and act strategically in building and sharpening their competitive edge.

j) **Exclusions and Exemptions**

i) The dynamic nature of the market environment dictates that exclusions and exemptions of certain economic activities and firms from the competition policy and its related legislation be granted conditionally taking into account factors such as:

- The economic activity's strategic importance and national interest to the country;
- The extent to which social benefits to be gained from exclusions and exemptions outweigh the costs;
- The extent to which the size of the market share affected will not substantially lessen competition;
- The extent to which efficiency and external competitiveness will be enhanced as a result of exclusions and exemptions;
- Convincing proof or evidence that a sector regulatory body acting within its powers expressly approved the firm or organisation's action in question (explicit exclusion and exemption); and
- Convincing proof or evidence that the application of the Competition Policy and/or its related legislation is displaced by sector specific

regulatory regimes or other manifestations of state ownership or directive (implicit exclusion and exemption).

ii) Taking the foregoing scenario into consideration, Government will grant the following conditional exclusions and exemptions from the Competition Policy:

a) Public Utilities

i) The provision of infrastructural facilities for public utilities such as land-line telecommunications, water, and electricity require huge capital outlays, which take long to recoup given the paucity of Botswana's population and the resultant small market base. Since this situation may constrain private sector investment in this sub-sector, Government may exclude and exempt the provision of some of the infrastructural facilities from this Policy.

ii) The aforementioned exclusions and exemptions notwithstanding, Government may include the provision of services such as public utility connections and distribution services within the ambit of this Policy.

b) Collective Bargaining

In order to prevent employers from exploiting workers under the pretext of free competition, Government will exempt and exclude collective bargaining by unionised workers from the ambit of this Policy. Furthermore, the Government's Policy of social protection for workers through the Labour Law and minimum wages shall remain in force.

c) Intellectual Property Rights

The Policy recognises the important role intellectual property (patents, trade marks and copyrights) plays in Botswana's human and economic development endeavours and the need to protect and safeguard the interests of intellectual property rights-holders. Therefore, as a way of protecting intellectual property rights from infringement and in order to promote the development of creations and innovations, intellectual property rights will be exempted and excluded from the ambit of this Policy.

Source: Republic of Botswana (2005).

Appendix 9.7: Competition Policy and Law and Regional Trade Policy Implementation Matrix in Tanzania

Policy	Objectives	Targets	Priority Activities	Responsibility
Competition Policy and Law	Create conducive environment for fair competition under a fully liberalised economy with free access to new entrants.	Update trade laws underlying effective consumer protection in a market economy; Create awareness of the Fair Competition Act of 2000 among consumers and other stakeholders	Eliminate restrictive business practices; Enact laws related to competition policy e.g. anti-dumping and other trade laws.	Ministry of Industry and Trade EWURA, SUMATRA, and Other regulators
Regional Trading Arrangements (RTA)	Capacity building for effective participation/ negotiation for both public and private sectors.	Reduce trade imbalances with regional partners Become a regionally competitive economy	Identify potential regional export opportunities Build capacity to access and take advantage of such opportunities	Ministry of Industry and Trade Business Associations

Source: United Republic of Tanzania (2003d: 83).

Appendix 9.8: Special Rules of the EU Competition Policy

- Regulation EC No. 1/2003 fundamentally modifies and simplifies the way in which the Treaty's antitrust rules are enforced throughout the EU.

- The first substantial modification is that companies no longer need notify their agreements to the Commission in order to obtain antitrust approval. It is now up to companies themselves to assess whether their agreements restrict competition, and if so, whether the restriction qualifies for an exemption under Article 81(3). Obviously, guidance from the Commission can be sought in cases of uncertainty.

- The second major thrust of the reform is that the task of policing anti-competitive behaviour and handling complains in no longer exclusive competence of the Commission. This task is now shared with the European Competition Authorities existing at national level. This implies that all competition authorities involved will co-operate closely in applying antitrust rules.

- This reform also extends to the case of mergers.

Source: Andreasso Jacobson (2005:498).

Notes

1. For details see, for instance, Sadoulet and Janvry (1995:3).
2. Compare this to the Price Control in Africa (Chapter 5).
3. For details see, for instance, Kakujaha-Matundu (2007), Kapunda and Akinkugbe (2008) and McCarthy (2008).
4. For details, see Sadoulet and Janvry (1995:4) and Weimer and Vining (2005:97).
5. See, for instance, Republic of Botswana (2000:3).
6. For details, see, for instance, Kapunda (2005).
7. For details, see, for example, United Republic of Tanzania (2003a).
8. See the list, for instance, in Sadoulet and Janvry (1995:3).
9. For details, see Sadoulet and Janvry, ibid.
10. For details on the classification of efficiency-oriented and non-efficiency-oriented government intervention see, especially Sadoulet and Janvry (1995:3).
11. For elaboration see, especially, Andreasso and Jacobson (2005:446).
12. The emphasis, henceforth, is ours.
13. See, Makoa (2008:64).
14. For details see Foreword by Vickers in Vickers, ed, (2008:7).
15. See, for instance, Andreasso and Jacobson (2005:470).
16. See, especially, Sutcliffe, (1971:248) and Andreasso and Jacobson (2005:470).
17. For details see, for instance, Kapunda and Akinkugbe (2008:47) and Mpabanga (2001:379).
18. See, Republic of Botswana (1998:1).
19. See, Kapunda and Akinkugbe (2008:48).
20. For further details on WHO's retrospective explanation see, for instance, Agbaje and Jerome (2000: 53).

21. For details see Kapunda and Akinkugbe (2008:48).
22. For details see Galebotswe (1999:3).
23. See, Makoa (2008:66).
24. See, Kingdom of Lesotho (1980:224).
25. Cf. Makoa (2008:66).
26. Adongo (2008:76).
27. Ibid, p.77.
28. Ibid.
29. For details see Kaplan (2008:33).
30. UNIDO & UNCTAD (2011:2).
31. Cf. Kaplain (2008: 41).
32. Ibid.
33. See, for instance, Rweyemamu (1971:123) and Kapunda and Mbogoro (1989:147).
34. See, for instance, Rweyemamu (1971:154), and Sutcliffe (1971:260).
35. United Republic of Tanzania (URT), 1980, *Budget Speech* 1979/80, Dar-es-Salaam, URT.
36. As per United Republic of Tanzania (1997) *Third Five Year Plan* (1976 – 1981).
37. Cf. United Republic of Tanzania, (2003a:9).
38. See, United Republic of Tanzania, (2003b:8).
39. For details, see, Kapunda and Akinkugbe (2008:50).
40. Ibid.
41. Ibid.
42. Cf. Vickers (2008:9).
43. Ibid, p.7.
44. For details see, Kapunda and Akinkugbe (2008), MacCarthy (2008) and Sentsho and Tsheko (2005) and Siwawa-Ndai (2001).
45. Ibid.
46. Cf. Kapunda and Akinkugbe (2008).
47. Vickers (2008:9).
48. See, Vickers [(ed), 2008].
49. Southern African Development Co-ordination Conference (SADCC).
50. Nine founder member of SADCC were Angola, Botswana, Lesotho, Malawi, Mozambique, Swaziland, Tanzania, Zambia and Zimbabwe.
51. Namibia was already an additional member to the 9 founder members. Namibia became a member when it attained independence in 1990.
52. For details see Oosthuizen (2006:101).
53. Year, henceforth, of joining SADC.
54. Cf. Oosthuizen (2006:94).
55. Ibid, p.95.
56. PTA was formed in 1981.
57. See, Oosthuizen (2006:61).
58. Ibid.
59. See, United Republic of Tanzania (1998:89).
60. Cf. Oosthuizen (2006:62). EU being European Union and EPA stands for Economic Partnership Agreement.

61. Years of joining the common market. Former COMESA members and the date of quiting are Lesotho (1997), Mozambique (1997), Tanzania (2000), Namibia (2004) and Angola (2007).
62. Cf. Jebuni and Yahya (2010:18).
63. Cf. Soludo (1995:6).
64. For further details see Jebuni and Yahya, op.cit.
65. See, Seck et al (2010: 84).
66. See, UNIDO and UNCTAD (2011:3).
67. For details see, Andreasso and Jacobson (2005:479).
68. Cf. Mulaudzi (2006:8).
69. Cf. Soludo (1995:6) and Oosthuizen (2006:97).
70. For details see, Oosthuizen (2006:96).
71. Cf. United Republic of Tanzania (2009:40).
72. For details see United Republic of Tanzania (2011:49).
73. Steers (1999).
74. OECD (1991).
75. Cf. Andreasso and Jacobson (2005:470).
76. Cf. Sentsho (2001:11).
77. Cf. Andreasso and Jacobson (2005:470).
78. Chowdhury and Islam (1993).
79. Cf. Mwaigomole (2012:98).
80. See Andreasso and Jacobson (2005:470).
81. For details, see, for instance, Sinha and Mogotsi (2009:3).
82. Cf. Andreasso and Jacobson (2005:467).
83. See, for instance, Galebotswe (2002:11).
84. For detail see, Republic of Botswana (2005: 1).
85. Cf. Galebotswe, op.cit.
86. Cf. Republic of Botswana (2005: 1).
87. Ibid.
88. Ibid, p.2.
89. Ibid, p.7.
90. United Republic of Tanzania (2003d:22).
91. United Republic of Tanzania (2003c:81).
92. United Republic of Tanzania (2003d:16).
93. See, for instance, Brusick *et al.* (2005) and Kakujaha-Matundu (2009).
94. Cf. Kakujaha-Matundu (2009:1).
95. Ibid.
96. Cf. *Weekend Post,* 17 – 20 April 2012, p.9.
97. For details, see Mazonde and Sigwele (2000: 1, 28 – 30).
98. EPA – Economic Partnership Agreement.
99. For details, see Oosthuizein (2006: 271).

100. Cf. Kakujaha-Matundu (2009: 11).
101. Ibid.
102. Weimer and Viking (2005: 2009).
103. See, Republic of Botswana (2000: 7).
104. These measures include *contracting-out, leasing, joint-venture,* and *liberalisation of entry* to public sector entrepreneurs. For detail see, for instance, Republic of Botswana (2000: 27).
105. Republic of Botswana (2000:7).
106. For details, see Andreasso and Jacobson (2005:462).
107. Cf Republic of Botswana (2000).

10

Industrial Development in Africa

Learning Objectives

The main objectives of this chapter are:

- To provide a retrospective explanation of industrial development in Africa;
- To explain the rationale for industrialisation in Africa;
- To examine performance of the industrial sector in Africa; and
- To look into constraints, opportunities, and the way forward for Industrial development in Africa.

Introductory Note

The traditional industrial economics underscores industrial performance through models like the S-C-P paradigm. In this chapter, the performance concept is examined broadly with reference to industrial development. Most African countries have been trying to promote industrial development since gaining independence mainly in the 1960s. As noted in the previous chapter, several industrial policies and strategies were formulated to guide industrialisation in Africa.

This chapter examines the performance of the industrial sector in Africa after presenting a retrospective explanation to industrialisation. The main constraints and opportunities are also outlined.

Retrospective Approach to Industrial Development in Africa

The 2011 UNIDO/UNCTAD *Report on Economic Development in Africa* identifies three broad phases or stages which industrial development in Africa has gone through since independence mainly in the 1960s. The first phase is the import substitution industrialisation (ISI) phase which began in the 1960s and ended in the late 1970s.[1] The second phase covered mostly the structural adjustment programmes (SAPs) from the early 1980s to the 1990s. The third phase, the poverty reduction strategy papers (PRSP) phase which began in 2000.[2]

The first phase started after most African countries got independence in the 1960s. African leaders regarded industrialisation as means of ensuring self-reliance and economic independence. It was also expected that industrial development would speed up the transformation of African countries from agricultural to modern economies, thereby creating employment opportunities, raising incomes as well as living standards, and reducing vulnerability to terms of trade shocks based on dependence on primary commodity exports.[3]

African governments were centrally involved in supporting ISI which emphasised production of consumer goods which were formerly imported to meet basically domestic demand. It was assumed that production of intermediate and capital goods would follow as a subsequent stage of industrial development.

In general, ISI involved (i) restriction of imports to intermediate inputs and capital goods required by domestic industries; (ii) extensive use of tariff and non-tariff barriers to trade and protection of infant industries; (iii) currency overvaluation to facilitate the import of goods needed by domestic industries; (iv) subsidised interest rates to make domestic investment attractive; (v) public ownership or participation in industry; and (vi) provision of direct loans to firms as well as access to foreign exchange for imported inputs.[4]

In the late 1970s, however, African economies were faced by economic crisis arising mainly from successive oil shocks and resulting debt problems. Imported inputs for ISI became more expensive than before. As noted in chapter 5, many countries tried to mitigate the crisis by opting for structural adjustment programmes (SAPs) guided by IMF and the World Bank. Industrial development was also to follow the SAPs. Anti-export biases were discouraged and export-oriented industrialisation was encouraged. Privatisation was another policy condition, among others.[5] Although these policy conditions were intended to have structural effects, the conventional view is that they did not boost industrial development in Africa.[6]

After 2000, African countries demonstrated renewed commitment to industrialisation as part of the broader agenda to diversify their economies, and develop productive capacity for high and sustained economic growth, creation of employment opportunities and substantial poverty reduction. This became the essence of phase three of industrialisation based on poverty reduction strategy papers (PRSP).7 As noted in section 9.6.1, NEPAD underscored the new phase of industrialisation in 2001.

The Rationale for Industrialisation in Africa

Despite the 3-phase evolution of African industrial development, the arguments for industrialisation have remained similar to those put forward during the early years of political independence in the 1960s. The rationale for renewed commitment to industrialisation include the following:

Firstly, the industrial sector[8] is expected to lead economic diversification. Some of the arguments for this line of thinking are (i) employment promotion especially for labour-intensive industrial activities; (ii) reduction of vulnerability, risk and uncertainty in production and export as is the case with the primary sector; (iii) provision of substantial forward and backward linkages with other sectors; and (iv) achievement of self-reliance and economic independence in the long run.

Secondly, industrialisation, via economic diversification and growth, economic and employment creation, is expected to raise people's incomes and living standards and reduce or eradicate poverty.

Thirdly, industrialisation has great possibilities for technological transfer and adaptation and creation of technology.[9]

Finally, industry leads to export market expansion. According to one version of Engel's law, whereas the share of agriculture in total household expenditure declines as per capita income rises, that of manufacturing increases. The implication is that manufacturing offers significant opportunities for export market expansion and therefore may be a driver of merchandise trade and growth.[10]

Performance of the Industrial Sector in Africa

Background Information

Africa is usually referred to as the least industrialised continent. With the exception of Egypt, Morocco, South Africa and Tunisia the continent's industrial sector performance is relatively low.

Apart from domestic problems,[11] African economies have been facing three interrelated external shocks: hikes in food prices, increase in energy prices and the global economic and financial crisis which originated from the United States in 2007.[12] As a result of the crisis, the growth rates of real output fell from an annual average of 5.2 per cent in the period 2000 – 2006 to 2.6 per cent in 2009. Similarly, the growth rate of real output per capita fell from 2.7 per cent to 0.3 per cent over the same period.[13] In 2009, most of the year over year changes of GDP growth rates in Africa were negative as shown in Appendix 10.1.

The performance of the industrial sector danced to a similar tune of the general economic performance as will be shown in the subsequent sub-sections. Furthermore, as pointed out elsewhere14 the crisis also eroded recent gains made by African countries in poverty reduction and reduced prospects of achieving the Millennium Development Goals (MDGs).[14]

Industrial Growth Rates

Between 2000 and 2009, the narrowly defined industrial sector (manufacturing) in Africa grew at a compound annual growth rate of 3.2 per cent (For details see Appendix 10.2).

Resource-based manufacturing (mainly consumer goods, and glass and other non-metallic minerals) grew by 2.6 per cent, while low-technology manufacturing (mainly textiles, apparel, and fabricated metal products) grew by

1.6 per cent. The growth of medium/high technology manufacturing (mainly chemicals machinery and equipment and vehicles) was 5.7 per cent. For details, see Appendix 10.2. In 2007/2008 manufacturing annual growth rate was 5.7 per cent. For country details, see Table 10.1.

The broadly defined industrial production (manufacturing, mining and construction) grew by an average of 1.9 per cent in 2009. Many countries, especially those which depend significantly on mining, experienced negative growth rates. Examples include Angola, Botswana, Namibia and South Africa. For details, see Table 10.1. This might be attributed to shrinkage in global demand for minerals like diamond because of the great intensity of the global crisis in 2009. In Botswana, for instance, the mining sector which accounted for about 70 per cent of the government revenue was hit hardest by the crisis. In

2009 the diamond giant, Debswana, succumbed to laying off some workers and some mining sub-sectors had to close down.[15]

However, in general rates of industrial growth in Africa have been impressive. Over the period 2001 – 2010, six of the 10 fastest-growing economies in the world were in Sub-Saharan Africa (UNIDO and UNCTAD 2011: 81).

Table 10.1: Industrial Production Growth in Some African Countries During the Global Crisis (percentage)

Country	Industry 2009	Manufacturing 2007/2008	Mining 2007/2008
Algeria	1.1	2.0	3.0
Angola	-2.4	17.1	36.5
Benin	2.8	8.4	8.0
Botswana	-19.9	17.5	-2.0
Burkina Faso	4.5	2.5	26.2
Burundi	2.0	5.0	4.2
Cameroon	1.0	0.5	-5.4
Cape Verde	1.5	5.8	9.1
Chad	1.5	-3.3	-12.7
Congo, Republic of the	13.0	18.9	7.1
Cote d'Ivoire	5.0	3.3	3.3
Egypt	5.1	5.3	8.9
Equatorial Guinea	5.9	20.6	5.2
Eritrea	4.0	-7.3	-

Ethiopia	9.9	7.1	6.8
Gabon	-4.3	9.5	-1.1
Gambia,	7.2	1.4	6.9
The Ghana	1.6	5.5	6.0
Guinea	-5.0	4.0	11.3
Kenya	3.7	6.2	12.9
Lesotho	1.5	-10.7	35.2
Libya	-4.4	7.6	1.7
Madagascar	-2.0	8.2	9.0
Malawi	9.5	26.0	8.3
Mauritius	1.7	1.8	-
Morocco	-0.3	3.8	9.1
Mozambique	8.0	1.3	34.4
Namibia	-12.4	7.2	-0.4
Nigeria	0.6	9.1	-5.7
Rwanda	7.0	6.9	37.5
Sao Toma and Principe	8.0	3.8	6.5
Senegal	1.5	-2.5	-19.4
Seychelles	-3.0	-4.3	-
South Africa	-7.2	4.5	0.0
Sudan	3.2	4.8	-
Swaziland	-3.5	2.0	15.8
Tanzania	7.0	8.7	10.7
Togo	1.0	9.1	2.9
Tunisia	-2.8	5.1	4.3
Uganda	0.7	8.9	5.0
Zambia	11.0	4.5	4.9
Zimbabwe	-2.0	3.8	1.3
Africa	1.9	5.7	7.0

Sources: CIA,2010, *The World Fact book by CIA*, for industry and 2009 *African Statistical Yearbook* 2009, for manufacturing and mining.

Industrial Contribution to GDP and Employment

The share of manufacturing value added (MVA) in Africa's GDP rose from 6.3 per cent in 1970 to a peak of 15.3 per cent in 1990 (Table 10.2). By 2000 it was only 12.8 per cent and fell further to 10.5 per ent in 2008. The sub-regional contributions to GDP followed a similar pattern as indicated in the table.

The African share in world manufacturing is relatively small and has recently been declining. It fell from 1.2 per cent in 2000 to 1.1 per cent in 2009 (Appendix 10.2). The great intensity of the global economic and financial crisis in 2008/2009 might have contributed partially to the decline.

Employment in the industrial sector is also relatively small. According to 2003 data from the African Development Bank, only 15 per cent of the workers were employed in the industrial sector.

Table 10.2: Contribution to industry to GDP, 1970-2008

	% share of GDP	1970	1980	1990	2000	2005	2008
World	Industry	36.9	38.1	33.3	29.1	28.8	30.1
	Manufacturing	26.7	24.4	21.7	19.2	17.8	18.1
	Mining & utilities	3.9	7.1	5.2	4.5	5.5	6.2
Developing economies	Industry	27.3	41.1	36.8	36.3	38.9	40.2
	Manufacturing	17.6	20.2	22.4	22.6	23.3	23.7
	Mining & utilities	5.7	14.7	8.9	8.3	10.1	10.9
African developing economies	Industry	13.1	35.6	35.2	35.5	38.8	40.7
	Manufacturing	6.3	11.9	15.3	12.8	11.6	10.5
	Mining & utilities	4.8	19.3	15.2	18.4	23.0	25.8
Eastern Africa	Industry	3.1	7.8	20.6	18.6	20.6	20.3
	Manufacturing	1.7	4.9	13.4	10.4	10.3	9.7
	Mining & utilities	0.8	1.5	3.3	3.1	3.6	3.7
Middle Africa	Industry	34.2	38.4	34.1	50.4	57.9	59.8
	Manufacturing	10.3	11.8	11.2	8.2	7.3	6.4
	Mining & utilities	19.1	21.2	18.9	39.3	47.9	50.5
Northern Africa	Industry	34.2	50.0	37.4	37.8	45.0	46.0
	Manufacturing	13.6	9.7	13.4	12.8	11.3	10.7
	Mining & utilities	15.7	33.0	17.2	19.5	28.2	29.8
Southern Africa	Industry	38.2	48.2	40.6	32.7	31.7	34.5
	Manufacturing	22.0	20.9	22.9	18.4	17.9	18.2
	Mining & utilities	12.0	24.0	14.3	11.7	11.2	13.1
Western Africa	Industry	26.7	43.3	34.5	39.8	36.7	37.4
	Manufacturing	13.3	16.8	13.1	7.8	6.0	5.0
	Mining & utilities	7.7	21.3	18.8	29.3	27.7	29.6

Source: UNCTAD and UNIDO (2011: 15)

Trends in the Manufacturing Exports.

The share of manufacturing exports in total exports in Africa fell from 43 percent in 2000 to 39 percent in 2008 when the global economic and financial crisis had started showing its impact on the African economies. This share is relatively lower than other developing economies.[16] In 2008, for instance, the share of manufacturing exports in total exports was 89 percent in low and middle income countries in East Asia and the Pacific, 61 percent in low and middle income countries in Latin America, and 85 percent in low and middle income countries in South Asia.[17]

However, the negative side should not completely hide the positive side of the trends. Africa's share of global manufacturing exports rose from 1 percent in 2000 to 1.3 percent in 2008.[18] Furthermore, the percentage of African countries' average manufacturing exports to GDP has been rising after trade liberalisation in 1980s. It rose from 3.3 in the 1980s to 4.3 in the 1990s; and increased again to 7.6 during the period 2000 – 2006. For country details see Table 10.3.

Table 10.3: African countries' average manufacturing exports ((GDP percentage)

	1980-1989	1990-1999	2000-2006
Benin	0.5	1.5	1.3
Botswana	..	..	35.7
Burkina Faso	0.5	..	1.4
Burundi	..	0.2	0.4
Cameroon	1.3	1.5	0.9
Cape Verde	..	1.3	1.4
Cote d'Ivoire	3.4	6.3	7.8
Egypt	2.4	2.3	2.1
Ethiopia	..	0.4	0.8
Gabon	2.8	1.4	4.0
Gambia	0.4	1.4	0.6
Ghana	0.3	3.1	4.5
Guinea	..	4.5	6.3
Kenya	2.0	4.6	3.5
Madagascar	0.8	3.1	6.3
Malawi	1.6	2.5	2.6
Mali	0.1	1.4	8.8
Mauritius	25.2	28.5	26.1
Morocco	6.0	10.0	14.0
Mozambique	..	0.9	1.1

Namibia	..	..	17.2
Niger	0.4	3.5	1.8
Nigeria	0.0	0.6	0.7
Rwanda	..	0.2	0.2
Senegal	3.5	7.2	7.5
Seychelles	1.2	2.3	2.3
Sierra Leone	3.8	..	0.4
South Africa	4.4	9.1	13.2
Sudan	0.2	0.3	0.3
Swaziland	..	..	46.9
Togo	2.5	4.0	13.7
Tunisia	11.7	21.6	25.9
Uganda	..	0.7	1.0
United Republic of Tanzania	..	1.2	1.9
Zambia	..	4.4	4.4
Africa	0.4	4.3	7.6

Source: UNCTAD, 2008.

Performance of Small Manufacturing Industries in Africa

African small and medium manufacturing industries are dominated by formal and informal small and medium enterprises (SMEs). These comprise over 90 per cent of African businesses and contribute to over 50 per cent of African employment and GDP.[19]

A significant proportion of the small or micro enterprises in Africa are informal as opposed to formal enterprises or firms. Informal firms are relatively small in size, unregistered and not taxed, produce to order, are run by managers with low human capital, do not have easy access to external finance, do not advertise their products and sell to largely informal clients for cash. Furthermore, informal firms rarely become formal as they grow.[20]

The informal economy in Africa was estimated to have been 42 per cent of GDP in 1999/2000. Zimbabwe, Tanzania, and Nigeria were at the high end with 59.4, 58.3 and 57.9 per cent respectively. At the lower end was Botswana with 33.4 per cent and Cameroon with 32.8 per cent. These are higher percentages compared to those from advanced economies such as USA (8.8 per cent) and Japan (11.3 per cent).[21]

Informal employment in Africa accounts for 72 per cent of non-agriculture employment in Sub-Saharan Africa.[22]

The dominance and non-formality of small firms in the manufacturing sector in Africa raises the question of access to inputs, credit and firm growth.

Performance of Industries through Regional Integration

The share of intra-African trade in Africa's total export is generally low. The bulk of Africa's exports go to more developed countries (MDCs). In 2009, for example, about 60 per cent of Africa's total merchandise exports were accounted for by MDCs. Asia accounted for 24.3 per cent, while Africa accounted for only 12.3 per cent.[23] Increasing intra-African trade in Africa may be promoted through intensifying regional integration for at least three reasons:

Firstly, regional integration has a big role to play in lifting some constraints such as high indirect costs stemming from poor infrastructure, high regulatory burden faced by African firms and political instability (UNIDO and UNCTAD 2011: 80). Some elaboration is in order: Regional co-operation in the development of infrastructure, for instance, would lower transaction costs, enhance regional markets, and make manufacturing production and exports more competitive.[24]

Regional harmonization policies can reduce the regulatory burden facing African firms. Furthermore, regional integration promotes peace and security effectively. The political crises in Liberia, Sierra Leone, Kenya and Zimbabwe are examples where regional institutions and measures played a key role in handling the crises.[25]

Security, regional integration can also facilitate the development of financial markets and improve access to credit, and competitiveness.[26]

Thirdly, given the relatively high growing population[27] in Africa, the continent should take advantage of the growing regional market.

Lastly, although Africa has relatively low per capita income, its purchasing power is rising and it has one of the fast-growing and dynamic consumer markets.[28]

In view of these and similar opportunities, the objectives of the West African common industrial policy (WACIP) under ECOWAS were set in 2010 as follows:[29]

- To improve intra-community trade from 13 per cent in 2010 to 40 per cent by 2030;
- To expand the volume of exports of manufactured goods from West Africa to the global market from 0.1 in 2010 to 1 per cent by 2030;
- To diversify and broaden the region's industrial production by progressively raising the processing of export products by an average of 30 per cent by 2030; and
- To progressively increase the manufacturing industry's contribution to regional GDP to an average of over 20 per cent in 2030 from an average of between 6 and 7 per cent in 2010.

Constraints and Opportunities for Industrial Development in Africa
Constraints for Industrial Development in Africa

An Introductory Note

As noted earlier in this chapter, the general problems of African economies are both external and internal. The main external problems or shocks have been hikes in energy prices and the resulting increase in food prices, and global economic and financial crisis. The internal constraints are many but some may directly or indirectly be related to the external problems. These are outlined in the next sub-section.

Constraints to General Industrial Development

The constraints to general industrial development may be put into seven categories as follows: Basic political-economic constraints; technological and entrepreneurship limitations; limited resource mobilisation and funding; relatively poor infrastructure and high factor costs; structural limitation of industries; restricted size of domestic market and relatively low ability to compete globally and diversify; and slow pace of regional integration and harmonisation. These are elaborated hereunder.

(i) Basic political-economic constraints

These include low level of good governance, political instability, inappropriate macroeconomic policies including fiscal and monetary policies, bureaucracy and high regulatory burden, and weak government capabilities and partial implementation of industrial policies.

Low level governance affects industrial development negatively, mainly in terms of lack of accountability, corruption, and injudicious use of resources away from industrial and general economic development projects.

Political instability and unresolved conflicts affect industrial development negatively. As the World Bank[30] maintains, improving good governance and resolving conflict is perhaps the most basic requirement for faster industrial and general development. The 2011 UNIDO and UNCTAD report[31] also underscores that political stability is a necessary condition for industrial development in Africa.

Inappropriate macro-economic policies including fiscal and monetary policies in Africa have also contributed negatively to economic development including industrialisation. The mix of fiscal and monetary policies has to be such that firms have better access to credit and real internet rate and at levels that do not deter industrial investment.[32]

Bureaucracy and high regulatory burden affect industrial entrepreneurs and investors adversely in both SMEs and large industries.

Weak public capabilities, especially in terms of weak state institutions, limits governments in Africa to implement successfully their industrial development programmes and policies.[33]

(ii) Technological and Entrepreneurship Limitation

Low-level scientific and technological innovation and limited number of industrial entrepreneurs with financial power form another set of constraints.

Low-level applied science, technology, innovation and research and development (R&D) affects industrial development negatively. Related to this is the limited number of industrial entrepreneurs and investors. Most of entrepreneurs in Africa are artisans in small and informal enterprises. There is serious scarcity of entrepreneurs and local investors in medium and large industries who have financial strength.

(iii) Limited Resource Mobilisation and Scarcity of Financial Resources

Limited resource mobilisation, scarcity of domestic and foreign financial resources and overdependence on foreign aid affect industrialisation adversely.

Limited mobilisation of resources to finance industrial investment is a constraint to industrialisation. As the 2011 UNIDO and UNCTAD report[34] underscores, there has been a tendency for African governments to focus on resource allocation as opposed to resource mobilisation issues in the conduct of industrial policy.

Scarcity of domestic resources affects industrial development adversely. Credit is also difficult to access, especially for the informal small enterprises. The general shortage of foreign exchange and exchange rate fluctuations create major obstacles and uncertainties to industrial investment in general.

Overdependence on foreign aid is also a problem to industrial and general development. High debt service and conditional requirements compound the constraint.

(iv) Relatively Poor Infrastructure and High Factor Costs

Relatively poor infrastructure and high factor costs are also major constraints for industrial development in Africa.

Indirect costs to firms stem largely from poor infrastructure in Africa. Furthermore, while unskilled labour costs are relatively low in Africa, shortage of skilled labour and capital leads to high cost of production.

(v) Structural limitation of industries

As noted in this chapter, most of African firms are small and informal. Furthermore, even the medium and large ones are basically consumer industries. African governments tend to focus perpetually on such industries and there is inertia to develop intermediate and capital good industries. This inertia may be regarded as a constraint to balanced industrial development involving production of consumer, intermediate and capital goods to ensure domestic industrial linkages and economic independence.

(vi) Restricted Size of Domestic Market and Low Ability to diversify and Compete Globally Small size of domestic market and low ability to diversify and compete globally form another set of constraints of industrial development in Africa.

Small size of domestic market tends to be an obstacle to the foreign industrial investors who predominantly seek access and expansion into new markets. It is also a hurdle to local investors as certain technologies and industrial units need a substantial market size to achieve economies of scale.[35]

Low level of economic diversification and international competition are also constraints to the industrial sector in Africa which is mainly composed of SMEs and is struggling to compete globally due to relatively low quality products and high prices.

(vii) Slow Pace of Regional Integration and Policy Harmonisation

Regional integration in Africa is often advocated as a desirable solution to restricted sizes of national markets. Other advantages of regional integration have been spelt out in this chapter. However, regional integration has not made very significant progress and there is need to accelerate it.

Constraints for SMEs

So far, the constraints to industrial development in general have been identified. The often cited traditional constraints or hurdles of (manufacturing) SMEs are listed hereunder:

(i)   Limited access to finance;

(ii) Lack of entrepreneurial skills;

(iii) Lack of marketing skills;

(iv) Inherent bias against SMEs;

 (v) Bias of the education system against self-employment;

(vi) Shortage of business premises;

(vii) Excessive government laws and regulations.

With the advent of globalisation, too much competition may be added as a new hurdle to SMEs.

Opportunities

Africa is expected to transform the constraints and challenges facing the industrial sector into opportunities.

Direct opportunities which should be exploited include:

(i) Dominance of small and informal firms or SMEs in general

This is an opportunity in the sense of developing entrepreneurship, creating employment and generating income and eventually reducing poverty especially in the short and medium terms. This is the essence of phase three of African industrial development.[36]

(ii) Fast population growth

This is an opportunity in terms of potential market of industrial products and potential source of industrial entrepreneurs and investors.

(iii) Vast resources

The vast natural, physical and human resources may be exploited further to contribute to industrial and general development in Africa.

(iv) Regional integration

As regional integration is strengthened, constraints such as small domestic markets and poor infrastructure are relaxed. This is positive to industrialisation.

Other issues worth considering in the short and medium terms include:

(i)   Improving governance and resolving conflicts as a requirement for fast industrial and general development.

(ii)   Adopting appropriate macroeconomic policies including fiscal and monetary policies.

(iii)   Minimising bureaucracy and regulatory conditions to promote industrialisation.

(iv)   Improving government capability and implementing industrial programmes and policies effectively.

(v)   Investing in human capital for accelerated industrial development.

(vi)   Making more significant effort in mobilising resources to promote industrial development.

(vii)   Improving infrastructure for industrial and general development.

In the long run, the following industrial development issues are worth considering:

(i)   Uplifting the technological and entrepreneurship constraint in the industrial sector.

(ii)   Establishing significant intermediate and capital goods industries.

(iii)   Increasing competitiveness and strengthening industrial linkages and economic diversification.

(iv)   Strengthening regional integration and harmonising regional policies towards Africa's industrial policy.

Conclusion

This chapter has provided a retrospective explanation of industrial development, including the rationale and phases of industrial development in Africa. Performance of the industrial sector has been shown to be relatively low in terms of manufacturing contribution to GDP, total employment and exports despite somewhat impressive growth rates. The chapter has finally outlined the main constraints and opportunities.

Review Questions

1. (a) Outline the stages or phases of industrial development in Africa.
   (b) Are these stages applicable to your country? Explain.
2. (a) Evaluate the industrial performance of Africa in terms of:
      (i) growth
      (ii) contribution to GDP or total employment or export.
   (b) Compare your evaluation with that of a specified country in Africa.
3. (a) Explain the main constraints of industrial development in: (i) Africa
      (ii) your own country
   (b) Suggest the way forward.

Appendix 10.1: Real GDP Growth Rates of Some African Countries

Country	2005	2006	2007	2008	2009	YOY 2008	YOY 2009
Benin	2.94	3.76	4.65	4.98	3.84	0.33	-1.14
Burkina Faso	7.10	5.51	3.60	5.00	3.54	1.40	-1.47
Burundi	0.91	5.31	3.58	4.53	3.53	0.96	-1.00
Central African Republic	2.40	3.80	3.70	2.20	2.40	-1.50	0.20
Chad	7.94	0.15	0.18	-0.41	2.83	-1.59	3.24
Congo, Democratic Republic	7.88	5.59	6.26	6.20	2.70	-0.06	-3.50
Cote d'Ivoire	1.90	0.73	1.59	2.33	3.70	0.75	1.37
Eritrea	2.57	-0.97	1.33	1.03	1.14	-0.29	0.11
Ethiopia	12.64	11.54	11.47	11.61	6.52	0.14	-5.09
Gambia,	5.11	6.55	6.31	5.86	3.98	-0.45	-1.87
The Ghana	5.87	6.43	6.10	7.16	4.50	1.07	-2.66
Guinea	3.00	2.50	1.76	3.96	2.55	2.20	-1.41
Guinea-Bissau	3.47	0.56	2.70	3.33	1.90	0.63	-1.43
Kenya	5.88	6.38	7.02	2.01	3.01	-5.01	1.01
Liberia	5.29	7.79	9.52	7.13	4.87	-2.38	-2.26
Madagascar	4.60	5.02	6.42	5.04	-0.18	-1.20	-5.22
Malawi	3.27	6.75	8.65	9.70	6.90	1.05	-2.81
Mali	6.14	5.25	4.30	4.99	3.88	0.69	-1.11
Mauritania	5.45	11.45	1.02	2.23	2.35	1.21	0.12
Mozambique	8.39	8.69	7.02	6.18	4.30	-0.85	-1.88
Niger	8.42	5.81	3.30	9.52	3.02	6.22	-6.50
Nigeria	5.39	6.21	6.45	5.29	2.86	-1.17	-2.43
Rwanda	7.20	7.29	7.94	11.23	5.60	3.29	-5.63
Senegal	5.62	2.44	4.75	2.49	3.12	-2.26	0.64
Sierra Leone	7.25	7.38	6.38	5.52	4.49	-0.87	-1.03
Tanzania	7.37	6.74	7.15	7.46	4.97	0.32	-2.50
Togo	1.18	3.95	1.94	1.10	1.69	-0.84	0.59
Uganda	6.33	10.79	8.59	9.53	6.20	0.95	-3.33
Zambia	5.31	6.25	6.26	6.02	4.04	-0.24	-1.98
Zimbabwe	-3.95	-5.42	-6.09	-	-	-	-

Note: The last two columns show year over year (YOY) changes as of 2008 and 2009 respectively.

Source: AERC African Economic Research Consortium – (2010: 12).

Appendix 10.2: African Manufacturing by Sector and Technological Classification, 2000-2009 (%)

ISIC rev. 3 manufacturing sectors	African MVA structure		African growth	African share in the world	
	Compound annual growth 2000-2009	2009 share of total MVA	2000 share of total MVA	Share in World MVA 2000	Share in World MVA 2009
15 – Food and beverages	1.1	16.6	20.0	2.4	1.9
16 – Tobacco	1.6	2.6	3.0	3.4	2.5
20 – Wood	-1.9	1.8	2.8	1.7	1.5
21 – Paper	2.9	3.0	3.1	1.3	1.5
23 – Refined petroleum and coke	3.6	6.1	5.9	2.0	2.1
25 – Rubber and plastics	4.1	2.9	2.7	1.0	1.1
26–Glass and other non metallic minerals	7.9	10.1	6.8	2.2	3.3
27 – Basic metals	0.4	5.6	7.3	1.7	1.0
Sub-total RBM (resource-based manufacturing)	2.6	48.8	51.6	2.0	1.8
17 -Textiles	-0.9	4.7	6.8	3.1	2.3
18 - Apparel	2.3	4.3	4.7	3.0	3.3
19 -Leather	0.8	1.2	1.5	2.7	2.3
22 - Publishing and printing	2.7	2.7	2.9	0.8	1.0
28 - Fabricated metal products	3.0	5.1	5.2	1.1	1.3
36 - Furniture and manufacturing	3.2	1.8	1.8	0.7	0.7
Sub-total LTM (low technology manufacturing)	1.6	19.9	22.9	1.5	1.5
24 - Chemicals	8.4	19.2	12.4	1.6	2.2
29 - Machinery and equipment	2.9	3.6	3.7	0.6	0.6
30 - Office machinery	3.9	0.3	0.3	0.1	0.1
31 - Electrical machinery	5.9	2.5	2.0	0.6	0.6
32 - Radio, TV and communication equipment	2.2	0.8	0.9	0.1	0.0
33 - Medical, precision and optical instruments	3.3	0.3	0.3	0.1	0.1
34 - Motor vehicles	0.4	3.8	4.9	0.9	0.7
35 - Other transport equipment	1.8	0.9	1.0	0.5	0.4

Subtotal MHTM (medium/ high technology manufacturing)	5.7	31.4	25.5	0.6	0.6
Total Manufacturing	3.2	100.0	100.0	1.2	1.1

Source: UNIDO and UNCTAD (2011: 19).

Appendix 10.3: Manufacturing Performance of African Countries

Country	MVA[a] per capita (Com- pound annual growth rate 1990-2010)	MVA per capita[b] (1990)	MVA per capita[b] (2010)
Algeria	-1.4	179	136
Angola	4.8	26	66
Benin	0.4	21	23
Botswana	1.6	124	171
Burkina Faso	1.9	26	37
Burundi	-2.9	16	9
Cameroon	0.8	126	148
Cape Verde	1.2	108	139
Central African Republic	-1.3	21	16
Chad	-1.8	22	15
Comoros	-0.9	14	12
Congo	1.5	62	83
Côte d'Ivoire	-0.6	112	99
Dem. Rep. of the Congo	-5.7	16	5
Djibouti	-3	37	20
Egypt	3.7	177	369
Eritrea	0.2	9	9
Ethiopia	0.3	8	9
Gabon	1	163	200
Gambia	-0.7	19	16
Ghana	1.6	20	28
Guinea	1.7	12	17
Guinea-Bissau	-2.2	26	16
Kenya	-0.3	49	47
Lesotho	4.3	44	103
Liberia	-3.6	34	17
Libyan Arab Jamahiriya	-1.5	237	319
Madagascar	-0.8	25	30
Malawi	-1	17	21
Mali	-3.3	7	13
Mauritania	-0.9	22	27
Mauritius	2.2	801	522
Morocco	1.6	246	180
Mozambique	6.2	52	15

Namibia	6.9	348	92
Niger	-1.5	10	13
Nigeria	2.4	24	15
Rwanda	-5.9	17	56
Sao Tome and Principe	1.9	50	34
Senegal	-0.3	54	57
Seychelles	2.8	1,193	692
Sierra Leone	-2.4	6	9
Somalia	-0.1	7	8
South Africa	0.3	581	551
Sudan	2.8	34	19
Swaziland	1.9	451	311
Togo	0.5	25	22
Tunisia	3.4	493	253
United Republic of Tanzania	2.2	29	19
Zambia	1.1	44	36
Zimbabwe	-5.5	34	106

Notes: a.   MVA – Manufacturing value added
            b.   MVA per capita (US$)
Source: UNIDO & UNCTAD 2011: 27.

Notes

1. Exceptional cases with period coverage exist. As noted in chapter 9, in Tanzania, for instance, ISI was replaced by basic industry strategy (BIS) in 1975. When SAP was introduced in 1986, Tanzania was in the middle of the long-term BIS (1975 – 1995).
2. UNIDO & UNCTAD (2011: 10).
3. bid, p.2.
4. UNIDO & UNCTAD (2011:11).   Also Mkandawire and Soludo (2003) and Wangwe and Semboja (2003).
5. For details, see for instance, Husain and Farugee (1994).
6. For further details on criticism of SAPs see, for instance, UNIDO & UNCTAD 2011, Soludo et al 2004, and Stein 1992.
7. Examples include the 2007 South Africa National Industrial Policy Framework (NIPF) which emphasised diversification of production and export and poverty reduction, among others; the national strategy for poverty reduction (NSPR) in Botswana; MKUKUTA (Mkakati wa Kukuza Uchumi na Kupunguza Umaskini Tanzania), Swahili for the National Strategy on Economic Growth and Poverty Reduction (NSEGPR) in Tanzania, and many others. For details see, for instance, Wollmuth et al (2009), New Growth and Poverty Alleviation Strategies for Africa.

8. Industrial sector is broadly viewed as manufacturing plus other supporting sectors such as public utility and construction. Traditionally, mining is considered a component of the industrial sector when coal and other energy providers are considered. Most of the arguments are based on narrowly defined industry (manufacturing). The United Nations Department of Economic and Social Affairs (DESA) defines manufacturing as the physical or chemical transformation of materials, substances or components into new products (UNIDO and UNCTAD 2011: 5).

9. See UNIDO and UNCTAD (2011: 5) and Kapunda and Akinkugbe (2005: 151).

10. Cf. UNIDO and UNCTAD (2011: 5).

11. This will be elaborated in the section dealing with constraints in industrial performance in this chapter.

12. For details, see for example, AERC – African Economic Research Consortium (2010), Osakwe (2010) and UNIDO and UNCTAD (2011).

13. Cf. UNIDO and UNCTAD (2011: 4).

14. See Osakwe (2010).

15. See, for instance, Kapunda et al (2010: 2).

16. See UNIDO and UNCTAD (2011: 17).

17. Ibid, pp.17 – 18.

18. Ibid, p.14.

19. UNIDO and UNCTAD (2011: 23).

20. Ibid, p.106.

21. Mwamba (2011: 27).

22. For details, see ILO 2002.

23. UNIDO and UNCTAD (2011: 80).

24. Ibid.

25. Ibid.

26. Ibid, p.81.

27. Between 1975 an 2009, for example, Africa's population grew at an average annual rate of 2.6 per cent, while the world average was 1.5 per cent. The United Nations projection of African population growth is 2.7 between 2009 and 2050 (UNIDO and UNCTAD (2011: 82).

28. UNIDO and UNCTAD (2011: 84).

29. Ibid, p.80.

30. World Bank (2000: 2).

31. UNIDO and UNCTAD (2011: 110).

32. Ibid, p.109.

33. Ibid, p.108.

34. Ibid, p.109.

35. See Hinzen, (1996: 19).

36. It will be recalled that phases or stages of industrial development were outlined earlier in this chapter.

References

Adongo, J., 2008, 'Development Integration and Industrial Policy in SACU: The Case of Namibia', in B. Vickers, ed, Industrial Policy in the Southern African Customs Union, Midrand, South Africa: Institute for Dialogue.

AERC (African Economic Research Consortium), 2010, The Global Financial Crisis: Implications for African Economies, Nairobi: AERC.

AfriBiz (citing), 2009, African Statistical Yearbook, AfriBiz.

Agbaje, A. and Jerome, A., 2010, 'Institutional Framework and the Process of Trade Policy Making in African Countries: The Case of Nigeria', in African Economic Research Consortium (AER) African Imperatives in the New World Trade Order, Nairobi: AERC, Vol. III.

Agu, C., 1992, 'Analysis of the Determinants of the Nigerian Banking Systems" Profits and Profitability performance', Saving and Development, 16(4): 353 – 69.

Alexander, J.W., 1984, 'The Basic, Non-basic concept of Urban Economic Functions', Economic Geography, 30: 246 – 61.

Allen, W.B., N. Doherty, K. Weigelt and E. Mansfield, 2005, Managerial Economics: Theory, Application, and Cases, 6th Edition, London: W.W. Norton Company Ltd.

Andreosso, B. and Jacobson, D., 2005, Industrial Economics and Organization: A European Perspective, London: McGraw-Hill Education.

Andrews, P.W.S., 1951, 'Industrial Analysis in Economics', in T. Wilson and P.W.S.

Andrews, eds, Oxford Studies in the Price Mechanism, Oxford: Clarendon Press.

Andrews, P.W.S., 1952, 'Industrial Economics as a Specialist Subject', Journal of Industrial Economics.

Arrow, K.J., 1962, 'Economic Welfare and the Allocation of Resources for Invention', in NBECR: The Rate and Direction of Inventive Activity, National Bureau of Economic Conference Report (NBECR), Princeton, NJ: Princeton University Press: 609 – 25.
Baah-Nuakoh, Amoah, 1997, Studies On the Ghanaian Economy, Legon: Ghana University Press, Vol. I.

Bain, J.S., 1956, Barriers to New Competition, Cambridge: Harvard University Press.
Bain, J.S., 1958, Industrial Organization, New York: John Wiley.

Bain, J.S., 1968, Industrial Organization, 2nd edition, New York: John Wiley. Barthwal, R.R., 1985, Industrial Economics, New Delhi: Wiley Eastern Limited.

Baumol, W.J., 1967, Business, Behaviour, Value and Growth, New York: Harcourt Brace Jovanorich.

Baye, M.R., 2010, Managerial Economics and Business Strategy, New York: McGraw-Hill. Berry, C.H., 1975, Corporate Growth and Diversification, Princeton: University Press. Besanko, D., Dranove, D., Shanley, M. and Schaefer, S., 2010, Economics of Strategy, Asia: John Wiley.

Bhagavan, M.R., ed, 1999, Reforming the Power Sector In Africa, New York: Zed Books Ltd. BIDPA (Botswana Institute for Development Policy Analysis), 2002 Economic Mapping for Botswana, Gaborone: BIDPA.

Bongenaar, B. and Szirmai, B., 2001, 'Development and Diffusion of Technology: The Case of TIRDO' in A. Szirmai and P. Lapperre, eds, The Industrial Experience of Tanzania, New York: Palgrave Publishers.

Botswana Competition Authority, 2013, Botswana Competition Bulletin, Vol. I, Issue 1:1 – 2).

Boyes, W., 2012, Managerial Economics, Markets and the Firm, Mason: South-Western. Brusick, P., Alvarez, A.M. and Cernat, L., 2005, Competition Provisions in Regional Trade Agreements: How to Assure Development Gains, Washington DC: UNCTAD.

Buxton, A.J., Davies, S.W. and Lyons, S.R., 1984, 'Concentration and Advertising in Consumer and Producer Markets', Journal of Industrial Economics, 32: 451 – 64. Carlton, D.W. and J.M. Perloff, S.M., 2005, Modern Industrial Organization, London:Pearson Addison.

Chamberlin, E., 1933, The Theory of Monopolistic Competition, Cambridge: Harvard University Press.

Chipeta, C., and Schade, K., eds, 2007, Deepening Integration in SADC: Macroeconomic Policies and Social Impact, Gaborone: Friedrich Ebert Foundation.

Chowdhury, A., and Islam, Y., 1993, The Newly Industrialising Economies of East Asia, London: Routledge.

Christaller, W., 1933, Die Zentralen Orte in Souddeutschland, translated by Baskin, C.W. (1966)

as Central Places in Southern Germany, Englewood Cliffs, N.J.: Prentice-Hall.

Church, J. and Ware, R., 2000, Industrial Organization: A Strategic Approach, London: McGraw-Hill.

CIA, 2010, World Factbook, New York: CIA.

Clark, J.M., 1940, 'Towards a concept of Workable Competition', American Economic Review, 30: 241 – 56.

Clarke, R., 2000, Industrial Economics, Oxford: Blackwell.

Curry, B. and George, K.D., 1983, 'Industrial Concentration: A Survey', Journal of Industrial Economics, 31: 2003 – 55.

Darby, M. and Karni, E., 1973, 'Free Competition and the Optimal Amount of Fraud', Journal of Law and Economics, (16) April: 67 – 88.

Devine, P.J., Lee, N., Jones, R.M. and Tyson, W.J., 1985, An Introduction to Industrial Economics, London: Allen &Unwin.

Dietrich, M., 1992, 'The Foundations of Industrial Policy', in K. Cowling and Sudgen, R., eds, Current Issues in Industrial Economic Strategy, Manchester: Manchester University.

Dornbusch, R., Fischer, S., Startz, R., 2001, Macroeconomics, London: McGraw-Hill, Irwin.

Douglas, E.J., 1992, Managerial Economics: Analysis and Strategy, London: Prentice-Hall International, Inc.

Edgmand, M. 1987, Macroeconomics: Theory and Policy, London: Addison-Wesley.
Englebert, P. and R. Hoffman, 1994, 'Burundi: Learning the Lessons' in I. Husain and R. Faruqee, eds, Adjustment in Africa: Lessons From Case Studies, Washington, D.C.: World Bank.

Faruqee, R., 1994, 'Nigeria: Ownership Abandoned', in I. Hussain and R. Faruqee, eds, Adjustment In Africa: Lessons from Country Case Studies, Washington D.C.: World Bank.

Fazzan, S.M., Hubard, R.G. and Bruce, C.P., 1988, 'Financing Constraints and Corporate Investment', Brooking Papers on Economic Activities, Activity 1.

Ferguson, P.R. and Ferguson, G.J., 1994, Industrial Economics: Issues and Perspectives, London: Macmillan.

Fetter, M., 1924, 'The Economic Law of Market Area', Quarterly Journal of Economics, 39. Florence, P.S., 1948, Investment, Location and Size of Plant, Cambridge: Cambridge University Press.

Freund, J.E., and Williams, T.A., 1983, College Mathematics With Business Applications, London: Prentice-Hall International, Inc.

Funjika, P., 2010, 'Deposit Dullarization and Monetary Policy In Zambia', MA (Economics Dissertation, University of Botswana.

Galbraith, J.K. 1952, American Capitalism, Boston: Houghton Mifflin.

Galebotswe, O., 1999, 'The Current Industrial Development Strategy of Botswana: Some Observations', Barclays Economic Review, June: 3 – 6.

Galebotswe, O., 2002, 'Competition Policy: A Threat to Competition and Economic Diversification?', Barclays Economic Review, Second Quarter: 11 – 14.

Geroski, P.A., 1991, 'Specification and Testing the Profits-Concentration Relationship: Some Experiments for the United Kingdom', Economica 48: 279 – 88.

Hay, D.A. and Morris, D.J., 1991, Industrial Economics and Organisation: Theory and Evidence, Oxford: University Press.

Hinzen, E., 1996, 'Promotion of Industry and Foreign Investment in Africa', Development and Cooperation (D+C), No. 1 Jan/February.

Hirschey, M., 2009, Managerial Economics, Mason: Thomson South-Western.

Hoover, E.M., 1937, Location Theory and Shoe and Leather Industry, Cambridge: Harvard University Press.

Hoover, E.M., 1948, Location of Economic Activity, New York: McGraw-Hill. Hotelling, H., 1929, 'Stability in Competition', Economic Journal, 39: 41 – 57.

Husain, I. and Faruqee, 1994, Adjustment in Africa Lessons from Country Case Studies, Washington DC: World Bank.

ICICI (Industrial Credit and Investment Corporation of India), 1980, Financial Performance of Companies, Bombay: ICICI.

ILO, 2002, Women and Men in the Informal Economy: A Statistical Picture, Geneva: ILO. IMF, 2005, CIA World Factbook, WEO Database, Washington DC: IMF.

Israd, W., 1960, Location on Space-Economy, Cambridge: MIT Press.

Jebuni, C.D., and Yahya, K., 2010, 'Institutional Framework and the Trade Policy Process in Ghana', in T. Oyejide and A. Fosu, eds, African Imperative in the New World Trade Order, Vol. III, Nairobi: African Economic Research Consortium.

Johnston, C., 1984, 'The Idea of Industrial Policy' in C. Johnston, ed, The Industrial Policy Debate, San Francisco: Institute for Contemporary Studies.

Kakujaha-Matundu, O., 2007, 'Competition and Infant Industry Protection Within SACU: The Case of UHT Milk in Namibia', Tralac Brief No. 4. Stellenbosch: US Printer.

Kakujaha-Matundu, O., 2009, 'Competition Policy and Growth in Southern African Customs Unions (SACU)', University of Namibia, Research Paper.

Kamien, M.J. and Schwartz, N.L., 1982, Market Structure and Innovation, Cambridge: Cambridge University Press.

Kaplan, D., 2008, 'Constraints and Institutional Challenges Facing Industrial Policy in South Africa', in B. Vickers, ed, Industrial Policy in the Southern African Customs Union, Midrand, South Africa: Institute for Global Dialogue.

Kapunda, S.M., 2005, 'The Role of Industry In Diversification and Sustainable Economic Development in Less Developed countries, in N. Narayana, ed, Economic Development Issues and Policies, Vol. I, New Delhi: Serial Publications, pp.175 – 89.

Kapunda, S.M., 2016, "Industrial Development and Economic Diversification in Botswana" N. Narayana (ed), Economic Diversification in Botswana, forthcoming

Kapunda, S.M. and Akinkugbe, O., 2008, 'Botswana's Industrial Development Policy and Policy Harmonisation Within SACU: Challenges and Opportunities', in B. Vickers, ed, Industrial Policy in the Southern African Customs Union, Midrand, South Africa: Institute for Global Dialogue, pp.47 - 59.

Kapunda, S.M. and Akinkugbe, O., 2005, 'Industrial Development in Botswana', in H. Siphambe, N. Narayana, O. Akinkugbe, and J. Sentsho, eds, Economic Development of Botswana: Facets, Policies, Problems and Prospects, Gaborone: Bay Publishing Ltd.

Kapunda, S.M., Magembe, B.A.S., and Shunda, J.P., 2008, 'Small and Medium Enterprises Finance In Botswana: Challenges and Prospects', Asian-African Journal of Economics and Econometrics, 8(1): 29 – 43.

Kapunda, S.M. and Mbogoro, D., 1989, 'The Economic and Industrial Development in Tanzania', in C.K. Omari, ed, Persistent Principles Amidst Crisis, Arusha: Evangelical Lutheran Church.

Kapunda, S.M., Magembe, B.A.S., and N. Tlotlego, 2010, 'The Impact of the Global Economic and Financial Crisis on SME Development in Botswana', Economics Departmental Research Report, University of Botswana.

Kapunda, S.M. and Molosiwa, T.K., 2012, 'An Assessmentof the Performance of Commercial Banks in Botswana: A Structure-Conduct-Performance Approach', International Journal of Economics and Business Studies, Vol. 2, No. 1, Spring, 3-12.

Kay, J., 2002, 'Business Economics' in W. Lazonick, ed., The IEBM Handbook of Economics, Thomson, London.

Keat, P.G. and Young, P.K.Y., 1996, Managerial Economics, New York: Macmillan Publishing.

Kingdom of Lesotho (KL), 1980, Third Five Year Development Plan, 1980 – 1985, Maseru: KL.

Koch, J.V., 1980, Industrial Organisation and Prices, New Jersey: Prentice-Hall. Krugman, P., 1991, 'Increasing Returns and Economic Geography', Journal of Political Economy, 99: 183 – 99.

Krugman, P., 1993, Geography and Trade, Cambridge: MIT Press.

Krugman, 1998, 'Whats New About the New Economic Geography?', Oxford Review of Economic Policy, 14(2), 7 – 18.

Leechor, C., 1994, 'Ghana: Frontrunner in Adjustment', in Husain and Fraquee, Adjustment in Africa: Lessons from Country Studies, Washington, D.C.: World Bank. Littlechild, S.C., 1978, The Fallacy of the Mixed Economy, Hobart Paper No. 80, London: Institute of Economic Affairs.

Lipczynski, J., Wilson, J.O.S., and Goddard, J., 2009, Industrial Organisation: Competition, Strategy, Policy, London: Prentice Hall.

Losch, A., 1940, (Germany), 1954 (English version), The Economics of Location, New Haven: Yale University Press: First Published in Germany in 1940.

Mabe, T.M., 2001, Determinants of Industrial Location In Botswana: Case Study of Gaborone and Maun, Research Project, Department of Economics, University of Botswana.

Makoa, F., 2008, 'Industrial Policy In the Kingdom of Lesotho', in B. Vickers, ed, Industrial Policy in the Southern African Customs Union, Midrand, South Africa: Institute for Global Dialogue.

Mans, D., 1994, 'Tanzania: Resolute Action', in I. Husain and Faruquee, Adjustment In Africa: Lessons from Country Case Studies, Washingon, D.C.: World Bank.

Mansfield, E., Allen, W.B., Doherty, N.A. and Weigelt, K., 2002, Managerial Economics: Theory, Applications, and Cases, London: W.W. Norton Co.

Marris, R., 1963, 'A model of the managerial enterprise', Quarterly Journal of Economics, No. 77, May, 185-209.

Marris, R., 1966, The Economic Theory of Managerial Capitalism, London: Macmillan.

Marshall, A., 1892, Elements of Economics of Industry, 3rd edition, London: Macmillan.

Marshall, A., 1898, Principles of Economics, London: Macmillan.

Marshall, A., 1899, The Economics of Industry, 3rd Edition, London: Macmillan. Martin, S., 1993, Advanced Industrial Economics, Oxford: Blackwell.

Mason, E.S., 1939, 'Price and Production Policies of Large-Scale Enterprise', American Economic Review, Supplement, 29: 61 – 74.

Mason, E.S., 1949, 'The Current State of the Monopoly Problem in the United States', Harvard Law Review, 62: 1265 – 85.

Mason, E.S., 1957, Economic Concentration and the Monopoly Problem, Cambridge, Mass: Harvard University Press.

Mazonde, I.N. and Sigwele, H.K., eds, 2000, Towards Policy on Agricultural Trade within SADC: Focus on Botswana, Gaborone: Printing and Publishing Company, Botswana.

McCarthy, C., 2008, 'The Challenge of Reconciling Revenue Distribution and Industrial Development in SACU', in B. Vicker's, ed, Industrial Policy in the Southern African Union: Past Experience, and Future Plans, Midrand, South Africa: Institute for Global Dialogue.

Millstein, I.M. and Cadbury, A., 2005, International Corporate Governance, Discussion Paper No. 1 for ECSN.

Ministry of Trade and Industries (MTI), 1979/80, Budget Speech, Dar-es-Salaam: MTI.

Mkandawire, T. and Soludo, C., 2003, African Voices on Structural Adjustment: A Compassion to Our Continent, Our Future, Trenton: Africa World Press, Inc.

Mpabanga, D., 2001, 'Constraint to Industrial Development', in J.S. Salkin, D. Mpabanga, D. Cowan, J. Selwe, and M. Wright, eds, Aspects of the Botswana Economy, Gaborone: Lentswe La Lesedi Publishers.

Mukras, M.S. 2004, Intermediate Mathematical Economics, Nairobi: African Centre for Contemporary Studies.

Mulaudzi, C., 2006, The Politics of Regionalism in Southern Africa, Occasional Paper, No. 51, Midrand, South Africa: Institute for Global Dialogue.

Mulikita, N.M., 2000, 'Public Policy Management and Strategic Planning In Zambia', Bulletin: Development Policy Management in Africa, 2 (November):13-15. Murphy, R.E., 1966, The American City, London: McGraw-Hill.

Mutasa, F.L., 2011, Principles of Economics; Banking Certificate, Dar-es-Salaam, The Tanzania Institute of Bankers.

Mwaigomole, E.A., 2012, 'Economic Trends and Public Policy in East Asia: Publications for the African Region', Tanzania Journal of Development Studies, Vol. 2, No. 1: 79 – 100.

Mwamba, N.E., 2004, 'Extension of Social Security in the Informal Sector in Tanzania", Tanzania Economic Trends, 17: 1 (June): 27 – 44.

Nelson, P., 1970, 'Information and Consumer Behaviour', Journal of Political Economy, (78), March/April: 311 – 29.

Nelson, R.R. and Winter, S.G., 1982, 'The Schumpeterian Tradeoff Revisited', American Economic Review, 73: 114 – 32.

O'Sullivan, M., 2000, Contests for Corporate Control: Corporate Governance and Economic Performance in the United States and Germany, Oxford: University Press.

OECD, 1991, Industrial Policy in OECD Countries, Annual Review, Paris: OECD.

OECD, 1994, Science and Technology Policy – Review and Outlook, Paris: OECD. Oosthuizen, G.H., 2006, The Southern African Development Community, Midrand, South Africa: Institute for Global Dialogue.

Osakwe, P.N., 2010, 'Africa and the Global Financial and Economic Crisis: Impacts, Responses, and Opportunities', in S. Dullien, D. Kotte, A. Marquez, and J. Priewel, eds, Financial and Economic Crisis of 2008 – 2009 and the Developing Countries, New York: United Nations and HTW Berlin University of Applied Sciences.

Pepall, L., D. Richards and G. Norman, 2011, Contemporary Industrial Organization. A quantitative Approach, New Jersey: J. Wiley & Sons, Inc.

Pepall, L., D. Richards and G. Norman, 2009, Industrial Organization: Contemporary Theory and Empirical Applications, 4th Edition, Oxford: Blackwell Publishing. Pigou, A.C., 1932, The Economics of Welfare, London: Macmillan.

Rawstron, E.M., 1958, 'Three Principles of Industrial Location', Transactions and Papers, 25: 132 – 42.

Regent Business School (RBS), 2007, MBA Managerial Economics, South Africa: RBS. Renner, G.T., 1947, 'Geography of Industrial Location', Economic Geography, 23: 167 – 89.

Renner, G.T., 1950, 'Some Principles and Laws of Economic Geography', Journal of Geography, 49: 14 – 22.

Republic of Botswana (RB), 1998, Industrial Development Policy For Botswana, Gaborone: RB Republic of Botswana (RB), 1999, Policy on Small Medium and Micro Enterprises in Botswana, Gaborone:RB.

Republic of Botswana (RB), 2000, Privatisation Policy, Gaborone: RB.

Republic of Botswana (RB), 2003, National Development Plan 9, 2003/2004 – 2008/09, Gaborone.

Republic of Botswana (RB), 2005, National Competition Policy for Botswana, Gaborone: RB.

Republic of Botswana (RB), 2014, Industrial Development Policy for Botswana, Gaborone: RB

Rhodgers, H., and Edmond, S., 2013, 'Corporate Governance and Code of Corporate Governance, A Case for Botswana', Challenges and Opportunities For Business Innovation and Development, Conference Proceedings, Faculty of Business, University of Botswana.

Robinson, J., 1933, The Economics of Imperfect Competition, London: Macmillan.

Robinson, E.A.G., 1958, The Structure of Competitive Industry, Chicago: University of Chicago Press.

Rouis, M., 1994, 'Senegal: Stabilization, Partial Adjustment, and Stagnation' in I. Husain and R. Faruqee, eds, Adjustment in Africa: Lessons from Country Case Studies, Washington D.C.: World Bank.

Rweyemamu, J., 1973, Underdevelopment and Industrialization in Tanzania, London: Oxford University Press.

SADC (2015) SADC Industrialisation Strategy and Roadmap, 2015-2063, Gaborone: SADC.

Sadoulet, E. and Janvry, A., 1995, Quantitative Development Policy Analysis, London: The John Hopkins University Press.

Salvatore, D., 2006, Managerial Economics, Oxford: Oxford University Press.

Schumpeter, J., 1928, 'The Instability of Capitalism', Economic Journal, 30: 361 – 86.

Schumpeter, J., 1950, Capitalism, Socialism and Democracy, New York: Harper & Row

Seck, C.S., Wade, O.T. and Ndoye, M., 2010, 'Institutional Framework and Trade Policy Formulation Process in African Countries: The Case of Senegal', in T.A. Oyejide and A. Fosu, eds, African Imperatives in the New World Trade Order, Nairobi: African Economic Research Consortium.

Semboja, H.H. and Kweka, J.P., 2001, "The Form and Role of Innovativeness in Enhancing Firms' Productivity: The Case of Selected Manufacturing Firms in Tanzania" in A. Szirmai and Lappere, P., eds., The Industrial Experience of Tanzania, New York: Palgrave Publishers.

Sentsho, J. and Tsheko, B.O., 2005, 'Botswana in the Context of Regional Economy', in H.K. Siphambe, N., Narayana, O., Akinkugbe and J. Sentsho, eds, Economic Development of Botswana, Gaborone: Bay Publishing.

Sentsho, J., 2001, 'Bringing the State In', Barclays Economic Review, end of year issue, 11 – 13. Sinha, N. and Mogotsi, I., 2009, Regional Integration, Economic Diversification and Small Resource-based Economy: Some Lessons for Botswana, Research Paper Department of Economics, University of Botswana.

Siwawa-Ndai, P.D., 2001, 'Industrialisation in Botswana: Evolution, Performance and Prospects', in J.S. Salkin, D. Mpabanga, D. Cowan, J. Selwe, and M. Wright, Aspects of the Botswana Economics, Gaborone: Lesedi Publishers.

Smith, Adam, 1776, An Inquiry Into the Nature and Causes of the Wealth of Nations, Reprinted 1976 by University of Chicago Press.

Smithies, A.F., 1941, 'Optimum Location in Spatial Competition', Journal of Political Economy, 49: 423 - 39.

Soludo, C., Ogbu, O. and Chang, H., 2004, The Politics of Trade and Industrial Policy in Africa, Trenton: Africa World Press.

Soludo, C., 1995, 'A Framework for Macroeconomic Policy Coordination among African Countries: The Case of the ECOWAS Sub-region', UNEGA, African Economic and Social Review: 1, No. 1 - 2, June and December: 1 – 31.

Steers, R.M., 1999, Made in Korea, Chung Ju Yung and the Rise of Hyundai, New York: Routledge.

Stein, H., 1995, Asian Industrialisation and Africa: Studies in policy alternatives to Structural Adjustment, London: Macmillan.

Stoneman, P., 1995, Handbook of the Economics of Innovation and Technical Change, Oxford: Blackwell.

Sutcliffe, R.B., 1971, Industry and Underdevelopment, London: Addison-Wesley Publishing Company.

Sutton, J., 1974, 'Advertising, Concentration and Competition', Economic Journal, 84: 56 – 69.

Swamy, G., 1994, 'Kenya: Patchy, Intermitted Commitment', in I. Hussain and R. Faruqee, eds, Adjustment in Africa: Lessons Form Country Case Studies, Washington, D.C.: World Bank.

Thompson, J.H., 1966, 'Some Theoretical Considerations for Manufacturing Geography', Economic Geography, 42: 356 – 65.

UNCTAD, 2008, Economic Development in Africa: Export Performance, New York, UNCTAD.

UNIDO & UNCTAD, 2011, Economic Development In Africa, Report 2011: Fostering Industrial Development in Africa in the New Global Environment, New York: UNIDO/ UNCTAD.

United Republic of Tanzania (URT), 1977, Third Five Year Plan (1976 – 1981), Dar-es- Salaam.

United Republic of Tanzania (URT), 1980, Budget Speech by Minister of Industry and Trade, Dar-es-Salaam.

United Republic of Tanzania (URT), 1982, First Five Year Union Plan (1981/82 – 1985/86), Dar-es-Salaam.

United Republic of Tanzania (URT), 1998, The Economic Survey, Dar-es-Salaam: URT. United Republic of Tanzania (URT), 2009, The Economic Survey, Dar-es-Salaam: URT. United Republic of Tanzania (URT), 2011, The Economic Survey, Dar-es-Salaam: URT. United Republic of Tanzania (URT), 2003a, Budget Speech by Minister of Industry and Trade, Dar-es-Salaam: URT.

United Republic of Tanzania (URT), 2003b, Small and Medium Enterprises Development Policy, Dar-es-Salaam: URT.

United Republic of Tanzania (URT), 2003c, National Trade Policy: Background Papers, Dar-es-Salaam: URT.

United Republic of Tanzania (URT), 2003d, National Trade Policy, Dar-es-Salaam: URT.

Uri, N.D., 1987, 'A Re-examination of the Advertising and Industrial Concentration Relationship', Applied Economics, 19: 427 – 35.

Uuman, E.L. and Dacey, M.F., 1960, 'The Minimum Requirement Approach to the Economic Base', Papers, Regional Science Association, 6: 175 – 94.

Vickers, B., ed, 2008, Industrial Policy in the Southern African Customs Union, Midrand: South Africa: Institute for Global Dialogue.

Waldman, D.E. and Jensen, E.J., 2007, Industrial Organisation: Theory and Practice, London: Pearson, Addison Wesley.

Wangwe, S. and Semboja, H., 2003, 'Impact of Structural Adjustment on Industrialisation and Technology in Africa', in T. Mkandawire and C. Soludo, eds, African Voices on Structural Adjustment: A Companion to Our Continent, Our Future, Trenton: Africa World Press, Inc.

Weber, A. 1909, Uber den Standort der Industrien i.e.Theory of the Location of Industries, Chicago: University of Chicago (Translated in English 1929).

Weimer, D.L., and Vining, A.R., 2005, Policy Analysis: Concepts and Practice, New Jersey: Pearson Prentice Hall.

Weiss, L.W., 1963, 'Factors in Changing Concentration', Review of Economics and Statistics, 45: 70 – 77.

Weiss, L.W., Pascoe, G. and Martin, S., 1963, 'The Size of Selling Costs', Review of Economics and Statistics, 65: 668 – 72.

WIPO (World Intellectual Property Organization), 2007, World Intellectual Property Organization, Geneva: WIPO.

Wohlmuth, K., Alabi, R., Burger, P., Gutowski, A., Jerome, A., Kneduk, T., Meyn, M. and Urban, T., 2009, New Growth and Poverty Alleviation Strategies for Africa – Institutional and Local Perspectives, Berlin: Transaction Publishers.

World Bank, 2000, Can Africa Claim the 21st Century?, Washington DC: World Bank.

Index

Printed in the United States
By Bookmasters